Reviews

What Top Management Is Saying about
Global Business Strategies for the Year 2000...

We believe that its encyclopedic scope and objective tone make Global Business Strategies for the Year 2000 an excellent choice as a primer or reference volume for the 21st century manager. William J. Warwick, President
AT&T Microelectronics

It is great news to have a book like Global Business Strategies for the Year 2000 that covers wide areas and can be used as a guidebook for international business people. Fujio Cho, Managing Director
Member of the Board
Toyota Motor Corporation

This is a very timely and definitive work that brings focus to a myriad of important, complex issues. This work is essential reading for the forward thinking MNC executive. Ira M. Rosenmertz, Partner
Arthur Andersen & Co.

Finally there is a book that covers globalization from A to Z. The others just talk around it. Jay M. Duffy, Manager
Miles, Inc.

Global Business Strategies for the Year 2000

Volume 2
461-919

Edited by

Dr. Phillip D. Grub
Dr. Robert T. Moran

Beacham Publishing, Inc.
Washington, D.C.

Global Business Strategies for the Year 2000

Editors

Phillip D. Grub
Robert T. Moran

Library of Congress
Cataloging-in-Publication Data

Global Business Strategies for the Year 2000
    Includes bibliographical references and index.
    Profiles key issues of concern to U.S. companies doing business abroad.
    1. International business enterprises—Management. 2. Strategic planning. 3. International business enterprises—Law and legislation. I. Grub, Phillip D., 1931-; II. Moran, Robert T., 1938-.
HD62.4.G543 1995   658'.049-dc20   94-48564
ISBN 0-933833-36-9

Copyright, ©, 1995, by Walton Beacham. All rights to this book are reserved. No part of this work may be used or reproduced in any form or by any means, electronic or mechanical, including photocopy, recording, or in any information or storage retrieval system, without written permission from the copyright owner, except in the case of brief quotations embodied in critical articles and reviews. For information write the publisher, Beacham Publishing, Inc., 2100 S Street, N.W., Washington, D.C. 20008.

Library of Congress Catalog Number: 94-48564
ISBN 0-933833-36-9

Printed in the United States of America
First Printing, January 1995

Contents

Introduction, *Elliot L. Richardson,* ix
Editors' Foreword, *Dr. Phillip D. Grub* and *Dr. Robert T. Moran,* xii

Volume 1

1. Global Market Opportunities

Entering Foreign Markets, *Dr. Robert J. Kuhne,* 1
Assessing Global Market Opportunities, *Dr. Roe Goddard,* 9
Locating Strategic Export Markets for Small Business,
  Dr. Galen F. Degraff, 22
Niche Marketing for Small Business Exporters, *Dr. Tung-lung Chang,* 44

2. Doing Business in . . .

China, *Dr. John Frankenstein,* 60
Vietnam, *Dr. Phillip D. Grub,* 87
Korea, *Dr. Phillip D. Grub,* 108
Japan, *Dr. Douglas K. Barry,* 131
Chile, *Dr. Sherry Tousley,* 152

Contents

3. Strategies for Global Operations

Global Vision—Implementation Challenges in an Era of Change,
  Dr. John R. Riesenberger, 167
Corporate Global Alliances, *Robert J. Radway*, 181
Countertrade, *Dr. Patricia J. Bost*, 190
Technology Transfer Across Borders, *Dr. Antonio Grimaldi*, 200
R&D Performed Abroad by U.S. Multinationals,
  Dr. Sherri Sweetman De Coronado, 210
Interfirm Collaboration for Technology Sharing, *Dr. Melanie Treviño*, 224
Managing International Science and Technology Transfer,
  Dr. Melanie Treviño, 261
Internationalization of the Small Firm, *Robert J. Radway*, 245
Managing Product Life Cycles in a Trans-global Environment,
  Dr. Nancy J. Adler and *Dr. Fariborz Ghadar*, 255

4. Establishing Overseas Operations

Programs of the Overseas Private Investment Corporation (OPIC),
  Julie A. Martin, 275
Licensing as an International Business Strategy, *Dr. Phillip D. Grub*, 290
International Franchising, *Robert J. Radway*, 303
Joint-ventures, *Karl William Viehe*, 314
Turnkey Operations, *Emilie Barton*, 333

5. Political Risk

Socio-Political Risk Analysis, *Dr. Llewellyn D. Howell*, 343

Contents

Political Instability, *Dr. Martin H. Sours,* 363
International Risk Analysis, *Dr. F. John Mathis,* 372
Tariff Barriers, *Dr. Sherry Tousley,* 380
Technology Controls, *Emilie Barton,* 394
Export Restrictions, *Dr. Robert J. Kuhne,* 401

6. Export Marketing in Developing Nations

The Public Sector Role in Export Marketing for Developing Nations,
   Dr. Mary Lou Egan, 411
The Private Sector Role in Export Marketing for Developing Countries,
   Dr. Kenneth L. Murrell, 431
Chinese Trading Companies in the U.S., *Dr. Min H. Lu,* 449

Volume 2

7. International Financial Management

Managing Profits from Foreign Operations, *Dr. Rodney W. Eldridge,* 461
Managing Transaction Exposure, *Dr. Ahmad Sohrabian,* 466
Emerging Equity Markets,
   Antoine W. Van Agtmael and *Bryan L. Sudweeks,* 477
An Overview of the Foreign Exchange Market,
   Dr. Francisco Carrado-Bravo, 489
Foreign Exchange Rates and Forecasting, *Dr. Chuck C. Y. Kwok,* 496
Spot Market Speculators, *Dr. Dale Vor Der Landwehr,* 518

Contents

8. International Tax

Taxation for U.S Corporations Doing Business Abroad,
  Donald T. Williamson and *Karl William Viehe*, 531
Taxation for U.S Citizens Doing Business Abroad,
  Donald T. Williamson and *Karl William Viehe*, 548
U.S Taxation of Non-resident Aliens and Foreign Corporations,
  Donald T. Williamson and *Karl William Viehe*, 556

9. International Law and Agreements

Treaties and Conventions, *Diane B. Macdonald*, 565
Patents and Trademarks, *Diane B. Macdonald*, 574
Management Contracts, *Robert J. Radway*, 586
Foreign Contract Agreements, *Robert J. Radway*, 594
Selecting and Managing Local Lawyers, *Robert J. Radway*, 603

10. Global Alliances

The Impact of GATT on the Global Business Environment,
  Dr. David Thornton, 613
Strategies for the European Union,
  Dr. Joel W. Cook and *Dr. Deborah Smith Cook*, 624
North American Free Trade Agreement (NAFTA),
  Dr. Robert T. Moran and *Dr. Jeffrey Abbott*, 646
Legal Standards Imposed by International Organizations,
  Dr. Isik Urla Zeytinoglu, 657

11. World Differences in Labor and Management Issues

European Labor Relations and Industrial Democracy,
 Dr. Beverly J. Springer, 669
Japanese Management by Consensus, *Dr. Martin H. Sours,* 681
Management Infrastructure in the Third World, *Dr. Kenneth L. Murrell,* 691
Nepotism in International Management,
 Dr. Youngho Lee and *Dr. Joe W. Lee,* 704
Cultural and Legal Advantages to Decentralizing Human Resources
 Management, *John O. Bigelow,* 721
The Global Reach: Headquarters and Foreign Subsidiary Communication,
 Dr. D. Robert Shuter, 729
Approaches to Alternative Dispute Resolution in International Business,
 Dr. Karen S. Walch, 742

12. International Personnel

An Overview to Selecting Expatriate Managers, *Dr. James E. Boyce,* 755
Systems for Selecting International Personnel,
 Dr. P. Christopher Earley and *Dr. C. Carstens Smith,* 765
Selecting Foreign Assignees, *Michael Troppe,* 775
Preparing Managers for Intercultural Assignments,
 Dr. P. Christopher Earley, 790
Compensation in International Settings, *Dr. P. Christopher Earley,* 800

13. The Impact of Culture on International Operations

Adapting Foreign Operations to Cultural Diversity, *Dr. Sue A. Miller,* 811

Contents

Ethical Dilemmas in Transacting Business Across Cultures,
 Dr. Joanna M. Banthin and *Dr. Leigh Stelzer,* 820
Profiling Your Negotiating Counterpart, *Dr. Robert T. Moran,* 830
Cultural Keys to Successful Negotiating, *Dr. Phillip D. Grub,* 840
Cultural Differences on Sexual Harrassment, *Dr. David Braaten,* 850

14. Evolving Issues in Global Business Operations

Developing Global Perspective, *Dr. Rosalie Tung,* 867
Strategic Planning for the MNC, *Dr. H. Charles Chase,* 877
International Market Analysis Through Electronic Databases,
 Dr. Zeinab A. Karake, 888
Corporate Philanthropy as Strategy, *Carole S. George,* 895

Index, 909

Global Business Strategies for the Year 2000

7.

International Financial Management

Managing Profits from Foreign Operations

OVERVIEW

A significant number of developing countries are faced with overwhelming external payment burdens resulting from international debt incurred over the past fifteen years. Some countries have been unable to generate hard currency to service these debts, causing defaults and renegotiation of terms. In this environment it has been necessary for governments to control hard currency carefully and to regulate access to foreign exchange. The compelling need for currency to reduce debt, and purchase essential imports overshadows the long-run and uncertain benefits expected from foreign investments. Profits from foreign companies become a tempting and highly visible target for restriction. When a firm undertakes operations in a foreign country, there is a risk that at some time during the life of the venture, the host government will take actions that may restrict the flow of funds, especially the remission of profits, from the foreign branch. Such risks are particularly pronounced in countries with immature economies and political instability. Careful planning and precommitment negotiations with the host government can reduce those risks.

IMPLEMENTATION

While numerous strategies are available to reduce the risk of government interruption of profit flows from foreign investment, the majority fall into two broad categories. The first can be called the "relocation of profits"—a profit, no matter where taken, is a profit. The second centers on the "renaming of profits"—a profit by any other name is a profit.

Relocation Strategy

The primary method of relocating profits with a complex organization, such as a multinational corporation, is the manipulation of transfer prices. The transfer price is the price charged by one unit of a complex entity for goods and services delivered to another international business within a single corporate headquarters. One result of the trend toward internalized decisions is the ability of complex organizations to bypass the discipline of the marketplace, which elevates the importance of transfer pricing decisions.

Profits (and losses) can readily be shifted from one unit of a firm to another by adjusting the transfer prices for goods and services exchanged by the units. The corporate entity's pricing theory holds that the profit maximizing transfer price is simply the marginal cost to the supplying unit. Taxing authorities, particularly those responsible for taxing profits, have long had a keen interest in transfer pricing because of its potential to move profits around, thus escaping taxation. Therefore, authorities have adopted a fairly standard rule concerning transfer prices. The rule requires that the transfer price be an "arm's length" price: that is, the price that would have normally been arrived at through negotiations between unrelated buyers and sellers—a market determined price.

Authorities responsible for administering foreign exchange controls also have a keen interest in monitoring international transfer prices. Shifting profits from one unit to another is a convenient route to bypass the host country and avoid restrictions on exporting profits. It is important to recognize, therefore, that the latitude to relocate profits through transfer pricing may be carefully controlled by government regulation. The benefits to be derived from the international business venture by the host country, however, may be sufficiently important to induce a waiver of transfer pricing regulations, but the foreign investor must negotiate these as part of the contract.

Profit Relocation via Transfer Pricing

Assume that an American firm producing fine leather goods has established a subsidiary in Argentina to acquire prime hides and convert them into leather. The leather is then shipped to the U.S. for final processing and fabrication. Further, assume the Argentine subsidiary's marginal cost per hide is the equivalent of $20 (marginal cost here defined to include a "normal" profit of $3 dollars per hide). In addition, assume that a price of $22 per hide could be defended as an "arm's length" or market price.

If the U.S. parent firm is faced or threatened with restrictions on its Argentine subsidiary in accessing U.S. dollars for purposes of remitting profits, it should consider establishing the transfer price at say $17 per hide. If acceptable to the Argentine authorities, profits can be eliminated from the Argentine subsidiary and shifted to the American parent. To make the agreement acceptable, the Argentine authorities must realize that restricting the profits could cause the parent company to shut down the subsidiary and deprive the host company of dollars ($17 per hide) which are sorely needed.

An alternative solution might be for the U.S. parent company to supply tanning equipment or other materials to the Argentine subsidiary and relocate profits from the subsidiary to the parent by charging a high arm's length market price for the equipment. The Argentine authorities would be likely to view this transfer price with a more jaundiced eye since the "manipulated" price creates an immediate increase in foreign exchange drain rather than simply a reduction in foreign exchange revenues.

Renaming Profits

In general, foreign exchange controls permit greater access to the markets for the purpose of meeting fixed obligations than for the remission of residual earnings as profits. In countries where nationalistic sentiment runs high, governments may be compelled to take a hard line on profits taken out of the country by multinational corporations. However, realistic officials might accept the lower profile, fixed obligation flows.

Interest payments are an example of a fixed obligation with a lower foreign exchange profile than profits. Where there is potential for the host government to block profits, the capital committed by the parent firm should be in the form of debt rather than equity. Interest payments, which represent the return to the debt capital supplied, are not threatened by restrictions on profits. Also, depending on the amortization schedule selected, the use of debt does provide for an orderly repatriation of the capital committed.

In addition to the substitution of interest payments for profit dividends, a variety of fees and charges can be included in the initial contractual agreement between parent and subsidiary. Examples of such contractual obligations include patent fees, licensing fees, royalty payments, management fees, and shared Research and Development expenditures. While "understandings" with governmental authorities concerning transfer pricing will be tacit and somewhat ambiguous, arrangements concerning fee structures and other fixed obligations can be explicit and contractual. It is important that they be negotiated with host government authorities prior to closing commitments.

EVALUATION

Frequently the restriction on the remission of profits takes the form of a "cap" on the rate of profit allowed; i.e., a maximum return on investment. It is important, therefore, that all capital committed by the parent to the venture be registered with host government authorities. It is desirable to establish as high a registered investment base as possible in order to reduce the perceived return on investment and perhaps escape imposed ceilings. One way to maximize the registered investment base is, again, to increase the transfer price for any commitment of capital in kind, such as real capital equipment.

Planners must recognize that the strategies suggested here can result in serious distortions of the financial statements. To rely on such distorted information for decision-making would lead to serious errors.

CONCLUSION

These strategies are designed to circumvent governmental controls and restrictions. It is appropriate to question the ethical bases of such strategies, especially those which technically violate regulations. As a general principle, negotiations and relationships between foreign investors and host governments need not and should not be a zero sum game.

International business ventures have the potential to generate benefits for all parties concerned. In international business ventures, as in domestic activities, there is an adversarial relationship between government and business; however, a longer planning and evaluation period reduces potential conflicts. An incorruptible, dedicated government official may well determine that the best interest of his government and his country are best served by a tacit waiver of certain regulations.

Dr. Rodney W. Eldridge
Professor of International Finance
The George Washington University

Managing Transaction Exposure

OVERVIEW

Transaction exposure exists when future cash transactions of a firm are affected by exchange rate fluctuations. There are three ways in which transaction exposure can occur if:

1. Currency has to be converted to make or to receive payment for goods or services.
2. Currency has to be converted to repay a loan plus the interest.
3. Currency conversion is needed to make dividend payments.

Multinational corporations (MNCs) often desire to avoid transaction exposure since they prefer to know the amount of their currency needed for future purchases. The management of transaction exposure centers on the concept of hedging. A hedge is a contract that provides defense against the risk of loss from a change in foreign exchange rates. The three most common methods to offset transaction exposure are a forward market hedge, a money market hedge, and an options market hedge.

EXAMPLES

Assume that a U.S. firm sells merchandise on open account to a French buyer for FF420,000 with payment to be made in 60 days. The exchange rate is FF6/$, and the U.S. seller expects to exchange the FF420,000 for $70,000 when payment is received. Exposure arises because of the risk that the U.S. seller will receive something other than $70,000 after the French franc receipts are exchanged for dollars. For example, if the exchange rate were FF7/$ when payment was received, the U.S. seller would receive only 60,000 (FF420,000 at FF7/$), some $10,000 less than was anticipated. If the exchange rate had gone to FF5/$, however, the U.S. seller would have received $84,000, an increase of $14,000 over the amount expected. Thus, transaction exposure is the chance of either a loss or a gain. Note that the U.S. firm could have avoided the exchange risk by insisting that payment for the merchandise be in dollars. This does not eliminate the risk but simply transfers the risk from the seller to the buyer.

The above example is from the perspective of a U.S. based MNC that needs a foreign currency to make payment. Its futures payables are exposed to exchange rate fluctuations. When considering a U.S. based MNC that will be receiving a foreign currency for which it will have no use, its futures receivables are exposed since it is uncertain of the dollars it will obtain when selling off the foreign currency received. Again, the MNC must deal with this transaction exposure.

BENEFITS

The basic value of hedging is to protect a company against unexpected exchange rate changes. A hedge allows a firm to reduce the variability of its future cash flows (in terms of home currency) which can then enhance corporate planning. A further benefit of reduced variability in cash flow is the possibility that an increase in the firm's debt capacity will arise because of lower financial risk.

Management's motivation to reduce variability is sometimes reinforced for cosmetic reasons if management believes it will be criticized more severely for incurring foreign exchange losses on the income statement than for incurring similar or even higher costs in avoiding the foreign exchange loss. The belief is reinforced by the firm's income statement, where foreign exchange losses may appear as a highly visible separate line item or footnote.

IMPLEMENTATION

The forward market hedge consists of offsetting an anticipated receivable/payable denominated in a foreign currency by concluding at the outset a forward contract to sell/buy that currency with delivery set at a determinate future date so as to coincide with the date of an anticipated receipt/payment of the foreign currency. In our previous example in which a U.S. firm had a receivable in French francs due in 60 days, a request for a forward sale of French francs is appropriate. By doing this, the U.S. firm locks in the rate at which it can sell these francs off for dollars. Many MNCs commonly implement the forward hedging technique. For example, Westinghouse Electric Corporation hedged its future receivables in French francs during 1983. The French franc depreciated during this period. Westinghouse saved millions of dollars since the forward contract hedged against such a movement. As another example, E.I. DuPont de Nemours often has the equivalent of $300 million to $500 million of forward contracts at any one time to cover open currency positions. Its forward sale contracts are designed to sell incoming foreign currencies at a specific rate, while its forward purchase contracts are designed to lock in a price for foreign currencies needed in the future.

The money market hedge consists of reversing the foreign currency receivables/payables by creating matching payable/receivables in the respective foreign currency through borrowing in the money markets. If a U.S. firm is committed to pay French francs in three months, it could hedge the exchange risk by borrowing U.S. dollars now, converting the dollars into French francs

Managing Transaction Exposure

at the spot rate, and investing the proceeds in French money market instruments. The proceeds of the instruments upon maturity in three months will be used to meet the French francs payable. The amount of the U.S. dollar loan depends on: (1) the spot exchange rate between dollars and French francs, and (2) the yield on the investment in French money market instruments. In this manner, the U.S. firm has substituted a fixed amount of obligation denominated in U.S. dollars for a commitment dominated in French francs which will translate into an unknown amount of dollars.

These are strategies for firms to hedge known foreign currency transaction exposures. Yet, in many circumstances, the firm is uncertain whether the hedged foreign currency cash inflow or outflow will materialize. For example, a U.S. MNC must submit a fixed price bid in a foreign currency without knowing until some later date whether its bid is successful. U.S. firms would like to guarantee that the exchange rate does not move against it between the time it bids and the time it gets paid, should it win the contract. The danger of not hedging happens when its bid is selected and the foreign currency declines in value, possibly wiping out the firm's anticipated profit margin. The apparent solution is for the U.S. firm to sell the anticipated receivable forward. But if the U.S. firm does that, and loses the bid on the contract, it still has to sell the currency (which it will have to get by buying on the open market, perhaps at a big loss).

Until recently, any company that bid on a foreign contract in a foreign currency and was not assured of success would be unable to resolve its foreign exchange risk dilemma. The advent of currency options has changed all that.

There are two types of options available to managing risk. A "put" option gives the buyer the right, but not the obligation, to sell a specified number of foreign currency units to the option seller at a fixed dollar price, up to the option's expiration date. Alternatively, a "call" option is the right, but not the obligation, to buy the foreign currency at a specified dollar price, up to the expiration date.

A call option is valuable, for example, when a firm has offered to buy some foreign assets, such as another firm, at a fixed foreign price but is uncertain whether its bid will be accepted. By buying a call option on the foreign currency, the firm can lock in a maximum dollar price for its tender offer, while at the same time limiting its downside risk to the call premium (cost of the option) in the event its bid is rejected. Given the advantages of a currency option relative to a forward contract when hedging future payables/ receivables, why don't all firms hedge with currency options? The answer is that a firm must pay to obtain a currency option. Some firms may believe the options are overpriced.

The general rules to follow in choosing between currency options and forward contracts for hedging purposes can be summarized as follows:

1. When the quantity of a foreign currency cash flow is known, buy the currency forward; when the quantity is unknown buy a call option on the currency.

2. When the quantity of a foreign currency cash inflow is known, sell the currency forward; when the quantity is unknown, buy a put option on the currency.

3. When the quantity of a foreign currency cash flow is partially known and partially uncertain, use a forward contract to hedge the known portion and a call option to hedge the maximum value of the uncertain remainder.

EVALUATION

Forward hedging must be balanced against the transaction costs (the spread between the bid and the ask prices). It must also be pointed out that the forward hedge is available only for major currencies and for certain maturities. The bulk of international transactions, however, is denominated in these currencies, and most maturity needs for MNCs are covered by available contracts in these forward markets. This aspect of the foreign exchange market renders exposure management more difficult for MNCs with substantial exposure in developing countries.

The structure of a money market resembles that of a forward exchange hedge. The difference is that the cost of the money market hedge is determined by differential interest rates, while the cost of the forward market hedge is a function of the forward rate quotations. In efficient markets, interest rate parity should ensure that these costs are nearly the same. The choice of which hedge to take will then depend on the opportunity cost of funds to the firm as well as whether local borrowing (in a case of hedging receivables dominated in foreign currency) is actually available. In situations where interest rate parity does not hold and interest rate differentials exceeding transaction costs exist, arbitrage operations are profitable. Whenever such opportunities exist, they should be taken by the MNC irrespective of its exchange exposure position or exposure management policies.

An option contract is more flexible than a forward contract for hedging payables/receivables. However, a firm must pay to obtain a currency option. A firm does not know for sure whether a currency option is more appropriate (less costly) than a forward contract until it knows the spot rate that exists at the time the payables or receivables are due. Of course, by this time the firm would already have decided on a hedging device.

For an MNC that has frequent exposure in many currencies, hedging every transaction is counterproductive, since the likely outcome of the gains and losses under an unhedged position will approach zero, particularly under a floating rate regime. Unless the exchange market is perceived to be grossly distorted, due to political risk or otherwise, a policy to hedge all exposures is likely to be as costly as the expected exchange rate changes. If hedging a large number of transactions will produce the same outcome as the unhedged position, then the overall gain from hedging operations is slightly negative because of the cost of arranging the protection.

APPLICATIONS TO SMALL BUSINESS

With small businesses increasing their international trade, forward contracts, money market hedges and currency option contracts will be utilized in minimizing transaction exposures. It is important that small business managers are aware of the uses and drawbacks to these methods for their operations. The gains/losses from hedging can lead to total success/failure of these firms.

CONCLUSION

A firm does not have the perfect foresight on future exchange rates to know whether hedging will be less costly than allowing the foreign currency position to remain exposed. However, it can lock in the maximum amount of its currency needed to cover foreign currency payables and/or the minimum amount of the local currency to be received when converting foreign currency receivables. A common method of deciding whether to hedge is to first forecast the future exchange rate. If hedging appears less costly or more lucrative than an unhedged position, then the firm should hedge. Even if it is not, then some firms may hedge anyway to avoid or reduce transaction exposure to exchange rate fluctuations.

Many types of future cash flows cannot be predicted with perfect accuracy. Thus, firms that desire to hedge may not be able to fully insulate against transaction exposure. In addition, the hedging techniques are normally available for only the most widely traded currencies. In these cases, other methods like investing/borrowing strategy or invoicing strategy should be used to reduce transaction exposure.

REFERENCES/SOURCES

Ankrom, Robert K. "Top Level Approach to the Foreign Exchange Problem." *Harvard Business Review* (July/August 1974): 79-90.

Antl, Boris, and Richard Ensor, eds. *Currency Risk and the Corporation.* London: Euromoney Publications, 1982.

―――. *The Management of Foreign Exchange Risk.* London: Euromoney Publications, 1982.

Babbel, David F. "Determining the Optimum Strategy for Hedging Currency Exposure." *Journal of International Business Studies* (Spring/Summer 1983): 133-139.

Batra, Raveendra N., Shabtai Donnenfeld, and Josef Hadar. "Hedging Behavior by Multinational Firms." *Journal of International Business Studies* (Winter 1982): 59-70.

Beidleman, Carl R., John L. Hilary and James A. Greenleaf. "Alternatives to Hedging Long-Date Contractual Foreign Exchange Exposure." *Sloan Management Review* (Summer 1983): 45-54.

Booth, Laurence D. "Hedging and Foreign Exchange Exposure." *Management International Review.* 22,1 (1982): 26-42.

Donaldson, J. A. *Corporate Currency Risk*. London: Financial Times Business Information, Ltd., 1980.

Dufey, Gunter and S. L. Srinivasulu. "The Case for Corporate Management of Foreign Exchange Risk." *Financial Management*. (Winter 1983): 54-62.

Eaker, Mark R. and Dwight Grant. "Optimal Hedging of Uncertain and Long-Term Foreign Exchange Exposure." *Journal of Banking and Finance* (June 1985): 222-231.

Fitzimons, Robert B. "Exposure Management is too Important to Be Left to the Treasurer." *Euromoney* (March 1979): 103-112.

Folks, William R., Jr. "Decision Analysis for Exchange Risk Management." *Financial Management* (Winter 1972): 101-112.

Giddy, Ian H. "Why It Doesn't Pay to Make a Habit of Forward Hedging." *Euromoney* (December 1976): 96-100.

———. "The Foreign Exchange Option as a Hedging Tool." *Midland Corporate Finance Journal* (Fall 1983): 32-42.

Hagemann, Helmut. "Anticipate Your Long-Term Foreign Exchange Risks." *Harvard Business Review* (March/April 1977): 81-88.

Herring, R. J., ed. *Managing Foreign Exchange Risk: Theory and Practice*. Lexington, MA: D.C. Heath, 1978.

———. "Management of Foreign Exchange Risk: A Review Article" *Journal of International Business Studies* (Spring/Summer 1981): 81-101.

Jilling, Michael. *Foreign Exchange Management in U.S. Multinational Corporations.* Ann Arbor, MI: UMI Press, 1980.

Kemp, Donald S. "Hedging a Long-Term Financing." *Euromoney* (February 1981): 102-105.

Korsvold, Paul. "The Futility of Currency Hedging Models." In Goran Bergendahl, ed. *International Financial Management* (Stockholm: Norstedts, 1982): 104-127.

Lassen, Richard. *Currency Management.* Cambridge, MA: Woodhead-Faulkner, 1982.

Levich, Richard M. and Clas G. Wihlborg, eds. *Exchange Risk and Exposure.* Lexington, MA: Lexington Books, 1980.

Mathur, Ike. "Managing Foreign Exchange Risks Profitably." *Columbia Journal of World Business* (Winter 1982): 23-30.

Naidu, G.W. and Tai Shim. "Effectiveness of Currency Futures Market in Hedging Foreign Exchange Risk." *Management International Review* 21,4 (1981): 5-16.

Reier, S. "The Boom in Long-Dated Forwards." *Institutional Investor* (October 1983): 353-354.

Rodrigez, Rita M. *Foreign Exchange Management in U.S. Multinationals.* Lexington, MA: Lexington Books, 1980.

———. "Corporate Exchange Risk Management: Theme and Aberrations."

Journal of Finance (May 1981): 427-439.

Soenen, Luc A. "Foreign Exchange Exposure Management." *Management International Review* 19,2 (1979): 31-38.

Soenen, Luc A. and F. G. F. van Winkel. "The Real Costs of Hedging in The Forward Exchange Market." *Management International Review* 22,1 (1982): 53-59.

Srinivasulu, S. L. "Strategic Response to Foreign Exchange Risks." *Columbia Journal of World Business* (Spring 1981): 13-23.

Tran, Vinh Quang. *Foreign Exchange Management in Multinational Firms.* Ann Arbor, MI: UMI Press, 1980.

Dr. Ahmad Sohrabian
Associate Professor of Finance
California State Polytechnic University, Pomona

Dr. Ahmad Sohrabian received his Ph.D. in Economics from the University of California at Santa Barbara. His areas of interest include econometrics and forecasting, international finance and corporate finance.

Emerging Equity Markets

OVERVIEW

International investing is not a new phenomenon. Early in the 20th century, issues of stocks and bonds, which at that time were more important than bank lending, financed the expansion of railways, utilities and other forms of economic development in the U.S. and Latin America. But economic depression and World Wars I and II cut back this flow of investment, although it continued on a more modest scale through the years with the Scottish, Swiss and Dutch investors playing particularly active roles. Major multinationals, and to a lesser degree, even stocks from "emerging" markets have been listed in London and the U.S. For many years, there was more trading in foreign than domestic stocks in both Holland and Switzerland. But during the 1960s and 1970s, the emphasis in international finance was on international lending by banks through syndicated loans, which was followed by rapid growth and increasing integration of the international bond markets. In recent years, however, the focus seems to have shifted from loans to securities and from debt to equity. A number of major developments have been behind this shift.

The first is the rise of the euro-equity markets. Many large multinational companies and even small high-tech firms are now offering their stocks, not just within their national boundaries, but to an international audience. Thanks to technological developments and less inhibition by regulatory constraints, trading of major (and even smaller) stocks is increasingly moving off the floors of national exchanges toward the trading rooms of the major commercial and investment banks. London's Big Bang is a major stimulus to this development.

Emerging Equity Markets

Today some 1,000 issues are said to be owned and traded internationally. By the turn of the century, the international equity markets may begin to rival the international bond and money markets in importance.

The second development is the growing role of pension funds. Pension funds in the U.S., Japan, and Europe have grown faster than the world economy over the past ten years. They are now estimated to have an aggregate size of over $2 trillion, second only in funds to international banks. Although smaller, investment funds have grown spectacularly to about $700 billion worldwide, not only in industrialized countries, but also in emerging markets such as Korea and India. This adds up to a rapidly growing pool of investible funds seeking diversification and, increasingly, higher returns.

Third, a greater understanding of the benefits of international diversification has emerged. There has been a steady trend toward internationalization in institutional investment. Although the actual percentages of investible funds in international markets is relatively small, the absolute amounts are becoming staggering, upwards of $100 billion in the U.S. alone. The upward trend is expected to continue, especially as regulatory and tax barriers are removed and the ease of trading increases. Internationalization has undoubtedly linked the markets, even though over a period as short as one year, investment returns are dramatically different from market to market due to local conditions as well as currency fluctuations.

Fourth, international equity markets have generally been doing well, although Black Monday, October 19, 1987, caused many investors to reconsider their investment strategies in favor of greater international diversification. However, some of this money invested in these markets may be looking for new horizons and some markets may have lower earnings potential as there are fewer prospects of currency appreciation in Europe and Japan for the international investor after the steady decline of the dollar.

Finally, viewed in combination, these developments put a spotlight on a fifth major trend, the growing importance of emerging capital markets. These markets have not only grown in size and activity, but they are also beginning to attract both institutional and individual investors. This article will discuss key developments in the international equity markets, the potential of emerging capital markets for international investors, potential problems and myths, and prospects of emerging capital markets in the next decade.

EXAMPLES

Despite the shock waves created by the devastating crash of Black Monday in many major and even smaller markets, 1987 was a surprisingly good year for most emerging capital markets. Among the ten best performing markets (in terms of U.S. dollars) were six emerging markets with returns over 30%. Taiwan, Korea, and Thailand outperformed even Japan, followed by the Philippines, Zimbabwe and Chile.

A number of emerging markets turned out to be relatively immune to the October crash, including Korea, the Philippines, India, Pakistan, Argentina, Jordan, Nigeria and Zimbabwe. Many of these markets had shown very little movement earlier in the year and, thus, were not vulnerable to a correction. Some were also insulated from foreign investors. The Philippines had undergone a major correction earlier in the year because of political uncertainties. Korea remained surprisingly unaffected by the worldwide crash and was one of the few markets to end the year higher than it stood on Black Monday.

Other emerging capital markets managed to outperform the U.S. market in 1987. In addition to the top performing markets mentioned earlier, Jordan (+13%), Pakistan (+11%), Malaysia (+6%), and India (+6%) ended the year above 1986 year-end levels.

At present, there are over 35 equity markets in developing countries and over 8,000 listings. In terms of size, many of the larger emerging markets are comparable to the medium-sized European markets, although they are much smaller than New York or Japan. Much room for growth remains. Whereas the GNP of the countries with emerging markets contributes approximately 10% to the world GNP, their financial markets still contribute less than 3% to world financial markets. Nevertheless, they have now reached a size and importance which can no longer be overlooked as demonstrated by the following examples:

- In recent years equity and bond markets have mobilized more funds for development through new issues than World Bank loan disbursements. In Korea and India alone, new issues amounted to over $5 billion in 1985. The amounts mobilized by the financial markets in developing countries should continue to grow as market activity increases.

- Many European markets have 100-500 listings, which is similar to the range found in most developing countries. There are more than 15 markets in the developing world with more than 100 companies. In India, over 5,000 companies are listed, which is larger than markets in the U.K. and Japan, although most of these companies are much smaller and much less actively traded.

- In recent years, there has been a boom in many emerging markets, especially various Asian markets. In 1987, of the top five performing markets, Taiwan, Korea, Thailand and the Philippines placed first, second, third, and fifth. Japan was the fourth best performing market.

- As developing country markets become more active, which has been the case in recent years, it is likely that new companies will list their shares and the market capitalization of companies listed will grow. By the year 2000, there could easily be 15,000 listings in the developing world of which some 500 would be traded in the international markets and held by institutional investors on a worldwide basis.

Additionally, clear evidence of a greater interest by international investors is the success of various country funds. For example, there have been at least four Korean funds or trust, four Taiwanese funds, two Thai funds, an Indian fund, and a Mexican fund. A number of years ago, several Brazilian funds and a Mexican fund were placed among international investors. The total market value of these funds is now in excess of U.S. $1.5 billion. There are also several diversified LDC (Less Developed Countries) funds.

BENEFITS

Many of the emerging markets have a respectable history of returns. Among ten of the top emerging markets tracked by the IFC Emerging Financial Markets Database since 1975, India, Korea, and Chile have outperformed both the index for the industrialized world (Morgan Stanley—Capital International World Index) and the United States (S&P 500). Mexico and Thailand, among others, are slightly below the international averages. Moreover, even with Black Monday, four of the top five markets in the world in 1987 were from emerging markets. Despite the debt crisis in the developing world and the recent boom in equity markets, the emerging markets have performed creditably in comparison.

In addition to high returns for individual assets, institutional investors are also concerned with diversification of assets among different countries and industries, which will either increase return for a given level of risk, or decrease risk for a given level of return. Risk for institutional investors is commonly referred to as the variance of returns (or the standard deviation). In addition to returns, investors are concerned with the correlation between country markets. Ideally, when one market is down, another market should be doing well, which should offset the lower returns in the first market, lowering portfolio risk (i.e. variability). Correlation coefficients in many emerging markets with the U.S. and other industrialized markets are close to zero. This provides excellent diversification opportunities for international investors. Moreover, current research has shown that the addition of a developing country's stocks to the set of U.S. and international assets generally results in greater returns from a U.S. dollar point of view, indicating that portfolio managers who are not considering these markets may be missing opportunities for higher returns. Good values can be found in many emerging capital markets as they have not yet been discovered by international and local institutional investors, although a few of the markets may be temporarily overvalued. For example:

- Price/earnings and price/book value ratios are often well below the ratios in the major international markets.

- Modern investment techniques and securities analysis are not yet used on a wide scale in these markets. This comparative inefficiency gives international investors with the skills the opportunities to find values which are no longer available through existing methods in the major markets.

- Some of the world's industrial leaders can be found in many developing countries. Many exporters to the industrialized world are quoted on local stock markets in the developing world. The demand for protection against their products is evidence of the threat they pose to competitors elsewhere.

- Many emerging capital markets are in countries which have fundamentally sounder economies than they did five or ten years ago. Many are benefitting from the recent alignment in major international currencies. Others are becoming more private-sector oriented; they have abandoned over-valued exchange rates and trimmed the fat off their corporate sectors during the recent shake-up of their economies.

IMPLEMENTATION

The appeal of investing in emerging markets is clear. Why has it not happened on a wider scale? The most important barrier in the past has been the lack of knowledge and information among international investors about the emerging capital markets. It was thought that these were small; that they lacked liquidity; were without significant disclosure, information and investor protection; and were restricted for foreigners and politically risky. Some of these problems do indeed exist, but perhaps on a smaller scale than expected.

Foreign portfolio investment in emerging markets is not exactly new. Earlier in this century, Argentina and Brazil benefited from international stock and bond issues. Since that time, there has been sporadic interest in certain markets:

- Many Malaysian stocks are listed in London, a few Philippine and Mexican stocks in New York, and Papua New Guinean stocks in Australia.

- Hong Kong and Singapore, whose markets are heavily dominated by Malaysian stocks, have attracted foreign funds for a long time.

- Several small British and Hong Kong based funds have invested in various Far Eastern markets for many years.

Emerging Equity Markets

Currently, international investors are showing an increasing interest in these emerging capital markets, especially in Brazil, Korea, Taiwan, Malaysia, Mexico, and India. Investment flows could reach between $500 million and $1 billion a year if many of the remaining barriers to foreign portfolio investment are removed. NAFTA alone ensures increased investments in Mexico.

The current size of pension and investment funds is around $2.7 trillion dollars. The managers of these funds are looking worldwide for attractive returns, diversification, and good values, areas where emerging capital markets are especially suited.

EVALUATION

On the whole, emerging markets are not very liquid in the sense that major blocks of stocks can be sold and bought without major price movements. But it should also be remembered that there are only about 100 stocks in the United States which are generally considered very liquid. In the week of Black Monday, institutional investors found it quite difficult to trade many of the smaller NASDAQ stocks.

Disclosure in most emerging markets is not comparable to practices in the U.S. but is often surprisingly good if compared with that of many companies listed in Europe and Japan. A sizeable number of companies quoted in the major emerging markets are audited by the "big eight" accounting firms.

Information on most emerging markets is becoming increasingly available. The IFC has a database which covers the top 18 markets in detail. It supplies aggregates, price indices and other relevant data for investors. Daily price quotations are now available on Reuters screens in more than 15 of the major emerging markets. Most of the major stock markets in developing countries can provide a wealth of market statistics and even company data. Many brokerage firms are now publishing regular reports on various Pacific markets and companies, while many private corporations provide a regular flow of economic, market and company data to its clients to keep them up-to-date.

Many, but not all, of the major emerging markets have securities legislation patterned after the U.S. securities laws, or, in a few cases, British laws. However, enforcement of investor protection and sanctions against insider protection are sometimes lax.

Although there are indeed investment restrictions in most developing countries, the trend is clearly toward gradual liberalization and internationalization of the markets. Among the top markets, Malaysia, Chile, Thailand, and the Philippines are already open. Brazil, India, Taiwan, Korea, and Mexico are now accessible through a variety of funds. In Mexico, a limited number of individual shares can be purchased. The most specific program of liberalization is in place in Korea. Among other countries there are signs that some may be opening up to international investors as well.

As for taxes, in most of these countries, withholding taxes are close to the international average or are likely to be brought in line very soon, although in Chile and Malaysia a heavy withholding tax on dividends has replaced a corporate income tax. It is clear that further improvement and liberalization are needed, but investment restrictions are no longer a serious reason for not being involved in emerging markets.

CONCLUSION

It is apparent that both domestic policy markets and international investors are viewing the financial markets in developing countries in a different and more attractive light. The combination of the new awareness of the importance of these markets with their demonstrable success in certain countries makes it certain that their role will expand rapidly in the coming years. There are some relatively sizeable emerging capital markets that offer attractive returns, excellent diversification alternatives, and good values, but also certain risks, including higher volatility.

As for the future, these emerging markets will gradually integrate with the euro-equity or, more broadly, the major international financial markets. Such an integration is inevitable in the long run, if countries, and, in particular, the major corporations in developing countries are to remain internationally competitive. Many of the companies in developing countries are increasingly forced to export and withstand competition as domestic protection erodes. As the real economy becomes more open, the financial world can no longer stay behind. In a more competitive world, a strong balance sheet and the ability to raise capital in a flexible and cost-efficient manner is becoming a crucial factor in being or not being internationally competitive, successful and viable.

Moreover, many of the top countries in emerging markets have outgrown their domestic markets. They cannot raise sufficient capital in their domestic markets, at least at competitive prices. Thus, whether they like it or not or whether their governments have hesitations or not, in the long run they will be forced by competitive pressures to go international.

From an analysis of the top companies in emerging markets, it is apparent that many are viable candidates for the euro-equity markets and would be among the selected list of first tier issuers. It must, in fact, be in their interest to enter this market earlier than later, to acquire some name recognition and establish their international reputation, especially if they are active international exporters.

A small number of emerging stocks are already listed on the major international stock exchanges. Several Korean companies have brought their first convertible debentures to the market. This will be the first step toward more frequent issues by the top corporations in the developing world of their convertible debentures, stocks and other financial instruments to international investors.

Gradually, the major pension funds, insurance companies, and investment funds will get used to the idea and will see the benefit of having a small number of the major corporations of the developing world among their stock holdings. This, in turn, will increase the demand for international trading and these companies will gradually become integrated into the international market place, as international investors develop a knowledge of emerging markets and major companies in these markets. More generally, it is unlikely the emerging capital markets will lead a separate existence. Just as the major markets of Europe and Japan are becoming integrated into the euro-equity market, the same development will take place for the emerging markets, although at a slower pace. Ultimately, local markets will establish electronic links with the euro-equity markets so that the major stocks will be traded as actively in the world markets as they are domestically.

Three trends will emerge in investment by institutional investors in the emerging capital markets. First, an increasing number of countries will bring forward country funds in an effort to make international investors more familiar with their market. This is a beginning step in the internationalization process. Second, major international investors will increasingly establish contact with local brokers and invest directly in a variety of the major stocks in these markets. Third, the top emerging country firms will gradually begin to involve themselves with international issues and list their shares on the world market as domestic and international markets become more integrated.

Emerging capital markets will be subject to increasing attention by investors, especially large institutional investors, in the future. Major developments over the coming decade will make these markets more attractive as they expand further, modernize, internationalize, and increasingly integrate into the world financial systems.

REFERENCES/SOURCES

Sudweeks, Bryan L. *Equity Market Development in Developing Countries.* New York: Praeger, 1988.

Antoine W. van Agtmael
President, Emerging Markets
Investors Corporation

Bryan L. Sudweeks
Director, Emerging Markets
Investors Corporation

The Foreign Exchange Market

OVERVIEW

The foreign exchange market refers to the organizational setting within which market participants buy and sell foreign currencies and other debt instruments. Unlike stock or commodity exchanges, the foreign exchange is not an organized structure. It has no centralized meeting place and no formal requirement for participation. Nor is the foreign exchange market limited to any country. The foreign exchange market for any currency is located in all major world capitals, including London, Zurich, Paris, Hong Kong, Singapore, and Tokyo.

The principal function of foreign exchange markets is the transfer of funds from one nation to another. This is usually accomplished by a telegraphic transfer from a domestic bank to a correspondent bank operating in a monetary center abroad. Through the wire, domestic banks can instruct their foreign correspondents to pay specified sums of foreign exchange to a person, firm, or account.

The most active participants in the foreign exchange market are 1) commercial banks, 2) multinational corporations, and 3) central banks. Individuals do not participate in the foreign exchange market because the transactions in this market are usually of a wholesale nature.

Commercial banks participate in the foreign exchange market as intermediaries for their corporate customers. The intermediation process usually leaves the commercial banks with a net position on each of the currencies traded. If the net position is different from the desired or ideal, then the banks deal on

The Foreign Exchange Market

their own to adjust their stock holdings of foreign exchange.

The involvement of business in foreign exchange markets originates from two primary sources: 1) international trade, which involves the payment or receipt of currency other than the one used in the home country of the corporation, and 2) direct investment, which involves not only the acquisition of assets (such as a plant) in a foreign country but also the generation of liability (such as foreign private debt) in terms of foreign currency.

Central banks are responsible for maintaining a stable value of the domestic currency vis-a-vis the foreign currencies. To perform this task, which is especially important under a system of fixed exchange rates, the central banks intervene in the foreign exchange market when the domestic currency is either in excess demand or excess supply.

EXAMPLES

International transactions either require the exchange of goods and services for foreign exchange or the exchange of one currency for another. If a Japanese firm imports wine from a French company, the invoice (bill) may be denominated in French francs or in Japanese yen. If the French company prefers receiving French francs, the Japanese company must exchange its Japanese yen for French francs to make the payment.

BENEFITS

Firms can profit from their participation in the foreign exchange market in two ways: 1) by arbitraging, and 2) by hedging. Exchange arbitrage is the simultaneous purchase and sale of a currency in different exchange markets to profit from exchange-rate differential in the two locations. For instance, if the

Swiss franc in terms of Canadian dollars is cheaper in Toronto than in Zurich, then foreign exchange traders would find it advantageous to purchase Swiss francs in Toronto for immediate resale in Zurich since a profit will be made.

Institutions that expect to make or receive payments in terms of a foreign currency at a future date are exposed to fluctuations in the exchange rate which could force them to make a greater than expected payment (in terms of the domestic currency), or receive less than expected (in terms of the local currency). To avoid, cover, or hedge for the exchange rate uncertainty, the firms can use any one of the following segments of the foreign exchange market: spot or money market, forward, futures, and options.

IMPLEMENTATION

If a German importer has a 90-day payable in terms of Japanese yen, he could hedge: 1) by immediately purchasing the present value of its payable in yen in the spot market and investing it in a Japanese bank (money-market hedge); 2) by pre-purchasing yen at today's forward rate. This transaction can be made for the exact day the yen are needed to meet the payment obligation without an immediate outlay of the importer's fund (forward hedge); 3) by pre-purchasing yen at today's futures rate, which can be made with a small outlay of the importer's funds (the margin requirement). Unlike forward transactions, the futures transactions cannot be tailored to the needs of the importer because futures transactions are standardized in terms of maturity and size; 4) by purchasing a yen "call option" which grants the importer the right to purchase yen at a specific price (the exercise or strike price) within a specific period of time.

EVALUATION

Forward contracts are better suited for participants who have specialized hedging needs given that 1) they can be tailored to meet the needs of individual corporations in terms of contract size and dates for delivery; 2) they do not require a security deposit (although some compensation balances or lines of credit may be required), and 3) the transaction costs are very low (transaction costs are usually restricted to the spread between bid and ask prices).

Futures and options markets are better designed to handle the needs of both speculators (individuals or institutions who are attempting to profit from their alleged superior knowledge of the foreign exchange market), and hedgers with open positions since the futures and options contracts allow a fast and low cost liquidation of open positions, mostly by offset.

APPLICATIONS TO SMALL BUSINESS

Forward contracts are set up by banks to accommodate the needs of large corporations and they are often valued at US $1 million or more. For this reason, forward contracts are not normally recommended for small businesses.

Both currency futures and currency option contracts appeal to small firms because of their standardized form and the relatively small purchase price of each type of contract. However, small businesses should restrict the use of both types of contracts to hedging. Speculative purposes should be discouraged given that even the experienced traders have difficulties in achieving consistent profits by taking speculative positions.

CONCLUSION

Corporations can use forward, futures, and options contracts to reduce their exposure to exchange rate movements and to lock in the price at which the firm can buy or sell specific currency in the future. These contracts are especially useful to aid in situations whereby a firm might receive in the future a foreign currency that is weakening over time, or need to purchase in the future a currency that is strengthening over time.

SOFTWARE/DATABASES

Compuserve Information Service, 5000 Arlington Centre Blvd., Columbus, OH 43220.

Dow Jones News/Retrival, P.O. Box 300, Princeton, NJ 08540.

Euromoney On Line, Nestor House, Playhouse Yard, London EC4V5EX.

MarkeTrader, BearClaw Software Systems, 16044 Napa St., Sepulveda, CA 91343. (818) 894-8790. Real time quote processor, provides bar charts, time and sales, stop alerts.

Portfolio Manager, Analytical Investment Management Inc., Bay 214, Union Wharf, Boston, MA 02109 (617) 523-0620. Uses probability theory and expectations to determine future values for securities and currencies.

Reuter News Service, 455 South Figueroa, Los Angeles, CA 90017.

Telerate, One World Trade Center, New York, NY 10048. This is an extensive data base of information on foreign securities, interest rates, and foreign currencies.

REFERENCES/SOURCES

Chrystal, K. A. "A Guide to Foreign Exchange Markets." *Federal Reserve Bank of St. Louis* Review. (March 1984). Provides an overview of the foreign exchange market for non-experts.

Folks, W. R. and R. Aggarwal. *International Dimensions of Financial Management.* Boston: PWS-Kent Publishing, 1988. Chapters 2, 3, and 5 provide a good description of the foreign exchange markets, hedging techniques, and international investment strategies.

Ketell, B. *A Businessman's Guide to the Foreign Exchange Market.* Lexington, MA: Lexington Books, 1985. Provides excellent coverage of the foreign exchange market and available investment techniques.

Kubarych, R. M. "Foreign Exchange Markets in the United States." Rev. ed. New York: Federal Reserve Bank of New York, 1983. Provides an excellent introduction to trading practices in the United States.

Madura, J. *International Financial Management.* St. Paul: West Publishing Co., 1986: 39-103. Chapters 3 and 4 of this widely used textbook provide a clear and comprehensive presentation of the most popular hedging and speculation techniques. Explanations of techniques are always supported with numerical examples.

Nix, E, and S. Nix. *The Dow Jones International Securities, Futures, and Options Markets* Homewood, IL: Dow Jones-Irwin, 1988. Provides a comprehensive coverage of foreign market investment strategies, market instruments, foreign exchange market practices in the most important foreign exchange centers of the world, and an explanation of how the international market functions worldwide.

Rhiel, H. and R. Rodriquez. *Foreign Exchange and Money Markets*. New York: McGraw-Hill, 1983: 3-80. Provides general information about the foreign exchange market and specific hedging techniques. It was written primarily for bank executives, traders, and treasurers of multinational corporations.

Tygier, C. *Basic Handbook of Foreign Exchange*. London: Euromoney Publications, 1983. Provides a description of bank dealing practices and an evaluation of the bank's foreign exchange positions.

Walmsley, J. *The Foreign Exchange Handbook*. New York: John Wiley, 1983. Provides a comprehensive treatment of all aspects of foreign exchange market practices.

Dr. Francisco Carrado-Bravo
Department of World Business
American Graduate School
of International Management

Foreign Exchange Rates and Forecasting

OVERVIEW

Foreign exchange is a key component of global business since cross-country commercial and financial transactions usually involve an exchange of currencies. The volume of transactions is continually increasing as financial markets around the world are becoming integrated. In order to deal effectively in global foreign exchange markets, corporate managers need to understand the meaning of special terms such as direct/indirect quotes, cross rates, spot/forward rates, forward premium/discount, outright/swap quotations, and depreciation/appreciation.

Besides understanding the market mechanisms, managers of multinational corporations also need exchange rate forecasts in making various business decisions. Such forecasts may be prepared in-house or obtained through subscription to commercial forecasting agencies. Different forecasting methods are employed by commercial agencies and can be grouped under three major categories: Fundamental Forecasting, Judgmental Forecasting and Technical Forecasting. The performance of exchange rate forecasts may be evaluated in various ways, depending on what forecast is used. Two common criteria of evaluation are "accuracy" and "correctness."

EXAMPLES

Most major banks around the world have their own foreign exchange trading rooms. The majority of foreign exchange transactions are conducted among these trading rooms via telecommunication systems. Banks deal both in the interbank or wholesale market (with other banks) and the retail market (with non-bank customers). As an example of a typical retail transaction, assume that a U.S. importing company needs to pay its Swiss supplier 1 million Swiss francs. The U.S. company calls the foreign exchange trading desk at Citibank in New York for a quotation on Swiss francs. The bank quotes the rate at Sf1.5030/$. If the importer agrees to deal at this rate, it pays the bank $665,336 (1,000,000/1.5030) and requests the bank to send the Swiss francs to the Swiss supplier. Citibank then instructs its subsidiary or correspondent bank in Switzerland to transfer Sf1 million to the bank account of the Swiss supplier.

Managers of multinational corporations require exchange rate forecasts to aid their decision making. Some prepare the forecasts in-house while most others subscribe to foreign exchange forecasting agencies. For example, Dixon, a UK retailing group, prefers in-house work to prepare short-term exchange rate forecasts. The forecasts are needed for currency exposure management since the company buys between #300 million to #350 million worth of electrical goods in yen and dollars for resale in sterling each year. The Director of the Treasury Department says, ". . . I have found it efficient to have a few programmes on some relatively sophisticated software to give me my currency outlook." An alternative example of commercial foreign exchange forecasting agency is Capital Techniques. Capital Techniques uses technical forecasting to project exchange rates for the Deutschemark, British pound sterling, Japanese yen, Canadian and Australian dollars. The agency also provides medium-term projections by using technical models which embody the Elliot Wave theory and bar charting patterns. Intraday technical commentaries are also available to interbank traders. Communication is via the Reuters and Telerate screen services. In 1988, the company, headquartered in New York, was charging $350 pm (per month) for the currency package, $350 pm for cross-rates and

$200 pm for the intraday service. It also has an independent sister company in London which provides a consultancy service in foreign exchange markets at a fee of £12,000 per annum.

BENEFITS

Over the years, the global foreign exchange market has developed its own system of terminology and conventions for foreign exchange quotations. Costly mistakes may be made if managers are not familiar with these terms and conventions. Conversely, managers who are familiar with the market mechanisms can utilize instruments available in the market to their advantage. For instance, in order to reduce exchange rate risk, they may use forward contracts to cover foreign currency receivables or payables. Occasionally, currency arbitrage opportunities may occur where riskless profits can be made by exploiting market disequilibrium.

Besides understanding the foreign exchange market mechanisms, managers of multinational corporations also need foreign exchange forecasts in making various business decisions—hedging future receivables or payables, short-term financing and investment decisions, formulating annual budgets, and establishing long-term strategic plans.

MNC managers often need to decide whether to hedge future payables and receivables denominated in foreign currencies. The foreign exchange forward market may be used if hedging is needed. To hedge or not depends on the comparison between the forecasted exchange rate and the forward rate as well as the risk-attitude of the manager. For example, if a US-based MNC is due to make a payment of DM 1 million in 30 days and the one-month forecasted value of DM is significantly lower than that of the forward rate, the MNC may decide not to hedge. If the forecast is accurate, the company will pay a smaller amount of dollars for the same DM 1 million than if a forward contract was used.

Foreign exchange forecasts are also required when managers of MNCs make decisions regarding which currency to borrow or invest in. The manager should not focus attention only on the nominal interest rates. The effective costs of capital or returns on investment depend also on the exchange rate changes between the foreign currency and the home currency. Exchange rate forecasts may be used as an estimate of the exchange rate changes to calculate the effective costs or returns in different currencies before a final decision is made.

In formulating annual operating budgets for overseas subsidiaries, MNCs also require exchange rate forecasts. Such budgets include monthly projections of foreign subsidiary income and expenses, assets and liabilities, profit or loss, and other financial and operating factors. Though the performance of a foreign subsidiary is usually evaluated in terms of local currency, monitoring of actual performance versus budgeted performance in home currency terms is an important component of effective management control.

Exchange rate forecasts are also needed for establishing long-term strategic plans. These international strategic plans usually adopt a five-year horizon and are updated annually. As part of the annual strategic plan review, MNCs evaluate existing overseas subsidiaries in light of the projected foreign exchange outlook. For example, if a subsidiary has a net asset foreign exchange exposure and continuing losses due to the depreciation of local currency expected, the company may adjust the subsidiary's pricing policy, product mix, asset and liability structure, capital structure, or may even decide to withdraw from the country. Similarly, when a company wants to open a new subsidiary overseas, it should examine whether the new operation is financially sound by going through a capital budgeting process. Forecasts of future cash flows are converted into home currency terms and thus exchange rate forecasts are needed.

IMPLEMENTATION

When a foreign exchange rate is quoted, the quotes may be direct or indirect. A *direct quote* is the number of units of home currency required to pay for one unit of foreign currency. Conversely, an *indirect quote* is the number of units of foreign currency required to pay for a unit of home currency. For example, the quotation of Sf 1.5030/$ is an indirect quote in the United States since it is expressed in terms of number of units of foreign currency (Swiss franc) per unit of home currency (U.S. dollar). To obtain the direct quote, simply take the reciprocal of the indirect quote: 1V Sf 1.5030/$ =$.6653/Sf. It should be noted that direct and indirect quotes are country-specific. In Switzerland, the same quote of Sf 1.5030/$ is direct since the Swiss franc is now the home currency.

In order to facilitate interbank trading between U.S. banks and banks in other countries, a convention was adopted in 1978 such that most currencies are quoted indirect in the U.S. and direct in most other countries. In this way, foreign exchange dealers are spared the trouble of taking reciprocals of foreign exchange quotes when they deal with foreign banks. Since the majority of currency transactions in the global foreign exchange market is between the U.S. dollar and other currencies, it is sensible for the U.S. to quote in one direction and the other countries in the opposite direction. However, exceptions to this convention are made for the U.K. pound sterling, Australian dollar, New Zealand dollar and Irish punt. In these latter cases, direct quotes are used by U.S. banks. For many centuries, the pound sterling was the key international currency and sterling was quoted in foreign currency price per pound. This practice remains unchanged today when the dollar is quoted against the pound. The other three currencies are also quoted direct in the U.S. because of their close historical ties with Great Britain.

When a bank asks another bank for a foreign exchange quotation, the other bank usually returns with a pair of quotes representing the bid and offer rates.

Normally, the quotes are given without currency signs which should be implicit from the context. For instance, Chase Manhattan may call Credit Suisse in Switzerland for a quote on the Swiss franc. In return, a quotation of 1.5030-40 is given on the video screen or spoken as "1.5030 to 40" or "1.5030 (pause) 40" on the phone. Though there are no currency signs, it should be obvious from the convention mentioned above that the rates are quoted in terms of number of units of Swiss francs per dollar. The first figure represents the bid rate. It indicates that Credit Suisse is willing to sell 1.5030 Swiss francs for one U.S. dollar. Alternatively, the full offer rate is obtained by substituting the last two digits of the bid rate (in this case, 30) with the digits of the offer rate (40). With this offer rate, Credit Suisse indicates that it is willing to sell a dollar for 1.5040 Swiss francs. The average of the bid and offer rates, 1.5035, is called the middle rate. The difference between the two rates, Sf.0010/$, is known as the *spread*. The profit earned by a bank is equal to the spread multiplied by the amount of currency transacted. Such profit is compensation to the bank for maintaining an active foreign exchange market and allowing the other side of the transaction to choose whether to buy or sell that foreign currency.

Since most currencies around the world are actively traded against the US dollar, it is easy to find exchange rate quotations between foreign currencies and the dollar. However, quotations may be difficult to find between currencies which are not frequently traded against each other. Under these circumstances, the exchange rate can still be obtained indirectly through a third currency that is commonly traded with both currencies. Exchange rates obtained indirectly in this manner are called *cross rates*. For instance, an exporter in Hong Kong who wants to export to Greece may find it difficult to obtain the foreign exchange rate between the Hong Kong dollar and Greek Drachma. Nevertheless, the exporter knows that both currencies are frequently traded and quoted against the US dollar. On that day, the quotations are HK$ 7.8090/$ and Dr 144.70/$. To get the exchange rate between the HK$ and Drachma, one simply divides the first rate by the second rate:

$$\frac{HK\$\ 7.8090/\$}{Dr\ 144.70/\$} = HK\$.05397/Dr$$

Sometimes, cross rates are computed to check for arbitrage opportunities even when exchange rates are directly available between the two currencies. Suppose that the Hong Kong currency market actually provides a quotation between the HK dollar and Drachma and the rate is HK$.05417/Dr. Checking the cross rate via the US dollar, the exchange rate is HK$.05397/Dr. An arbitrageur can make money by using one million Hong Kong dollars to purchase US$128,057 (1,000,000/7.8090). He then uses the U.S. dollars to buy 18,529,901 Drachmas ($128,057 multiplied by Dr144.7/$), and then the Drachmas to buy back 1,003,765 Hong Kong dollars (Dr18,529,901 multiplied by HK$.05417/Dr). By following this circuitous path, an arbitrage profit can be made and HK$3,765 is earned for each million Hong Kong dollar transacted. Even after deducting transaction costs, a net profit may still exist. Although opportunities like this occur, they will be quickly exploited by astute arbitrageurs and the discrepancy between the direct currency price and the cross rate will be corrected within a matter of minutes if not seconds.

When a foreign exchange contract is made, the actual delivery of the currency may take place at different times. The date on which the foreign currency is delivered is called the *value date*. In this respect, foreign exchange rates are differentiated into spot and forward rates. The *spot rate* is the price at which foreign currency can be bought or sold with delivery and payment completed on the second following business day. (However, one-day settlement is normal between the U.S. and Canadian dollar.) For example, a spot transaction entered on Friday between banks in Paris and New York will not be settled until the following Tuesday. If faster delivery is needed, banks can make special arrangements so that delivery can be made on the next business day (value tomorrow) or even on the same day (value today).

Alternatively, the *forward rate* is the price of foreign currency quoted today for delivery at a fixed future date. This is the rate specified on a foreign exchange forward contract, which is often used by companies to cover future payables or receivables denominated in a foreign currency. Banks routinely quote prices for forward contract maturities of one, two, three, six, and twelve months. Prices for intermediate, or broken, dates are also available but the rates are adjusted slightly since banks cannot easily adjust these odd-date forward positions with transactions in the interbank market. In recent years, long-term forward contracts have emerged which allow customers to cover forward payments of longer maturities. In some cases, the date of maturity may be as far out as ten years.

In the interbank market, abbreviations are often used in quoting forward rates. Dealers frequently express forward rates in terms of "points" (or sometimes known as "*swap rates*") which represent the differential between the forward rate and the spot rate. A "*point*" refers to one unit of the last digit of a quotation. Convention dictates how many decimal points to be used in a quotation. For instance, the Deutschemark and French franc are quoted with four decimal points against the dollar. On the other hand, Japanese yen is quoted with two decimal points. To obtain the full quotation of forward rates, the points are either added to or subtracted from their corresponding spot rates. When the bid in points is smaller than the offer, the points should be added to the spot rates. Conversely, when the bid in points is larger than the offer, the points should be subtracted. The following table expresses the forward rates of the Swiss franc as both swap rates and outright rates:

Table 1: Forward Rates of Swiss Franc Expressed as Swap and Outright Rates

	Swap Rates Bid-Offer	Outright Rates Bid-Offer
30-Day Forward	62-58	1.4968 1.4982
90-Day Forward	174-168	1.4856 1.4872
180-Day Forward	341-333	1.4689 1.4707

Spot Rates: 1.5030-40

The 30-day forward swap rates are 62 and 58. Since the bid in points is larger than the offer, the bid rate 62 should be subtracted from the spot bid rate 1.5030 to get the full quotation of 1.4968. To get the 30-day offer rate, 58 is subtracted from the spot offer rate 1.5040 to get 1.4982. These full quotations are called *outright rates* or outright quotations as contrasted with the abbreviated swap rates or point quotations.

The forward rate quoted in the market is usually different from the spot rate; it may be higher or lower than the spot rate. For example, suppose that the spot rate for Swiss francs is Sf1.5035/$ (the middle rate between the bid and offer rates of the example above) while the 30-day forward rate is Sf1.4975/$. The forward Swiss franc is more expensive since the exchange of one US dollar would result in .0062 less Swiss francs in the forward market than in the spot market. In this case, the forward Swiss franc is said to be selling at a *premium*. Alternatively, since the forward dollar is less expensive from the Swiss franc perspective, the dollar is said to be selling at a *discount*.

Forward rates are sometimes quoted in terms of percentage premium or discount per annum. To get the percentages, simply apply the following formula:

% Forward Premium or Discount (Per Anum)

$$= \frac{Forward\ Rate - Spot\ Rate}{Spot\ Rate} \times \frac{12}{No.\ of\ Months\ Forward} \times 100\%$$

In using this formula, one needs to differentiate between the two currencies involved: the target currency and the reference currency. The target currency is the currency one is asking about. The reference currency is the opposite currency which is used as the reference in measuring the value of the target currency. Before applying the formula, the quotations should be expressed in terms of the direct exchange rate of the reference currency (i.e., number of units of reference currency per unit of target currency). For instance, if we are asking for the percentage of premium or discount on the 30-day forward Swiss franc, the target currency is the Swiss franc and the US dollar is the reference currency. The above quotations need to be reversed and expressed in terms of $/Sf before applying the formula:

$$\frac{\frac{1}{Sf\ 1.4975/\$} - \frac{1}{Sf\ 1.5035/\$}}{\frac{1}{Sf\ 1.5035/\$}} \times \frac{12}{1} \times 100\% = +4.81\%$$

The result shows that the 30-day forward Swiss franc is selling at a premium of 4.81% per annum. Conversely, if the question is how much the percentage of premium or discount on the 30-day forward US dollar is, the target currency

505

Foreign Exchange Rates and Forecasting

is the US dollar and the Swiss franc is the reference currency. The quotations used should be in terms of Sf/$:

$$\frac{Sf\ 1.4975/\$ - Sf\ 1.5035/\$}{Sf\ 1.5035/\$} \times \frac{12}{1} \times 100\% = -4.79\%$$

The negative number shows that the 30-day forward dollar is selling at a discount of 4.79% per annum. It is obvious that when one currency is selling at a forward premium, the opposite currency is selling at a discount and vice versa. Furthermore, the percentage of premium is usually different from the percentage of discount.

In the foreign exchange area, it is also common to discuss the change in value of a foreign currency. The term appreciation or revaluation represents an increase in value of a currency with respect to a reference currency while depreciation or devaluation represents a decrease in value. Appreciation and depreciation are terms used under a floating exchange rate system while revaluation and devaluation are used for a fixed rate system. The formula for calculating the change in the exchange rate is as follows:

$$\%\ of\ Appreciation = \frac{New\ Rate - Old\ Rate}{Old\ Rate} \times 100\%$$

The formula is similar to the one for calculating the forward premium or discount. The differences are that the forward rate is replaced by the new rate while the spot rate is replaced by the old rate. Furthermore, the percentage change is normally not annualized. Again, when the formula is applied, the quotations should be expressed in terms of the direct exchange rate of the reference currency. For instance, assume that the exchange rate between the

Foreign Exchange Rates and Forecasting

Mexican peso and the US dollar was Ps2000/$ a year ago and it has now dropped to Ps2500/$. The question is how much the peso has devalued. Since the target currency is the peso and the US dollar is the reference currency, the exchange rates need to be expressed in terms of $/Ps before using the formula:

$$\frac{\frac{1}{Ps\ 2500/\$} - \frac{1}{Ps\ 2000/\$}}{\frac{1}{Ps\ 2000/\$}} \times 100\% = -20\%$$

The negative figure indicates that the peso has devalued 20% against the US dollar. The next question is how much the US dollar has appreciated against the peso. Applying the formula with the appropriate quotations:

$$\frac{Ps\ 2500/\$ - Ps\ 2000/\$}{Ps\ 2000/\$} \times 100\% = +25\%$$

The result indicates that the dollar has appreciated 25% against the peso. In fact, if one knows the percentage of appreciation of one currency without knowing the exact new or old exchange rates, it is still possible to calculate the percentage of depreciation of the opposite currency by using the following formula:

$$y = \frac{-x}{1 + x}$$

where x stands for the amount of appreciation of one currency expressed in decimal terms and y is the amount of appreciation of the opposite currency. Using the same example above, if we know that the peso has devalued 20% against the dollar, x is equal to -.20. Applying the formula to solve for y, the dollar is found to have appreciated by 25% against the peso.

$$y = \frac{-(-.20)}{1 + (.20)} = +.25 = +.25\%$$

In fact, with some modifications, the same formula can be used to find the percentage of forward premium of one currency when the percentage of forward discount is known for the opposite currency. Since the forward premium percentage is in per annum terms, it needs to be de-annualized first (divided by 12/n, where n is the number of months forward) before applying the formula to solve for y. When y is obtained, the figure needs to be re-annualized (multiplied by 12/n) to obtain the percentage in per annum terms. Using the earlier example, it was stated that the 30-day forward Swiss franc was selling at a premium of 4.81% or .0481 per annum. This figure is de-annualized by dividing it by 12/1 to get x=.004008. Applying the formula, y becomes -.00399. This number is re-annualized by multiplying it by 12/1 which results in -.0479 or -4.79% per annum.

When a corporate treasurer needs to buy or sell foreign exchange, it is advisable to call several banks for rates before deciding on which bank to deal with. It is true that rates offered by different banks tend to be close to each other due to competition. On occasion, however, the rates of a bank may deviate from the norm if the bank wants to alter its position in a foreign currency by adjusting the rates to encourage (or discourage) buying or selling of that currency.

As in other financial markets, there are arbitrageurs who check exchange rates from different sources to search for riskless profit-making opportunities.

There are three common types of currency arbitrages—locational arbitrage, triangular arbitrage and covered interest arbitrage. When two banks offer different rates on the same currency and it is profitable enough for an arbitraguer to buy low from one bank and sell high to the other bank, this kind of profit is known as locational arbitrage. Triangular arbitrage refers to a profitable opportunity that arises when the cross rate of a currency differs from the rate that is quoted directly. Finally, covered interest arbitrage occurs when the interest rate differential between two countries does not agree with the forward premium or discount between their currencies.

In the preparation of currency forecasts, different methods are used by commercial forecasting agencies or corporate treasurers. While there may be a large variety of approaches, these methods can be classified into three major categories: fundamental forecasting, judgmental forecasting and technical forecasting.

Fundamental forecasting, sometimes known as the econometric method, predicts the exchange rate from other economic variables. A simple illustration of this approach is to use the difference in inflation rates between a foreign country and the home country to predict the percentage of appreciation or depreciation of that foreign currency. However, fundamental forecasters rarely rely on only one economic variable. Instead, sophisticated economic models consisting of from one to many equations are used. The model coefficients are estimated with historical data. Since the coefficients are based mainly on historical data, economic models are slow in capturing the effects of more recent shifts in the economic structure. Empirical evidence shows that fundamental forecasting is sometimes outperformed by technical forecasting in the prediction of short-term exchange rate movements. Nevertheless, fundamental forecasts provide some distinct advantages. Since the forecasts are based on the performance of the economy in general, when long-term strategic plans are decided, managers can relate the forecasted exchange rates to the economic system in which the subsidiaries operate.

Judgmental forecasting takes into account not only economic variables, but also behavioral variables which are hard to quantify (e.g., impact of political elections, changes in tax policy, over-selling or under-selling of currencies and so forth). The forecasters view these factors in light of past experiences and may canvass experts in the field before agreeing upon a certain forecasted rate. This method is better than fundamental forecasting in capturing the effects of recent environmental changes and is more appropriate for currencies that are closely managed by their governments. In some less developed countries where the currency rates are fixed, governments tend to procrastinate the devaluation of their currencies to maintain a good image even when economic indicators show that the local currencies are much over-valued. Judgmental forecasters take such governmental behavior into consideration and predict when and by how much the devaluation will be.

Instead of predicting exchange rates from other variables, *technical forecasting* observes the recent movements of the exchange rate itself to forecast the rate in the future. Different versions of the technical method are used in the forecasting industry. One of these versions is the use of filter trading rules. When the exchange rate rises above a certain percentage (a filter), the forecasting agency will recommend that the subscriber buy that foreign currency; when the rate falls below certain percentage, the agency will recommend selling that currency. Normally, commercial agencies will not disclose the details of their forecasting rules to clients. They are afraid that once the method is disclosed, the clients may apply the rules themselves rather than pay for the forecasters' advice. Empirical evidence indicates that technical forecasting is good at predicting short-run movements in exchange rates. However, technical forecasts are more often used by speculators than corporate treasurers. The forecasts are good usually for a brief period of time (one or two days) which may be too short for most corporate decisions. Furthermore, technical forecasting agencies usually provide buy or sell signals instead of precise exchange rate estimates to the subscribers. The buy-sell signals are not directly applicable to corporate decisions such as budgeting or long-term strategic plans.

The three forecasting methods mentioned above have different strengths and capture different information. To arrive at a better forecast and to reduce overall forecasting errors through diversification, researchers suggest the use of *composite forecasting* to combine these forecasts. The forecasts may be combined in various ways. One of the approaches is the confirmation method where the reliability of one forecast is cross-checked with another forecast. For instance, a buy/sell signal generated by one technical forecast is only acted upon if the signal is confirmed by another technical forecast or forecast derived from another method (such as fundamental or judgmental). Another way of blending forecasts is to assign weights to different forecasts which are then summed up as a composite estimate. The assigned weights may be arbitrarily chosen or estimated using multiple regression techniques. Recently, a more sophisticated composite technique has been suggested that combines forecasts across currencies, maturities and forecasting services. Instead of minimizing the variance of one composite forecast, the objective of this approach is to minimize errors of a portfolio of forecasts.

EVALUATION

Since exchange rate forecasts may be used for different purposes, it is impossible to find one single criterion of evaluation that applies to all circumstances. For corporate treasurers, two commonly used criteria are "accuracy" and "correctness."

The "accuracy" criterion measures the deviations between the forecasted rates and the rates that actually occur later. Included in this category are measures such as mean absolute errors, mean squared errors, mean percentage errors and mean squared percentage errors. This criterion is more appropriate for corporate planning. For example, a U.S.-based multinational corporation wants to estimate the amount of cash flows of its German subsidiary in US dollar terms. It requires a 6-month exchange rate forecast of the Deutschemark. Forecasting Agency A provides a forecast of DM1.9000/$ while the forecast of Agency B is DM2.0100/$. After 6 months, the actual rate turns out to be DM2.0000/$. Based on the "accuracy" criterion, Agency B outperformed Agency A since its forecast is closer to the actual rate.

Under some circumstances, however, the "accuracy" criterion may not be appropriate. For instance, the same U.S. MNC has a 6-month payable of DM1 million to an independent German supplier. The corporate treasurer needs to decide whether to hedge this future payable with a forward contract. The 6-month forward rate quoted by the bank is DM2.0050/$. According to Agency A, the Deutschemark after 6 months will be DM1.9000/$ and therefore more expensive than the forward rate; the company should hedge. Alternatively, Agency B recommends no hedging since the forecasted rate, DM2.0100/$, is lower than the forward rate. After 6 months, the actual rate turns out to be DM2.0000/$. Though Agency A is less accurate than Agency B, it makes the correct hedging recommendation since the market price of the Deutschemark is still higher than that of the forward contract. Under these circumstances, an alternative criterion—"correctness"—should be used to evaluate different forecasts. The "correctness" criterion examines how frequently a forecast correctly predicts the direction of change of the exchange rate relative to the forward rate; it is more appropriate for decisions regarding whether to hedge a currency exposure in the forward market.

Besides the "accuracy" and "correctness" criteria, there are additional measures for evaluation. Examples of these are "return of capital at risk", "greatest loss" and "return of currency portfolio." The choice of criterion depends very much on what that forecast is used for and it is difficult to derive a universal criterion. There have been empirical studies which measure the performance of commercial forecasting agencies. The findings are somewhat mixed. While it is true that forecasts of some agencies may lead to better results, their performance may not be consistent over years. A year of good performance does not necessarily imply good performance in the following year.

APPLICATIONS TO SMALL BUSINESS

Small firms may also need to deal with foreign currencies at times. Some of their inputs may be sourced from foreign suppliers. Part of their sales revenue may also be generated from foreign markets. When small companies want to buy or sell foreign currencies, they can contact the banks directly. It is important to know, however, that the quotations published in the media—newspapers, newsletters or electronic messages—are wholesale quotes which are for transactions of large sizes. For these wholesale transactions, the minimum amounts that would be traded in the United States would be pound sterling .5 million, Deutsche mark 2 million, French franc 6 million, Japanese yen 200 million or Italian lira 1500 million. If the amounts bought or sold by companies are smaller than these figures, they need to contact the retail customer foreign exchange desk instead of the wholesale dealer. The bid and offer rates quoted at the retail desk will have a larger spread in order to make the service profitable to the bank.

While the daily operations of multinational corporations are affected by exchange rate changes, small companies are not totally immune from the effects of currency rate changes. Exchange rate forecasts may also be useful to small firm management at times. However, small companies may consider the thousands of dollars needed to subscribe to commercial services too expensive. Furthermore, they may not have the knowledge or resources to establish their own forecasting systems. Under these circumstances, they may use market indicators such as forward exchange rates or spot exchange rates as forecasts of future exchange rates. These rates are readily available in daily newspapers.

CONCLUSION

As the role of currency exchange is increasingly important in global business, corporate managers need to be familiar with different conventions and quotations of foreign exchange rates in order to deal effectively in the market. In the United States, the indirect quotation of foreign currencies is the norm while direct quotation is used in most other countries around the world. To save time, exchange rates are sometimes given in abbreviated terms. It would be helpful to understand how the abbreviated 'point quotation' can be converted back to the full 'outright quotation'. Furthermore, forward contracts can be used by corporations to cover future receivables or payables in foreign currencies. Forward rates are often given in terms of swap rates or percentages of premium per annum. Several formulae were provided for computing forward premium percentages, converting premium percentage into discount, and calculating the appreciation or depreciation of a currency.

Alternatively, managers of multinational corporations need foreign exchange forecasts to make various business decisions. Many of them subscribe to commercial forecasting agencies for the forecasts. Nevertheless, there are mixed reviews about the performance of these commercial forecasts. While some managers think that they benefit substantially from the forecasts, others complain that the performance is not consistent and is not really worth the money. In recent years, an increasing number of large corporations have developed their own sophisticated forecasting systems. In order to survive in the changing environment, commercial forecasters have begun to offer new additional services—such as helping companies to actively manage their currency portfolios, offering short-term forecasts and providing forecasts of exotic currencies such as Korean won and Hong Kong dollar.

SOFTWARE/DATABASES

Foreign exchange rate quotations can be obtained from various sources. Newspapers such as the *Wall Street Journal* and *Financial Times* (London) publish exchange rates of major currencies from the previous business day. Some of the major banks also publish weekly reviews on spot and forward exchange rates together with brief commentaries on recent market trends. Examples of these are Harris Bank's "Weekly Review" and the "Foreign Exchange Review" by First Wachovia Bank. For more current data on prevailing exchange rates, bank dealers, brokers and corporate treasurers subscribe to the Reuters Market Report. Quotations are transmitted electronically to the monitors of subscribers who can read the most recent quotes of dozens of banks from the screen.

It should be noted, however, that the exchange quotes listed in the newspapers, newsletters or the electronic information services (Reuters Market Report and Telerate) are not rates of offer. They are only indicative rates reflecting the current market situation. To obtain a firm quote, one needs to contact the bank's foreign exchange trader directly.

If companies want to establish their own forecasting systems, they can make use of common software packages (such as SAS and SPSS) to formulate their own economic or time-series models. Past data of exchange rates and other economic variables are available from the *International Financial Statistics* from the International Monetary Fund.

If companies want to subscribe to commercial forecasting agencies, some basic information about these services can be found in the annual August issue of the *Euromoney* magazine. The magazine provides a list of forecasting agencies and briefly describes the forecasting methods, annual fees and addresses of these services.

REFERENCES/SOURCES

Bilson, J. F. O. "The 'Speculative Efficiency' Hypothesis." *Journal of Business*. July 1981: 435-451. Discusses the portfolio approach to composite forecasting.

———. "The Evaluation and Use of Foreign Exchange Forecasting Services." In Richard Herring, ed. *Managing Foreign Exchange Risk*. New York: Cambridge University Press, 1983: 149-179. Discusses the various criteria for evaluating exchange rate forecasts.

Dufey, Gunter and Rolf Mirus. "Forecasting Foreign Exchange Rates: A Pedagogical Note." *Columbia Journal of World Business* (Summer 1981): 53-61. Describes the major forecasting methods and contrasts the uses of the "accuracy" and "correctness" criteria in evaluating forecasts.

Ensor, Richard, ed. *The Management of Foreign Exchange Risk*. 2d ed. Euromoney Publications, 1982. Provides a good selection of articles on the various aspects of foreign exchange management.

Euromoney Inc. *Euromoney*. August (annually). Provides a list of commercial forecasts and a brief description of their methodologies, annual fees and correspondence addresses. There are also articles discussing recent trends in the forecasting industry.

Frenkel, Jacob and Harry Johnson, eds. *Economics of Exchange Rates*. Reading, MA: Addison Wesley, 1978. A collection of articles on foreign exchange rates by a group of well-known economists.

Goodman, Stephen. "Foreign Exchange Rate Forecasting Techniques:

Implications for Business and Policy." *Journal of Finance* (May 1979): 415-427. Evaluates the performance of several commercial forecasts using different criteria.

Kubarych, Roger. *Foreign Exchange Markets in the United States.* Rev. ed. New York: Federal Reserve Bank of New York, 1983. Provides a good introduction to foreign exchange trading practices in the United States.

Levich, Richard M. "Exchange Rate Forecasting Techniques." *International Financial Handbook.* Abraham George and Ian Giddy, eds. New York: John Wiley, 1983. Section 8.1. Provides a good survey of issues related to foreign exchange forecasting.

Tygier, Claude. *Basic Handbook of Foreign Exchange.* London: Euromoney Publications, 1983. Describes bank dealing practices and the evaluation of bank positions.

Walmsley, Julian. *The Foreign Exchange Handbook.* New York: John Wiley, 1983. Provides a comprehensive explanation on various aspects of foreign exchange trading.

Dr. Chuck C. Y. Kwok
School of International Business
University of South Carolina

Dr. Chuck C. Y. Kwok earned his doctorate in International Business at the University of Texas at Austin in 1984. His research and publications concentrate in international finance and Asian business studies.

Spot-market Speculators

OVERVIEW

The most familiar market in foreign exchange and the one with which international managers have the greatest concern is the spot foreign exchange market. The movement in the spot foreign exchange rate can dramatically change the home currency value of sales, costs, accounts receivable, or accounts payable, for example, when these items are denominated in foreign currency terms.

There are also markets for agreements involving future delivery of foreign exchange. The largest such market is comprised of a network of large financial institutions and is termed the market for *forward* exchange. This market is characterized by customized contracts, lack of a secondary market, and few if any overt speculators.

Another market, established in 1972, which involves the future delivery of foreign exchange but which encourages the participation of speculators is the *futures* foreign exchange market. In this market standardized contracts are used, there is an active secondary market, and procedures used for trading are similar to those used for commodity futures. For example, one currency futures contract traded on the International Monetary Market (IMM) of the Chicago Mercantile Exchange (The Merc) requires the buyer to take delivery of 12.5 million Japanese yen on a specified date for a number of U.S. dollars agreed upon in advance. Only the U.S. dollar per yen price of the transaction is negotiated by the market participants involved; all other terms are standard. Closing procedures allow positions to be covered by reverse transactions, and only a small percentage of contracts result in the actual delivery of foreign currency.

The establishment of futures markets results in publicly available financial market signals which, when properly interpreted, allow insights into speculators' beliefs (forecasts) regarding the likelihood of future economic events. For example, the current price of a foreign currency futures contract is a signal which when deciphered provides the expectation (forecast) of speculators' consensus assessment of the distribution of spot exchange rate movements for some period in the foreseeable future.

Specifically, suppose that in the U.S. dollar/yen futures market the setting of the futures price is dominated by risk. Professional speculators will be forced by competition to set the U.S. dollar/yen futures price relative to the spot at a percentage premium (or discount) approximately equal to their consensus expectation (forecast) of the yen's appreciation (or depreciation) against the U.S. dollar in the spot market. That is, when the percentage rate of the yen's premium (or discount) against the U.S. dollar is observed publicly, speculators' consensus expectation (forecast) of the yen's appreciation (or depreciation) is also being observed. In this sense the private mind of market speculators is being read.

EXAMPLES

There are seven currency futures contracts on the IMM of the Chicago Mercantile Exchange. Derived from the prices on these contracts and shown in Figure 1 are six examples of one month speculators' consensus expectations forecasts for the percentage rates of appreciation (or depreciation) for six exchange rates. There were no French franc contracts open for the month shown.

Figure 1

**Market's Consensus Expectation (Forecast)/
Actual Rate of Appreciation (Depreciation)
of the Major Currencies Against the U.S. Dollar**

For Month 10/17/88 to 11/14/88

	Forecast	Actual
Japanese Yen	4.11%	27.06%
W. German Mark	3.94%	35.14%
Canadian Dollar	(2.00%)	(31.28%)
British Pound	(2.05%)	34.63%
Swiss Franc	5.02%	39.70%
Australian Dollar	(5.73%)	47.44%

BENEFITS

The mind reading of market speculators' technique for currency futures markets can open up to view almost instantly the most recent thoughts and opinions of professional speculators, something that could not be accomplished using normal means of communication. Assuming that speculators act swiftly on their beliefs, the lag between market thought and the view of that thought is only constrained by the delay with which the view accesses information regarding foreign currency futures and spot prices. Newspapers, for example, provide an overnight lagged view, and telephone calls to brokers and market information accessed in real-time mode supplies an almost immediate view.

In addition to providing an almost immediate view of speculators' thinking, the mind reading approach furnishes a precise view of their thinking. That is, this approach unveils speculators' implied beliefs about the future movement of spot exchange rates for any specific number of days within a time horizon extending out to the maturity date of each foreign currency's newest contract.

The mind reading of market speculators approach is also inexpensive. It requires no market analysts, econometric models or databases, yet it provides the evaluated, precise thoughts and opinions of market speculators which can be used as guidance and direction by international managers when forming their own judgments about future exchange rate activity.

Finally, the technique is suited to formal evaluation. As is discussed in the next section, the beliefs of foreign currency futures speculators can be evaluated for bias and forecasting efficiency.

IMPLEMENTATION

The IMM quotes the currency futures prices for the Australian dollar, British pound, Canadian dollar, Deutsche mark, French franc, Japanese yen and Swiss franc. All currency futures prices are quoted directly, or in "American Terms," which is the U.S. dollar price of each foreign currency unit. The IMM futures price activity and spot exchange rates can be monitored daily in the business pages of most major newspapers. The following display of the Japanese yen is an example of the way these prices are shown in the *Wall Street Journal*. The yen is the foreign currency which will be used to demonstrate implementation and evaluation procedures.

Figure 2

Currency Trading
Monday, October 17, 1988

Futures

Japanese Yen (1mm) 12.5 Million Yen - $ per Yen

	Open	High	Low	Settle	Change	Lifetime Hi Low	Open Interest
Dec 88	.7902	.7931	.7900	.0015	.8530	.7115	45,802
Mar 89	.7968	.8002	.7968	.0017	.8590	.7439	1,656
Jun 89	...	...	...	.8082	.8400	.7500	800
Sep 89	.8140	.8150	.8155	.0019	.8150	.7690	155

Exchange Rates

	U.S. $ Equiv. Mon. Fri.	Currency/U.S. $ Mon. Fri.
Country.....		
Japan (Yen)...	.007870 .007895	127.05 126.65

Note that for convenience the currency futures market states the U.S. dollar price of yen as 100 times its actual size but the yen spot market does not. The convenient approach of the futures market is followed in this article.

To implement the technique of reading the collective mind of market speculators requires the derivation of an implied futures rate for the yen for 11-14-88 because settlement prices on 10-17-88 were set for December, March, June, and September contracts only; that is, for contracts due on 12-19-88, 3-18-89, 6-19-89, and 9-18-89 (the last day of trading for contracts is two business days before the third Wednesday of the delivery month).

An implied futures rate could be calculated for every point between 10-17-88 and 11-14-88 by fitting a polynomial equation to the spot and all the futures prices set on 10-17-88. This method is shown in the evaluation section of this article. Generally, however, there is only a slight difference in the value of an implied futures rate when calculated using the polynomial approach and when using a simple linear interpolation. Therefore, for demonstrating the implementation of market mind reading, the interpolated value is used.

For example, the interpolated value for the implied yen futures rate set on 10-17-88 for 11-14-88 is .7897. Therefore, the percentage premium at an annual rate of the yen against the U.S. dollar is 4.12% and the continuously compounded annual rate is 4.11%. These values can be interpreted to mean that the speculators' consensus expectation (forecast) of a yen appreciation over the month 10-17-88 to 11-14-88 was approximately 4.11% at a continuously compounded annual rate.

EVALUATION

Reading the collective mind of speculators in the foreign currency futures market is the faculty of perceiving a consensus expectation (forecast) of the future movement in spot foreign exchange rates. But the precise way in which this forecast is incorporated into the judgement of an international manager will depend upon the manager's perception of the effectiveness of the speculators' forecast.

To measure their forecasting effectiveness it is necessary to compare actual spot exchange rate results with those that are forecast. For example, the actual results for the speculators' forecasts were shown earlier. The forecasting skills of speculators, however, may or may not be called into question by the results in this single example. What is needed is a comprehensive evaluation where speculators' forecasts may be compared with actual results on the basis of at least two broad evaluation criteria: 1) forecast bias and 2) forecast efficiency.

Two common forms of forecast bias are the expected forecast error bias and serial forecast error bias. The expected forecast error should be zero if speculators have chosen a correct forecasting model. A comprehensive evaluation should examine forecast errors and if speculators have chosen a correct forecasting model, it is likely that the average forecast error will be near zero.

There are several statistics used to estimate the expected forecast error. One such statistic is calculated by simply taking the average of past errors. This approach treats past errors as a sample from an infinite population of possible errors and is referred to as the sample mean of errors. At any time this sample mean will undoubtedly differ from zero. There are two possible explanations: 1) the forecasts are unbiased and the deviation from zero is due to random variation; and 2) the forecasts are biased and the deviation is due to a combination of bias and random variation. To distinguish between these two cases, what is needed is a measure of the natural random variation in the sample mean of errors about its population mean. The standard error of the mean of errors provides this information.

For example, a sample mean of error .0117 and a standard error of .0062 were calculated for the thirty-seven months of speculators' U.S. dollar/yen rate of exchange forecasts starting in January 1986. At a 95% confidence level the hypothesis that the expected forecast error is zero cannot be rejected. Over this period, speculators seemed to be free of expected forecast error bias.

In the last section it was argued that a desirable evaluation characteristic for speculators' forecasts is that the expected value of their forecast error be zero. This condition suggests that speculators correctly use available information to formulate a consensus expectation of the future movement in spot exchange rates when setting the foreign currency futures rates (discount or premium). Part of the information available to speculators at the setting of the value of the futures rate is the time series of historical values of speculators' forecast errors. The condition that speculators' expected forecast error to be zero implies that there is no way to use the time series of past forecast errors as the basis for formulating a nonzero expected value of forecasting errors.

One consequence of this is that speculators' forecast errors should be serially independent; that is, that the autocorrelations of the forecasting errors are zero for all time lags. Again, using the U.S. dollar/yen case for thirty-seven months starting January, 1986, this proposition is tested in Figure 3:

AUTOCORRELATIONS
TWO STANDARD ERROR LIMITS •

LAG	AUTO. CORR.	STAND. ERR.
1	-0.138	0.156
2	0.008	0.153
3	0.017	0.151
4	-0.078	0.149
5	-0.078	0.147
6	-0.068	0.144
7	-0.037	0.142
8	0.117	0.139
9	-0.018	0.137
10	-0.046	0.134
11	-0.091	0.132
12	0.119	0.129
13	0.074	0.126
14	-0.175	0.123
15	0.212	0.121
16	-0.142	0.118
17	0.018	0.115
18	-0.137	0.112
19	-0.012	0.109
20	0.012	0.105
21	0.101	0.102
22	0.044	0.098
23	0.109	0.095
24	0.050	0.091
25	-0.056	0.087

Figure 3

As can be seen for twenty-five lags, there are no statistically significant autocorrelation coefficients. Clearly this forecast evaluation cannot reject the hypothesis that speculators' forecasting errors were serially independent. Speculators, therefore, were not subject to serial forecast error bias.

Even though speculators' forecasts of the future foreign currency rate of depreciation or appreciation may be right on target on the average and their forecast errors may show no sign of serial dependence, these forecasts can be off on many occasions. Therefore, an evaluation of the forecasting skill speculators have should include a measure of the variability of forecast errors. For example, if the variability of forecast errors is large or inefficient by professional speculators, an international manager may want to take this as a general indication of spot exchange rate forecasting difficulty and avoid the impacts of exchange rate volatility by hedging.

Referring once more to the thirty-seven month period starting in January 1986, the variance and standard deviation of speculators' forecast errors over the period were .0014 and .0369 respectively. These values are large relative to the forecasts for 10-17-88. Speculators' forecasts for the period examined show no bias but do show substantial variability in forecast errors.

APPLICATIONS TO SMALL BUSINESS

One of the constraints facing small businesses when entering the international business arena is the expense associated with acquiring the expertise of skilled specialists. The mind reading of market speculators technique can supply small businesses with the opinions of skilled forecasting specialists at a very low cost. In addition, the forecast evaluation procedures presented here are found in most standard statistics textbooks and are easily accessible by small businesses.

CONCLUSION

International managers constantly face the disturbing prospect of making international financial decisions in a climate of volatile exchange rates. For most international managers, part of the process of formulating this judgement includes the input of skilled forecasting specialists.

Foreign currency futures speculators represent one type of skilled forecasting specialist. Their forecasts, however, are not generally available through normal means of communication. It is possible, nevertheless, to access speculators' forecasting opinions by interpreting the financial signs which they leave in the market place and, therefore, inferentially read their collective mind.

Even though speculators are skilled forecasting specialists, forecasting spot exchange rates may be so inherently difficult that they may be subject to forecasting bias and unacceptably large forecast errors (from a manager's point of view). By applying comprehensive evaluation methods designed to detect flaws in forecasting opinions of speculators, the international manager can decide precisely how to use speculators' opinions.

SOFTWARE/DATABASES

Both mainframe and microcomputer software packages are available to implement the evaluation phase of the mind reading of market speculators technique. Three of the most popular statistical packages available for mainframe and microcomputers are: MINITAB, SAS, and SPSS.

REFERENCES/SOURCES

Francis, J. C. *Investments: Analysis and Management.* 4th ed. New York: McGraw Hill, 1986

Kolb, R. W. *Understanding Futures Markets*. Glenview, IL: Scott, Foresman, 1985.

Schway, E. W., J. M. Hill, and T. Scheeweis. *Financial Futures: Fundamentals, Strategies, and Applications*. Homewood, IL: Dow Jones-Irwin, 1986.

Seidel, A. D. and P. M. Ginsberg. *Commodities Trading*. Englewood Cliffs, NJ: Prentice-Hall, 1983.

Tossigian, A. M. *Foreign Exchange Futures*. Homewood, IL: Dow Jones-Irwin, 1981.

Dr. Dale Vor der Landwehr
Jack Keane
Arthur Morgan
Cesar Roberts
American Graduate School
of International Management

8.

International Tax

Taxation for U.S. Corporations Doing Business Abroad

OVERVIEW

When a U.S. corporation engages in international operations, new dimensions are added to the already difficult tax rules applicable to U.S. citizens described previously. Besides making the difficult decision of whether to operate in a foreign country as a branch or as a subsidiary, the U.S. corporation must confront special rules regarding limitations on its foreign tax credit. Also, the U.S. corporation must contend with restrictions which disregard its business dealings with related foreign entities when those dealings are not at arm's length. Finally, as in the case of individuals, bilateral tax treaties between the U.S. and the host jurisdiction where a U.S. corporation conducts business may modify any or all of these tax rules.

EXAMPLES

If the U.S. corporation elects to operate as a branch, foreign taxes are subject to the same rules and limitations as applicable to individuals. Where the U.S. corporation elects to create an offshore subsidiary, special rules govern the ability of the U.S. corporation to credit foreign taxes paid by the subsidiary. These rules provide that a U.S. corporation may credit not only foreign taxes paid directly by the U.S. taxpayer (e.g., foreign withholding taxes on dividends) but also those foreign taxes "deemed" paid indirectly by the U.S.

corporation (e.g., foreign income taxes paid by the foreign subsidiary).

In order to claim a credit for foreign taxes paid by its subsidiary, the U.S. corporation must own at least 10% of the foreign corporation's voting stock at the time the U.S. corporation receives a distribution from the foreign corporation. The foreign source income is grossed up in the same manner as for the individual except that the gross income includes all foreign taxes deemed paid by the U.S. corporation on its includable foreign income.

This rule also extends to foreign taxes paid by foreign corporations owned by the foreign subsidiaries of the U.S. parent corporation receiving the dividend. In such cases, the U.S. corporation must own at least 5% of the foreign corporation paying the foreign tax and each foreign corporation must own at least 10% of the voting stock of the next lower-tier corporation. The deemed paid foreign tax credit does not extend beyond the third tier.

As an example, X, a U.S. corporation, owns 40% of foreign corporation A (first tier). A owns 30% of foreign corporation B (second tier) and B owns 80% of foreign corporation C (third tier). The 10% test is met at all levels and X has an indirect ownership of at least 5% in each tier as determined below:

$$X \text{ owns } 40\% \times 30\% = 12\% \text{ indirectly of B}$$
$$X \text{ owns } 12\% \times 80\% = 9.6\% \text{ indirectly of C}$$

Thus, X may claim a portion of the foreign taxes incurred by A, B and C. If, however, B owned only 35% of C, X would not be entitled to credit any portion of C's foreign taxes because the 5% test would not be met, i.e. X would then own only 4% indirectly of C.

If A only owned 8% of B, the 10% test between A and B is not met, which breaks the chain of required ownership altogether.

If the foreign operation is a branch, rather than a subsidiary, total foreign source income and total foreign taxes for the year are included in the U.S. corporation's calculation of its foreign tax credit limitation regardless of how much income is received currently by the U.S. corporation. However, to prevent perceived abuses, the law provides for separate foreign tax credit "baskets" in which separate foreign tax credit limitations are established for different types of foreign source income.

IMPLEMENTATION

A U.S. corporation may establish one or more separately taxed entities in conducting its business overseas. When a company exports products from the United States, it may be possible to reduce U.S. tax on such sales by channeling them through a special corporation known as a "foreign sales corporation" (FSC).

Foreign Sales Corporation

Most industrial nations provide tax incentives to exporters. However, the General Agreement on Tariffs and Trade (GATT) places restrictions on the type of tax incentives the signatory nations may provide. Primarily, GATT members may not exempt exports from direct taxes. In order to remain "GATT-legal," the United States, unlike its major trading partners, has centered its export tax incentives upon special corporations, namely, the Domestic International Sales Corporation (DISC) and the Foreign Sales Corporation (FSC).

After 1984, the DISC could be used to defer tax on income attributable to no more than $10 million of "qualified export gross receipts." In addition, the shareholders are charged interest on their potential tax that would be assessed if the deferred DISC income were distributed at the end of the current year.

Requirements for a FSC

In lieu of structuring export sales through a DISC, a U.S. exporter will probably want to use an FSC, whereby a portion of the taxable income of the entity attributable to export sales is entirely exempt from U.S. income taxation. However, in order to qualify for the exemption, the FSC must:

1. Be created or organized under the laws of a U.S. possession (other than Puerto Rico) or a foreign country which has an exchange of information agreement with the United States.

2. Have no more than 25 shareholders.

3. Have no preferred stock.

4. Maintain permanent books of account at an office outside the United States and keep all records at a U.S. office.

5. Have at least one non-U.S. resident (who may be a U.S. citizen) on its board of directors.

6. Not be a member of a controlled group that includes a DISC.

7. Make a timely FSC election.

8. Adopt the taxable year used by the shareholder with the greatest percentage of voting stock.

In addition to meeting the above requirements the FSC must meet certain foreign management and foreign economic tests in order to exempt its income from income tax. The foreign management test is met if the FSC holds the following outside the United States:

1. Formal meetings of the directors and shareholders.

2. The principal bank account which is used to pay all dividends, legal and accounting fees and officer and director salaries.

The foreign economic processes test is met if:

1. The solicitation (other than advertising), negotiation or contracting related to an export sale is performed outside the United States.

2. The foreign direct costs of an export sale are at least half of total direct costs or are 85% of any two of the following five categories: (1) advertising and sales promotion, (2) processing customer orders and arranging for delivery, (3) transportation from the time the property is acquired by the FSC until delivery to the customer, (4) determination of a final invoice or statement of account and its transmittal and collection and (5) assumption of the credit risk.

Exporters are not subject to either the foreign management or the foreign economic test if they elect "small FSC" status. The small FSC's annual tax-exemption is limited to the taxable income attributable to no more than $5 million of foreign trading gross receipts. However, the small FSC must still satisfy these tests in order to use the statutory pricing rules described below.

Excludable Income of FSC

If the FSC meets all the above requirements, a portion of its "foreign trade income" is exempt from U.S. tax. Generally, if the FSC is owned by a U.S. corporation and utilizes certain statutory pricing formulas described below, 15/23 (approximately 65%) of its foreign trade income is tax exempt. In calculating the FSC's foreign trade income, the U.S. supplier/shareholder may select a transfer price which results in FSC taxable income that does not exceed the greater of: (1) 23% of the combined taxable income that the U.S. supplier/shareholder derives from the export sales or (2) 1.83% of such export sales limited to twice the amount determined in the combined taxable income method.

For example, FSC purchases qualifying export property from a shareholder/supplier and resells it to an unrelated foreign buyer for $1,000. The FSC's expenses are $230 and the shareholder/supplier's cost of goods sold is $520 and its selling expenses are $110. The statutory transfer price is determined as follows:

Gross receipts	$1,000
Cost of goods sold	(520)
FSC's expenses	(230)
Shareholder/supplier selling expenses	(110)
Combined taxable income	$140

	23% Method	1.83% Method
Sales price	$1,000	$1,000
FSC expenses	(230)	(230)
FSC taxable income		
23% x $140	(32.20)	
1.83% x $1,000		(18.30)
Transfer price	$737.80	$751.70

Thus, the 23% method would be selected because it results in a greater amount of income attributable to the FSC. The exempt income then is $21 ($32.20 x 15/23). The remaining amount of $11.20 ($32.20 - $21) is taxable to the FSC. The U.S. shareholder/supplier is then taxed on $107.80 ($140 - 32.20).

Assuming a 34% corporate tax rate, the tax savings from utilizing the FSC is

$7.14 ($140 x .34) -[($11.20 x. 34) + ($107.80 x .34)].

The Possessions Corporation

The possessions corporation (PC) is a tax-advantaged U.S. corporation generally intended to encourage U.S. organizations to establish active business operations in U.S. possessions, most notably in Puerto Rico. If the PC qualifies, it receives a special tax credit equal to the U.S. tax attributable to its possession source income. Because of this tax credit and other special tax exemptions granted by the Puerto Rican government, PC's have extremely low effective tax rates (generally less than 10%).

A U.S. corporation may elect to be taxed as a PC if, during the three preceding years, it earned at least 80% of its gross income in a U.S. possession and at least 75% of its gross income is from active business operations conducted in a U.S. possession. An election cannot be revoked for at least 10 years without permission from the IRS, usually granted for hardship reasons where tax avoidance is not a factor.

In the past, U.S. corporations abused this incentive for doing business in Puerto Rico by transferring their intangible property (patents, copyrights, etc.) to a PC after deducting all research and development expenses attributable to the intangible assets. The law now provides that the PC's income from such intangibles is treated as U.S. source income to the corporation's shareholders rather than possession source income, thereby eliminating the tax credit on such income. There is an exception for income from intangibles held by a PC with a significant business presence (generally measured in terms of local employment) in the possession whereby the U.S. parent and its PC share in intangible income received by the PC based upon a cost sharing or profit splitting formula.

Controlled Foreign Corporations

U.S. multinational corporations may indefinitely defer U.S. tax on income earned outside the United States by their foreign subsidiaries by not repatriating those earnings to the U.S. To counter this technique, the U.S. has created the concept of the "controlled foreign corporation" (CFC). The objective of the CFC rules is to prevent corporations from establishing subsidiaries in tax-haven countries for the sole purpose of tax avoidance. The law provides that U.S. stockholders are taxed on their *pro rata* share of certain types of income (called "Subpart F" income) earned by a CFC regardless of when the U.S. shareholder of the CFC receives the income. However, the shareholders are not taxed again on that income when it is actually distributed to them.

Definition

A foreign corporation constitutes a CFC and its U.S. shareholders currently taxed on its "Subpart F income" if more than 50% of its voting power or value is controlled directly or indirectly at any time during the year by U.S. shareholders. U.S. shareholders, for this purpose, are U.S. persons who own at least 10% of the foreign corporation's voting power. Thus, if 46% of a foreign corporation's stock is owned by one U.S. shareholder and the remaining 54% is owned equally by six unrelated U.S. persons (9% each), it cannot be a CFC. However, if any one of the six U.S. persons acquires an additional one percent, directly or indirectly, the foreign corporation becomes a CFC. This change in status occurs because the 46% shareholder and the 10% shareholder together meet the 50% and 10% requirements.

Subpart F Income

Subpart F income includes those types of income earned by CFC's that had been frequently shielded from U.S. taxation through artificial arrangements with subsidiaries in tax-haven countries. The major types of Subpart F income include:

1. Income earned from providing insurance protection for U.S. property or residents.

2. Passive income, such as dividends, interests, rents, royalties, and gains from sale of stock.

3. Sales commissions, fees and profits earned as a result of buying and selling goods which are neither produced nor used in the CFC's country.

4. Income for management, maintenance, and other services performed outside the CFC's country for the benefit of a related party.

Generally, if Subpart F income is less than the lesser of 5% of gross income or $1,000,000, none of the income is taxed to the U.S. shareholders. On the other hand, if Subpart F income exceeds 70% of the CFC's total income, 100% of the CFC's income is treated as Subpart F income. Finally, if a CFC's Subpart F income cannot be repatriated to the United States because of currency restrictions, it is not taxable to the U.S. shareholders until the restrictions are removed.

Foreign Personal Holding Company

U.S. shareholders of a foreign corporation may avoid taxation under the CFC rules yet still be taxed under the "foreign personal holding company" (FPHC) rules. FPHC shareholders, like CFC shareholders, are deemed to receive constructive dividends equal to their interest in undistributed FPHC income. The shareholders are not taxed again when these dividends are actually distributed.

A foreign corporation is an FPHC if at least 50% of its gross income (or 60% if it was not an FPHC in the previous year) is FPHC income and more than 50% of the voting power or value of its outstanding stock was owned at any time during the taxable year directly or indirectly by five or fewer U.S. citizens or residents.

FPHC income consists of passive income such as dividends, interests, royalties, annuities, net gains from assets which generate passive income, passive leasing and licensing income and rents that do not constitute at least 50% of the gross income of the corporation. FPHC income also includes income from personal service contracts and payments for the use of its property by a shareholder who owns directly or indirectly at least 25% in value of the FPHC's outstanding stock.

Passive Foreign Investment Companies

The Tax Reform Act of 1986 added the passive foreign investment company (PFIC) to the panoply of specially defined foreign corporations that receive special U.S. income tax treatment. The object is to deprive U.S. taxpayers of the economic benefit of deferral of U.S. tax on a U.S. taxpayer's share of the undistributed income of a foreign investment company which has predominantly passive income—no matter how small that interest might be.

A PFIC is a foreign corporation 75% or more of whose gross income for the tax year is passive income, or at least 50% of the average value of whose assets during the tax year produce, or are held for the production of, passive income.

The advantage of deferral is negated by requiring U.S. taxpayers owning shares in a PFIC to pay tax plus an interest charge based on the value of tax deferred at the time the shareholder disposes of his PFIC investment or on receipt of an "excess distribution." An excess distribution for a year is any distribution in respect of stock to the extent that it represents a ratable portion of the total distributions on the stock during the year that exceeds 125% of the average distributions during the three prior years. In lieu of this treatment, shareholders of a PFIC may individually choose "qualified electing fund status" for the PFIC. This method allows the U.S. shareholder to include in gross income his share of the PFIC's earnings and profits each year.

Allocating Income and Deductions Among Affiliated Companies

Section 482

Few business decisions have greater impact on the operations of multinational organizations than those involving pricing policies between affiliated companies located in different countries. Transfer prices between units of the same organization will be respected for U.S. tax purposes only if such prices are at "arm's length;" i.e. prices that are based on market values between unrelated businesses. In the event that transfer prices are not at arm's length, the IRS is authorized to reallocate income and deductions between affiliated companies.

Specifically, Section 482 of the IRS code regulates five types of transactions: (1) interest on inter-company loans, (2) services performed for a related party, (3) use of tangible property by a related party, (4) inter-company transfers of intangible property, and (5) inter-company sales of tangible property. The law also prohibits importers from using a transfer price for federal income taxation which exceeds the comparable U.S. customs value assigned to that property.

As might be expected, the law in this area is vague and therefore allows the IRS and the courts considerable interpretative latitude. However, it is the responsibility of the taxpayer to convince the IRS and, if necessary, a court, that its pricing policies with its foreign affiliates are the same as those with unaffiliated companies. Simply showing that the company's pricing method is based on sound business reasons will not prevent the IRS and the courts from adjusting income between related parties. Where such an adjustment results in double taxation of the same income by the U.S. and another country, the taxpayer may seek relief if the U.S. has an income tax treaty with that other nation which provides for the competent authority of each treaty country to pursue an equitable solution to the double taxation problem.

Allocation of Deductions

United States Treasury Regulations provide rules governing the allocation of deductions between U.S. companies and their foreign affiliates. These regulations list 15 different classes of income to which deductions may be allocated, including business income, rents, interest and dividends. The deductions, once allocated to a class of income, are then apportioned between U.S. source and foreign source income.

Even though a multinational's taxable income from all sources usually remains unchanged regardless of whether deductions are allocated to foreign or U.S. sources, many firms pay higher taxes when deductions are allocated to foreign source income. This is because the reallocation lowers the multinational's foreign tax credit limitation. This deduction reallocation is complicated even further if, after a tax audit, the IRS reallocates income under section 482, which results in a change of gross income relationships to the extent that deductions must be reallocated and reapportioned between U.S. and foreign sources.

For example, during 1990, U.S. corporation A reports $10,000 of foreign source taxable income and accrues $3,200 of foreign taxes. A's worldwide taxable income is $20,000. This results in a tentative U.S. tax of $3,000 ($20,000 x 15%) and a $1700 ($3,200 - $1,500) excess foreign tax credit. Upon audit, the IRS allocates $1,000 of expenses from the U.S. to A's foreign activities. Although the adjustment does not change A's $3,000 (20,000 x 15%) tentative U.S. income tax liability, it does reduce A's foreign tax credit limitation as follows:

Pre-audit limitation

$$\$3{,}000 \times \frac{\$10{,}000}{\$20{,}000} = \$1{,}500$$

Post-audit limitation

$$\$3{,}000 \times \frac{\$9{,}000}{\$20{,}000} = \$1{,}350$$

This changes A's net U.S. tax liability from $1,500 to $1,650 and results in a $1,850 ($3,200 - $1,350) excess foreign tax credit.

Foreign Currency Gains and Losses

Although U.S. individuals and corporations conduct business in many currencies, in most instances, they must report U.S. taxable income in U.S. dollars. The exchange rate from a particular currency to dollars may change over time, producing taxable gains or losses attributable to those price fluctuations. Whether these foreign currency exchange gains and losses are ordinary or capital depends upon the nature of each transaction; i.e., gains and losses that arise in the normal course of business are ordinary, while those that arise from investment or personal transactions produce capital gain or loss.

Appropriate Exchange Rate

With certain exceptions that are beyond the scope of this article, U.S. taxpayers must use the U.S. dollar for recording international transactions.

Where the taxpayer has no physical location in a foreign country, exchange gains or losses in that country are determined on a transaction-by-transaction basis. Gain or loss for each transaction is determined in the foreign currency and then translated into U.S. dollars at the exchange rate in effect on that date. The difference between this amount and the actual amount received is the exchange gain or loss. This gain or loss is reported when collection (or payment) is made regardless of whether the accrual or cash method of accounting is used.

In the case of a U.S. corporation with a foreign branch, the profit or loss of the branch for the year is computed in the foreign branch's currency and then translated into U.S. dollars at the weighted average exchange rate for the taxable year. When distributions are made from this income, any exchange gain or loss (i.e., the difference between the exchange rate at the date of distribution and the weighted average rate used to report the income) is recognized as ordinary income or loss. Translated branch losses are deductible by the U.S. taxpayer only to the extent of the U.S. taxpayer's dollar basis in the branch.

Generally, dividend income paid in a foreign currency by a foreign corporation to a U.S. taxpayer is based on exchange rates in effect when the dividends are received. Subpart F income and FPHC income are translated in the same manner as income from a branch. When distributions are made from this income, any exchange gain or loss (i.e., the difference between the exchange rate at the date of distribution and the weighted average rate used to report the income) is recognized as foreign source ordinary income or loss.

Block Currency Rule

When taxpayers are unable to convert foreign currencies into U.S. dollars because of exchange restrictions imposed by the host government, they may elect to defer the U.S. taxation on such income until the blockage restrictions

Taxation for U.S. Corporations Doing Business Abroad

are removed. The deferral elections for blocked currency generally are not available for income that is includable regardless of whether distributed to the taxpayers, such as FPHC income or income from a foreign partnership. The deferral also is unavailable when the taxpayer is able to use the funds in the foreign country.

APPENDIX: INCOME TAX TREATIES IN FORCE

Some of the countries the United States has income tax treaties with include:

Aruba	Japan
Australia	Korea
Austria	Luxembourg
Barbados	Malta
Belgium	Morocco
Bermuda	Netherlands
Canada	New Zealand
Cypress	Norway
Denmark	Pakistan
Egypt	People's Republic of China
Finland	Philippines
France	Poland
Germany	Romania
Greece	Socialist Republics
Hungary	Sweden
Iceland	Switzerland
Ireland	Trinidad & Tobaga
Italy	United Kingdom
Jamaica	

Donald T. Williamson
The American University

Karl William Viehe
The George Washington University

Donald T. Williamson is Assistant Professor of Taxation at the Kogod College of Business Administration of The American University, Washington, D.C. and is Counsel to the law firm of Wickham & Associates, Washington, D.C. His degrees include a B.A., M.B.A., J.D., LL.M., and CPA.

Karl William Viehe is Adjunct Professor of International Law at The George Washington University and a practicing international attorney with the firm of Tighe, Curhan, Viehe & Rogala in Washington, D.C. His degrees include a B.A., M.A., J.D., and M.L.T.

Taxation for U.S. Citizens Doing Business Abroad

Overview

Most industrial nations reserve the right to tax their citizens on income earned within their territorial borders. The United States approaches taxation from an even broader jurisdictional principle, as outlined by the Sixteenth Amendment of the U.S. Constitution.

"The Congress shall have the power to lay and collect taxes on income, *from whatever source* derived without apportionment among the federal states, and without regard to any census or enumeration." (emphasis added)

Consequently, U.S. taxpayers are subject to U.S. taxation on their *worldwide income*. Thus, with few exceptions, the United States exerts its taxing jurisdiction over the income of U.S. citizens and U.S. corporations regardless of their place of residence and regardless of where their activities legally and/or economically occur. This chapter will briefly review the U.S. tax rules affecting U.S. citizens investing and doing business abroad with special emphasis on rules that alleviate the potential of double taxation by the U.S. and the host jurisdiction where the income was earned.

EXAMPLES

Foreign Tax Deductions or Credits

U.S. taxation of the worldwide income of its citizens and residents often results in the same income being taxed at several levels. First, foreign-earned income of a U.S. person is usually taxed by the jurisdiction where it was earned, usually by means of a withholding tax. Second, such gross income (income before foreign income taxes and withholding taxes are deducted) is taxable in the United States when it is constructively received by a U.S. citizen or corporation. Finally, this income may be subject to state and possibly local income taxes in both the host country and the United States.

To alleviate the burden of multiple taxation on U.S. citizens on their earnings in foreign countries, direct foreign income taxes may be either deducted against U.S. taxable income or credited against U.S. income tax. Whether a U.S. individual elects to deduct or credit foreign income taxes against his U.S. income tax, the amount of foreign source income he reports must be "grossed up" (i.e. increased) by the foreign taxes paid on that income. In most cases, a tax credit provides more benefits than a deduction. However, because a deduction is not subject to the foreign tax credit limitations described below, cases may arise where deducting foreign taxes would be more advantageous.

When the foreign effective tax rate does not exceed the U.S. effective tax rate, foreign taxes may be claimed as a credit without limit. However, when the foreign tax rate *exceeds* the U.S. rate, the foreign tax credit is limited to the U.S. effective rate. In other words, foreign taxes may be used to offset U.S. taxes up to, but not beyond, the amount of U.S. taxes attributable to foreign source income. The formula for the tax credit limitation is:

$$\frac{Foreign\,Source\,Taxable\,Income}{Worldwide\,Taxable\,Income} = U.S.\,Tax$$

For example, for the taxable year 1990 individual A has income of $10,000 from Country X which imposes a 15% tax and $20,000 from Country Y which imposes a 50% tax. A has taxable income of $70,000 from within the United States. Assume the U.S. tax on $100,000 of taxable income before the credit is $22,500. The overall limitation is as follows:

$$\frac{\$30,000}{\$100,000} \times \$22,250 = \$6,750$$

Thus, taxpayer A has an excess foreign tax credit of

$4,750 ($1,500 + $10,000 - $6,750)

Excess foreign tax credits may be carried over to years where the foreign tax credits are less than U.S. taxes on foreign source income. The carryover credit is limited to a two-year carryback and a five year carryforward.

Only foreign income taxes, war profits taxes and taxes on excess profits (or taxes paid in lieu of such taxes) qualify for the credit. U.S. criteria are applied to determine whether or not the foreign tax qualifies for the credit. Thus, value-added taxes, severance taxes, property taxes, and sales taxes do not qualify because they are not regarded in the U.S. as taxes on income. Such taxes, however, may be deductible against U.S. taxable income.

Foreign-Earned Income Exclusion

As an alternative to a deduction or credit for foreign taxes on foreign earned income, U.S. citizens or residents may elect to exclude foreign earned income from U.S. taxation up to certain statutory limits. Specifically, qualifying individuals who live or perform work outside of the U.S. (who meet either the *bona fide* resident or the physical presence tests discussed below) may elect to exclude up to $70,000 of foreign-earned income as well as any employer-provided foreign housing allowance.

IMPLEMENTATION

Foreign Earned Income

Besides salaries, the term "earned income" includes professional fees, commissions, employee benefits, and reimbursements. Whether a taxpayer's earned income is from U.S. or foreign sources is based solely upon the place where the work is actually performed. This determination is unaffected by either the location of the employer or the method of payment. For example, salary received by a U.S. citizen for work performed in Saudi Arabia is foreign source income even if payment is made by a U.S. corporation to the employee in his U.S. bank accounts.

Qualifying Individuals

U.S. citizens may qualify for the foreign-earned income exclusion under either the *bona fide* resident or physical presence tests. Citizens of another country may qualify only under the physical presence test unless a U.S. tax treaty with their country provides otherwise. The individual must receive the foreign income no later than the year following the service, and be paid by an entity other than the U.S. government or one of its agencies or instrumentalities.

Bona Fide Resident

The *bona fide* resident test requires the individual to maintain the status of a *bona fide* resident in one or more foreign countries for an uninterrupted period that includes an entire tax year. *Bona fide* resident status is not necessarily jeopardized if taxpayers continue to own a home in the U.S. or make brief business or personal trips to the U.S.; however, there must be a clear intent to return to the foreign tax home or a new one without unreasonable delay. The *bona fide* foreign resident generally is expected to work outside the U.S. for an extended or indefinite period and establish a permanent family residence in the work area. An intention to eventually return to the United States is not relevant to the test.

For purposes of this test, foreign residency status is denied to any taxpayer who makes a statement to authorities in the foreign country that he is not a resident and, consequently, is exempt from being taxed as a resident in that country.

Physical Presence Test

To qualify under the physical presence test, the taxpayer's tax home must not only be in a foreign country, but also the individual must have been present in one or more foreign countries for at least 330 days during *any* 12 consecutive months. Taxpayers are allowed considerable freedom in selecting the 12 months. They may be any consecutive 12 months and two periods may overlap.

For example, the taxpayer's trips to and from a foreign country in connection with his work were as follows:

Arrived in Foreign County	Arrived in United States
March 10, 1990	February 1, 1991
March 7, 1991	June 1, 1991

During the 12 consecutive months ending on March 10, 1991, the taxpayer was present in the foreign country for at least 330 full days (365 days less 28 days in February, 1991 and 7 days in March, 1991). Therefore, all income earned in the foreign country through March 10, 1991 is eligible for the exclusion. Income earned from March 11, 1991 through May 31, 1991 is also eligible for the exclusion because the taxpayer was present in the foreign country for 330 days during the 12 consecutive months ending on May 31, 1991.

If either the *bona fide* resident or physical presence tests are not met because the taxpayer was forced to leave the foreign tax home because of war, civil unrest, or other adverse conditions, the minimum time requirement may be waived. Such waivers are granted by the Treasury Department based on information provided by the State Department.

Excludable Amounts

In addition to their salaries, many U.S. corporations provide housing or housing allowances for their expatriate employees. Basically, these employer-provided housing allowances constitute foreign-earned income. Individuals may exclude that portion of the employer housing costs equal to the "housing cost amount" — computed as "qualifying foreign housing expenses" less 16% of the GS-14, (Step 1) salary level of a U.S. government employee (prorated on a daily basis if the taxpayer does not qualify for the exclusion the entire year).

Qualifying foreign housing expenses include all reasonable costs incurred to house an employee and, where appropriate, the spouse and all dependents living with the employee. Examples of acceptable expenses are rent, insurance, utilities, repairs and other costs related to the housing and its furnishings, plus parking fees and local telephone charges. Acceptable expenses do not include capital expenditures, depreciation, domestic help or expenses that can be claimed as itemized deductions, such as interest and property taxes.

To qualify for the exclusion, the housing must generally be near the foreign work place, but where living conditions in the area are dangerous, unhealthy or otherwise adverse, housing expenses also include costs of maintaining a separate foreign home for the spouse and the dependents.

Taxpayers who pay qualifying housing expenses and are not reimbursed by their employer may deduct the expenses. This deduction, however, may not exceed the taxpayer's includable foreign income. Any excess expenses may be carried forward one year and deducted to the extent there is taxable foreign earned income in that year.

Finally, a special exclusion is available to employees living in employer-provided camps, generally located in hardship areas. These individuals qualify as living and eating on the business premises at the convenience of the employer, and, as a result, the value of their employer-provided meals and lodging are excluded from income.

CONCLUSION

In many instances, U.S. citizens working abroad are subject to dual taxation, not only on their income earned in one country but in both. Additionally, taxes may be levied on fringe benefits, such as housing provided by the citizen's corporation. U.S. tax law allows for certain deductions or credits, but these may not offset the amount of total tax. While many corporations compensate employees for a potential tax loss, the circumstances should be evaluated and the extent of the liability calculated when an employee is contemplating an assignment abroad.

Donald T. Williamson
The American University

Karl William Viehe
The George Washington University

Donald T. Williamson is Assistant Professor of Taxation at the Kogod College of Business Administration of The American University, Washington, D.C. and is Counsel to the law firm of Wickham & Associates, Washington, D.C. His degrees include a B.A., M.B.A., J.D., LL.M., and C.P.A.

Karl WIlliam Viehe is Adjunct Professor of International Law at the George Washington University and a practicing international attorney in the firm of Tighe, Curhan, Viehe & Rogala in Washington, D.C. His degrees include a B.A., M.A., J.D., and M.L.T.

U.S. Taxation of Nonresident Aliens and Foreign Corporations

OVERVIEW

While U.S. citizens and corporations are subject to U.S. tax on their worldwide income, nonresident aliens and foreign corporations in general are only subject to U.S. taxation on income earned in the U.S. Basically, if nonresident aliens and foreign corporations conduct a trade or business in the U.S. at some time during the year, they will be taxed in the same manner and at the same rates as U.S. citizens and domestic corporations on all income that is "effectively connected" with that U.S. trade or business. If no such trade or business is conducted in the U.S., nonresident aliens and foreign corporations are taxed only on their investment income derived in the U.S.

IMPLEMENTATION

Nonresident Alien Defined

While a foreign corporation is simply a corporation incorporated outside the U.S., a nonresident alien is more difficult to define. Generally, a nonresident alien is any individual who is neither a citizen nor resident of the U.S. A "resident" includes an individual lawfully admitted for permanent residency (i.e., one who holds a green card) or an individual who meets a "substantial presence" test.

The substantial presence test requires the individual to be present in the U.S. on at least 31 days during the current year. Also, the sum of the number of days on which the individual was present in the U.S. in the current and the two preceding calendar years, when multiplied by a fraction (one third in the case of the first preceding year and one sixth for the second preceding year) must equal or exceed 183 days. There are certain exemptions from these residency rules for diplomats, students, and individuals in the U.S. for medical treatment.

An individual will not meet the substantial presence test with respect to any one year if the individual is present in the U.S. on fewer than 183 days in that year and the individual can establish that he or she has closer connections to a tax home in a foreign country.

Taxation of Non-resident Aliens and Foreign Corporations

Gross income of a nonresident alien individual or foreign corporation includes only income from U.S. sources or income effectively connected with a U.S. trade or business. In the case of U.S. source income not connected with a U.S. trade or business, payments of such income to a nonresident alien is subject to a 30% withholding tax. A 30% withholding tax is also imposed on the net capital gain of a nonresident alien individual present in the U.S. for a period or periods aggregating 183 days or more during the taxable year. These withholding taxes may be reduced by treaty between the U.S. and the foreign investor's jurisdiction.

An exception from the withholding tax applies to interest paid to foreign persons on certain portfolio debt obligations. This exception is intended to permit U.S. multinational corporations and the U.S. government to issue debt instruments on the Eurobond market at interest rates less than would be required if the interest were subject to withholding tax.

Income effectively connected with a U.S. trade or business of a nonresident alien individual or foreign corporation during the taxable year is taxed at the same graduated rates as apply to citizens and residents of the U.S. For purposes of computing effectively connected taxable income, deductions are allowable to the extent that they are connected with such income as determined by an apportionment and allocation procedure set out in Treasury regulations. Certain deductions, however, are permitted without allocation, the most important of which is personal casualty losses on property located within the U.S. To be entitled to any deductions or credits, the nonresident alien must file a true and accurate income tax return.

Where a nonresident alien individual or foreign corporation derives income during the taxable year from an interest in U.S. real property held for the production of income, the foreign person alien may elect to treat all such income as effectively connected with the conduct of a trade or business within the U.S. even though the taxpayer's activities with respect to the property does not constitute a U.S. trade or business. Although such an election is generally irrevocable, foreign persons should consider this option to offset income derived from other U.S. trades or businesses of the taxpayer where the property is operating at a loss.

Sourcing of Income

Whether income is derived from sources within the U.S. depends upon the type of income received by the nonresident alien or foreign corporation. In general, the following constitute U.S. source income, the receipt of which by a nonresident alien or foreign corporation is subject to a withholding tax described below:

- Interest paid by U.S. obligors

- Dividends paid by U.S. corporations or by foreign corporations to the extent that at least 25% of the foreign corporation's gross income over the three prior years is effectively connected with a U.S. trade or business

- Compensation for personal services performed in the U.S.

- Rents and royalties from property located in the U.S.

- Dispositions of "U.S. real property interests"

- Sales or exchanges of personal property within the U.S.

Expenses, losses and other deductions are apportioned and allocated to such income in arriving at taxable income from sources within the U.S.

Effectively Connected with a U.S. Trade or Business

For purposes of the "effectively connected" test, it is unclear what constitutes a "U.S. trade or business" by a foreign person. However, in determining whether U.S. source income from interest, dividends, and other fixed or determinable annual or periodical gains is effectively connected with the conduct of trade or business within the U.S., the following factors are required to be taken into account: (1) whether the income was derived from assets used in or held for use in the conduct of U.S. trade or business; or (2) whether the activities of such business were a material factor in the realization of the income. Income from sources without the U.S. is effectively connected with a U.S. trade or business if the nonresident alien individual or foreign corporation receiving the income has an office or other fixed place of business within the U.S. to which the income is attributable.

A nonresident alien individual or foreign corporation is deemed to have an office or other fixed place of business in the U.S. if the foreign person, corporation, or its agent has the authority to negotiate and conclude contracts in the name of the nonresident person or corporation within the U.S. and regularly exercises that authority.

Conduit Treatment Required of Partnerships

Any foreign person who is a partner in a partnership which is engaged in a trade or business within the U.S. is also considered to be so engaged. Thus, membership by a nonresident alien individual or foreign corporation in a partnership which has income effectively connected with a trade or business within the U.S. is taxed *pro tanto*, notwithstanding the fact that the nonresident alien individual or foreign corporation may have no direct income effectively connected with a trade or business within the U.S. This follows the standard approach of U.S. tax law treating the partnership as a conduit and imposing tax not on the partnership but on the partners individually.

Where a U.S. partnership has any income effectively connected with the conduct of a U.S. trade or business, the partnership or other withholding agent is required to withhold 28% of each non-corporate foreign partner's share of the effectively connected income and 34% of each corporate foreign partner's share of the effectively connected income.

Branch Profits Tax

A U.S. subsidiary of a foreign corporation pays not only U.S. income tax on its earnings, but also a withholding tax when those earnings are distributed to the foreign corporation. Previously, a foreign corporation was able to avoid the withholding tax simply by operating as a branch in the U.S. In order to equalize the treatment of U.S. branches of foreign corporations with the treatment of U.S. subsidiaries of foreign corporations, Congress enacted the "branch profits tax." Thus, in addition to the regular income tax imposed upon a U.S. branch of a foreign business, a 30% withholding tax must be paid by the branch upon its post-1986 U.S. effectively connected earnings and profits.

As an incentive to induce foreign corporations not to repatriate U.S. earnings, the tax is not imposed if the branch profits are reinvested in a U.S. business. The branch profits tax may also be reduced or eliminated if the United States has a treaty with the foreign corporation's domicile and the foreign domicile permits a withholding tax on the dividends paid by the foreign corporation.

Taxation of U.S. Real Property Dispositions by Foreign Sellers

Capital gains realized by foreign corporations not engaged in a U.S. trade or business are exempt from U.S. tax. Similarly, capital gains of a nonresident alien individual not engaged in a U.S. trade or business and present in the U.S. for less than 183 days in the taxable year are exempt from U.S. tax. These exemptions have one major exception where the foreign person disposes of a "U.S. real property interest" (USRPI), in which case the disposition is treated as effectively connected with a U.S. trade or business and consequently taxable at the same rates applicable to U.S. persons.

Generally, a USRPI is an interest in real property located in the U.S. or the Virgin Islands, and any interest (other than that as a creditor) in any domestic corporation unless the taxpayer establishes that the corporation was not a "U.S. real property holding corporation," at any time over the five year period ending on the date of the disposition of such interest. A USRPI does not include any interest in a corporation if, as of the date of disposition, the corporation did not hold any USRPI and any USRPI's held during the five year period prior to disposition of the stock were disposed of in transactions in which the full amount of the gain, if any, was recognized.

Donald T. Williamson
The American University

Karl William Viehe
The George Washington University

Donald T. Williamson is Associate Professor of Taxation at the Kogod College of Business Administration of The American University, Washington, D.C. and is Counsel to the law firm of Wickham & Associates, Washington, D.C. His degrees include a B.A., M.B.A, J.D., LL.M., and CPA.

Karl William Viehe is Adjunct Professor of International Law at the George Washington University and a practicing international attorney with the firm of Tighe, Curhan, Viehe, & Rogala in Washington, D.C. His degrees include a B.A., M.A., J.D., and M.L.T.

9.

International Law and Agreements

Treaties and Conventions

OVERVIEW

The legal environment surrounding companies engaged in international commercial transactions is shaped and defined by the agreements negotiated between and among governments. While individual businesses enter into private contracts that govern a particular transaction or series of transactions, to a large extent the effectiveness and enforceability of such contracts are dependent upon the cooperation and agreement between the sovereign nations of which those businesses are citizens. Matters negotiated at the governmental level but which impact private contracts include taxation, the transferability (including expatriation) of assets, enforcement procedures and remedies in the event of contract disputes, protections afforded investments and assets situated in a foreign state from the hostile actions of the government of that state, and the imposition of tariffs and other import or export restrictions.

Treaties are one kind of agreement between sovereign states. Under U.S. domestic law, the term "treaty" has a particular meaning, to wit, an agreement between the United States and other sovereign states made by the President with the consent of two thirds of the Senate (U.S. Constitution, Article 2, Section 2). In the parlance of international law, however, the term "treaty" is synonymous with the terms "convention," "covenant," "pact," "charter," or "protocol." All refer to an agreement between two (bilateral) or more (multilateral) sovereign states, which agreement generally becomes effective upon acceptance, adoption or ratification by the respective governments. The terms "sovereign states" and "states" both refer to those countries that are indepen-

Treaties and Conventions

dent and self-governing. While treaties are intended to bind specific states to specific agreements designed to promote that state's particular needs, the principles encompassed in the agreement may become so widely accepted that they in effect become part of international law.

At the international level, the law of treaties has been codified in the Vienna Convention on the Law of Treaties (1969), which entered into force in 1980. Although the U.S. is not yet a party to it (President Richard Nixon signed the Convention in 1970, but the Senate has not ratified it), the Vienna Convention is recognized by most countries, including the U.S., as a statement of the customary and generally accepted principles of the international law of treaties. At the domestic level, the American Law Institute's Restatement of the Foreign Relations Law of the United States analyzes the relationship between public international law, including the law of treaties, and U.S. domestic law and summarizes the way in which international law is applied by U.S. courts. For example, once ratified by the Senate, treaties take precedence over state law and over federal laws passed prior to the treaty. In the event of a conflict between a treaty and a federal law passed after the treaty was signed, however, the U.S. court must give effect to the statute even though it may violate the treaty obligations. At all times, a conflict between a U.S. treaty obligation and the U.S. Constitution must be resolved in favor of the Constitution.

Executive agreements are another kind of international agreement to which the U.S. may be a party and by which it may be bound, but which do not reach the level of a treaty as defined in the Constitution. Executive agreements refer to agreements made by the President in the exercise of his independent constitutional power to conduct foreign policy. Some executive agreements are in fact authorized by Congress either through specific legislation or through a provision in a ratified treaty. Others are made solely on the President's initiative. For all practical purposes, executive agreements have the same force, under international and U.S. law, as treaties. They are increasingly favored by Presidents as a way to strengthen executive power to conduct foreign affairs and as an effective means by which to resolve disputes with other states. Executive agreements are more flexible, faster, and easier to negotiate than treaties since the Senate ratification process is avoided. Treaties and executive agreements attempt to accomplish on an international level what domestic law accomplishes within a particular country. While treaties have traditionally dealt with the relationship and conduct between sovereign states alone, more modern treaties also address the concerns of individual citizens, including corporations and other businesses, and their relationships to citizens and governments of foreign host states. These concerns range in diversity from the definition of human rights to methods of resolving private disputes to the protection of investments.

EXAMPLES

Two examples will illustrate the interplay of private contract and public international law. In the first, assume that a Swedish manufacturer of glassware has agreed to sell 200 goblets to a specialty retailer in Chicago, Illinois. The parties have entered into a short and sketchy contract which recites the basic price and delivery information but fails to specify product warranties or remedies available in the event of a breach by one of the parties. Furthermore, the parties do not specify which law will apply in interpreting or enforcing the contract, the laws of the U.S. or the laws of Sweden. While the goods were to be delivered at the buyer's place of business by November 1st, they do not arrive until December 15th and, upon inspection, it is clear that the goblets do not conform to the sample which was shown to the buyer at the time of the contract. The buyer now wants to know what rights and remedies are applicable.

Although the parties may not realize it, the buyer's contract problem is governed by a treaty, the United Nations Convention on Contracts for the

Treaties and Conventions

International Sale of Goods. The treaty applies to all contracts for the sale of goods if the buyer and the seller have places of business in different countries and those countries have ratified the Convention. The Convention has been ratified by both Sweden and the U.S. (effective in the U.S. on January 1, 1988). The provisions of the Convention provide a uniform framework to resolve disputes concerning contracts for the sale of goods. The provisions of the Convention automatically apply to covered transactions, even though the parties are not aware of the Convention or its provisions. Private contracts may contain provisions superseding the Convention provisions, but the parties must clearly intend to do so. Following the rules set out in the Convention, the parties will be able to determine whether or not furnishing the sample glass constituted a warranty as to the quality of the product, and the buyer will know his options with respect to remedies for the late delivery.

In the second situation, imagine a British and an American manufacturer entering into a joint venture agreement to manufacture a line of women's clothing for sale in the United States and the United Kingdom. Part of the agreement calls for the joint development of a network of retail stores. The two parties want to provide for a method to resolve disputes that may arise, but neither wants to resort to the courts. The British manufacturer is particularly wary of the U.S. courts and the manner in which the U.S. antitrust laws are applied, and both are concerned with the time and cost involved in attempting to resolve international commercial disputes through the court system of either country. The parties may agree to use arbitration as the method of dispute resolution. Because of the wide acceptance of the 1958 United Nations Convention on the Recognition and Enforcement of Foreign Arbitration Awards, both parties can be confident that any judgment awarded in an arbitration proceeding will be enforced by the courts of their respective countries.

BENEFITS

It is impossible for business to adequately plan for future international trade without being aware of the structure, climate and restrictions imposed through international agreements. For example, U.S. companies must be aware of what is going on in the European Economic Community if they expect to be players in the world market. What started as six states signing the Treaty of Rome in 1957 has now grown to twelve states with a population that well exceeds 300 million people and more countries sure to join in the future. Under the Single European Act (1987) and the Maastricht Treaty (1992), the EC formed a single European trade market. While barriers continue to fall between the member nations, it is still unclear how non-member countries will be treated. U.S. companies that anticipated the European plan increased operations within member states to establish a strong presence or are teamed up with or bought out European partners. Those companies that were unaware of the unification plan are finding themselves locked out of the market.

IMPLEMENTATION

Each company engaging or intending to engage in international transactions must carefully study its operation and the type of transactions usually involved to identify all areas that may be subject to treaty provisions. Private contracts should be drawn to take advantage of applicable treaty protections as well as protections afforded by general principles of international law. In some instances, a party may want to opt out of treaty principles in favor of privately negotiated legal standards.

EVALUATION

Preprinted contracts, purchase orders and other forms should be periodically reviewed to reflect changes in the international legal environment as they occur. To help keep track of treaty developments, each year the Department of State makes available a publication called: *Treaties in Force: A List of Treaties and Other International Agreements of the United States.* The list names and provides a subject index for all of the agreements to which the United States is a party and which have been ratified or are otherwise enforceable. *Treaties in Force* is supplemented between annual revisions by the "Treaties—Current Actions" section of the Department of State Bulletin, a monthly publication.

The forward-looking company must be knowledgeable of world agreements beyond those to which the U.S. is a party; the scope of expertise must extend to include agreements affecting those countries that are part of the market served by the company. The question is not whether such knowledge is desirable. It is essential. Whether the expertise will be developed in house or by outside counsel is the more pertinent question, and one that can be answered only after analyzing the cost, the scope of operations, the expected profit and the long term outlook for growth.

APPLICATIONS TO SMALL BUSINESS

Developing expertise in international transactions is a problem for small business where time demands and budget constraints limit in-house involvement. Treaties are continually changing because of the addition of new parties, amendments to provisions, or because they come into effect in different countries at different times. Consequently, staying knowledgeable about the subject requires a commitment of personnel, time and resources. The best alternative for a small business that cannot afford to retain outside counsel is to take advantage of available government and industry resources. For example, the U.S. Department of Commerce operates the U.S. Foreign Commercial Service to offer export assistance and information. The Small Business

Administration likewise offers help through its various programs and seminars. Trade associations generally keep current on international matters affecting the specific industry in question. State governments have become increasingly more involved in aiding small business. Each operates some sort of economic development board or commission that provides information, if not direct assistance, in matters affecting international trade.

CONCLUSION

Perhaps the word "treaty" still conjures up to some the idea of mutual defense pacts or peace treaties ending an international conflict. While treaties have traditionally been limited to defining the relationship between sovereign states, they now also define rights accruing to and obligations of citizens of those states. Treaties touch every aspect of commercial life in the international sphere. They attempt to simplify the complexity of international dealings by providing a framework in which business must operate and in some cases provide protection so that business can operate with confidence and without interference by the host country.

SOFTWARE/DATABASES

There are two computerized database research systems available for international legal research. LEXIS is owned by Mead Data Central and WESTLAW is a service of the West Publishing Company. Both systems provide access to a broad range of databases including U.S. court decisions, statutes, and articles in law journals and other legal periodicals. A wide range of international law materials is available and new databases are continually being added.

REFERENCES/SOURCES

Reference materials fall into two categories: looseleaf services, which are updated on a regular basis to provide the most current information regarding the status of treaties, and other international agreements and treatises that give a general overview of the subject along with particulars of treaties and other international agreements in effect as of that publication date. In addition, business, trade and legal periodicals frequently provide articles discussing the legal environment of international business and the particulars of various treaty agreements. Periodicals that stress the legal aspects include *The Business Lawyer* and *The International Lawyer*, published by the Business Law Section and the International Law Section, respectively, of the American Bar Association. Both publications are written for practicing attorneys. Those who wish to explore this area from the layman's perspective should consult recent articles in the major business and industry specific periodicals, including: *CCH Congressional Index* - see for actions on pending treaties, *Digest of the Commercial Law of the World* (Oceana), *Doing Business in Europe* (CCH), *Encyclopedia of European Community Law* (Sweet & Maxwell; Bender), *Investment Laws of the World* (Oceana), *International Trade Reporter's Export Shipping Manual* (BNA), *International Trade Reporter's U.S. Export Weekly* (BNA).

Litka, Michael. *International Dimensions of The Legal Environment of Business*. Boston, MA: 2d ed. PWS-Kent Publishing Company, 1991. Clear, concise introduction to the international aspects of business, written for the business student.

Parry, Clive, John Grant, Anthony Parry, and Arthur Watts, eds. *Encyclopaedic Dictionary of International Law*. New York: Oceana Publications, 1986. Contains definitions and short explanations of international law terms and related topics.

Ruergenthal, Thomas, and Harold G. Maier. *Public International Law in a Nutshell*. St. Paul, MN: West Publishing Co., 1985. Overview of the sources of international law and the workings of the agencies which administer it. Chapter 10 contains many other research sources. Written for the nonpractitioner.

Diane B. MacDonald
Associate Professor
School of Business
Pacific Lutheran University

Diane MacDonald, MBA, JD, is a practicing attorney and an Associate Professor in the School of Business at Pacific Lutheran University. She has been teaching undergraduates for seven years and has practiced business law for over thirteen years, concentrating on small and mid-size business clients. Professor MacDonald's publications include articles in *Employment Relations Today, Journal of Professional Services Marketing,* and *The Journal of Legal Studies Education*. In addition to academic writing, she has published numerous articles on legal issues affecting small and closely held businesses.

Patents and Trademarks

OVERVIEW

Many companies engaging in international trade rely on the protections afforded by patent and trademark law. New inventions, unique designs, widely recognized products—all represent valuable proprietary interests which the owner wishes to profitably, and exclusively, exploit. The United States patent and trademark laws seem to be quite explicit, yet application of the laws can be unpredictable. A trademark is more likely to receive statutory protection when it is a suggestive rather than descriptive term. Distinguishing between what is suggestive ("Speedi Bake" for frozen dough) and what is descriptive ("Park 'N Fly" for airport parking) is difficult and subjective. A trademark may be federally registered, but unusable in a state where there is prior local registration or established common law rights. A patent application must pass the rigors of the Patent and Trademark Office review, subjected to the objections raised in the opinion of the patent examiner. A patent, though granted, may be challenged and overturned in the courts on the grounds of invalidity or antitrust. As complex and unpredictable as the U.S. law may be, its problems pale in comparison to the problems raised in securing multinational patent and trademark rights. The rights evidenced by a patent or trademark must be protected in accordance with the substantive law of each country in which it is or will be used. Failure to secure these rights will result in a loss of rights.

A U.S. patent may be one of three types: a utility patent (any new and useful process, machine, product, or composition of matter or any new and useful improvement thereof); a design patent (any new, original and ornamental design for an article of manufacture); or a plant patent (any asexually reproduced distinct and new variety of plant). A patent is effective for 17 years (design patents for 14 years) and grants its owner the right to exclude others from making, using or selling the patented invention. To be patentable, an invention must be useful, novel and unobvious to a person of ordinary skill in the art.

At the international level, treaty agreements, particularly the Paris Convention for the Protection of Industrial Property Rights (known as the Paris Convention), the Patent Cooperation Treaty, and, relative to the members of the European Economic Community, the European Patent Convention, have simplified procedures for the registration of patents on an international basis and clarified the rights of patents owners during the registration process. Under the Paris Convention, each member country agrees to give foreigners the same patent rights as its own citizens. The Convention provides for a single registration in the inventor's home country as a basis on which to protect ownership and proprietary rights in other member countries and establishes a priority period during which the registrant may file for protection within any member country, in accordance with that country's laws, without loss of rights. The Patent Cooperation Treaty provides for an international patent application and examination process. The patent applicant has twenty months from filing under the Patent Cooperation Treaty to file patent applications in accordance with the patent laws of member nations. The U.S. is a member of both the Paris Convention and the Patent Cooperation Treaty. The European Patent Convention provides for a single application and a single examination which is accepted by all member countries. Once patentability of the invention is established, individual applications must be filed in each country where patent protection is desired.

Progress has been made in the international patent procedure, but significant problems remain with differences in the way countries evaluate and award patents, particularly in the areas of prior publication, confidentiality and determination of priority. Under U.S. law, a patent may be awarded even if the invention has been described in a publication, so long as application is made within one year of publishing. Canada allows two years, Japan six months and the European Patent Convention allows no prior publication. U.S. patent information is kept confidential until the patent is granted, after which time the patent may be challenged by third parties. Under Japanese law, a patent application is made public after eighteen months to allow objection prior to its approval. In the U.S., priority to patent rights is determined by the date of invention, unlike most other countries where the filing date determines priority. All of these differences complicate the process of securing patent rights in multiple countries and in coordinating the application process and may lead to conflicting patent awards.

Even under U.S. law, the area of trademark protection has less certainty than that of patents. A trademark is any word, name, symbol or device, or any combination of these, adopted and used by a manufacturer or merchant to identify his goods and distinguish them from others. Trademarks identify the source of the product and convey certain product characteristics such as quality, character and reliability. The federal Lanham Act provides national registration for trademarks used in interstate or foreign commerce. States also have trademark registration and unfair competition statutes which attempt to prevent undue confusion about the source of a product and, depending on the jurisdiction, trademark users may acquire common law rights.

At the international level, trademark owners have frequently had to contend with governmental policy of ignoring trademark misappropriation and infringement, particularly in developing countries. As with patents, the Paris Convention is the most widely accepted agreement providing for trademark protection, requiring member nations to register and protect trademarks of other member nations to the extent that domestic trademarks are protected and again allowing a priority period during which a trademark may be filed in a member nation. In addition to the Paris Convention, trademark protection is granted under the Madrid Agreement Concerning the International Registration of Trademarks which requires registration with the World Intellectual Property Organization (WIPO). WIPO is an organization responsible for administering a number of international patent and trademark treaties, including the Paris Convention. As a result of WIPO's efforts to harmonize international trademark law, in 1989 a multinational committee drafted a new treaty, the Madrid Protocol Relating to the Madrid Agreement Concerning the International Registration of Trademarks. The Madrid Protocol calls for protecting trademarks in multiple countries through a central filing procedure. Although a separate treaty, the Madrid Protocol adopts many of the general principles contained in the Madrid Agreement. While the U.S. has never been a party to the Madrid Agreement, changes in U.S. trademark law increase the likelihood that in the future the U.S. will join the Madrid Protocol. Most notably, U.S. trademark law now permits filing for trademark protection using an "intent-to-use" application, rather than requiring actual use in commerce prior to filing. However, actual use must still occur before a registration will issue, unlike most other countries which do not require use before home country registration.

The U.S. is also a member of the Pan American Convention which gives the owner of a trademark the right to prevent use or registration of an infringing mark in another member country. The one asserting the claim of infringement has the burden of proving the infringer acted in bad faith.

As with patents, the international community has made progress regarding the procedural aspects of filing and registration of trademarks, yet significant differences remain in the substantive law, particularly the "use" requirement under U.S. law, and in the enforcement measures taken by various governments. The U.S. has increasingly tied its economic aid packages, such as to China and the Commonwealth of Independent States, to increased enforcement and protection of intellectual property rights.

EXAMPLES

Despite the attempts at creating international uniformity in protecting intellectual property rights, the disparities between substantive requirements of each country lead to confusion and assertions of unfairness in the awarding of patents and trademarks. A number of publications have cited the case of Tokyo University beating IBM in filing for a patent on the high temperature superconductor discovered by Georg Bednarz and Alex Muller at IBM Zurich. Tokyo University filed its patent in Japan based on its confirmation of the IBM discovery, which IBM announced before filing for its patents. IBM Zurich filed a similar patent application in Europe shortly after the filing by Tokyo University. Given the priority period under the Paris Convention, the IBM filing is open to challenge if Tokyo University files in Europe based on the Japanese filing within the required time period. Unlike U.S. law which awards patent priority based on the first to invent, Japanese and European laws award priority based on the first to file.

Similar disparities were highlighted in a situation where Stanford University could not obtain a patent in Europe on the early genetic engineering discoveries of Stanley Cohen and Herbert Boyer because application was made after the research results had been published. Stanford was awarded a patent in the U.S. which allows publications within one year of application.

Likewise with trademarks; international protections are in place, but the trademark owner must ensure that all appropriate and required steps are taken to comply with the requirements of each country. Thus, although Nike Inc. paid millions to be an official sponsor of the 1992 Barcelona Olympic Games, it was unable to use the NIKE trademark on its clothing in Spain because a Spanish court upheld a prior trademark registration, filed in 1932, which included the word "NIKE." When McDonald's allowed its Venezuelan registration to expire, a Venezuelan company registered the McDonald's name and claimed first rights to its use in Venezuela. From time to time trademark awards have been used to keep competitors out of a market, as when the major Japanese tobacco companies registered trademarks of U.S. tobacco products, making the trademarks unavailable for use in Japan by the U.S. companies.

U.S. laws have been strengthened to penalize those who infringe trademarks and enforcement actions have increased to stop the flow of counterfeit imports. While infringement is clearly illegal, a related problem, the importation of gray market goods, is not so clear and has been hotly contested in the courts. A gray market good is a foreign manufactured good, bearing a valid U.S. trademark, that is imported without the consent of the U.S. trademark holder. Often the goods are imported by discounters who then compete with the U.S. trademark owner's authorized distributors. While the term "gray market" connotes a certain shadiness in the business, some of the best known discounters, such as K-Mart Corporation and 47th Street Photo, Inc. are major gray market importers.

Rather than try to pursue individual defendants in an infringement action, the owners of U.S. trademarks try to stop the goods from reaching the U.S. market by using the U.S. Customs Service to bar entry to gray market goods. Section 526 of the Tariff Act of 1930 prohibits importing

> any merchandise of foreign manufacture if such merchandise . . . bears a trademark owned by a citizen of, or by a corporation or association created or organized within, the United States and registered in the Patent and Trademark Office . . . unless written consent of the owner of such trademark is produced at the time of making entry.

The U.S. Customs Service through its regulations has exempted imports from Section 526 if: a) the foreign and U.S. trademarks are owned by the same person or business entity; b) the foreign and domestic trademark owners are parent and subsidiary or otherwise subject to common ownership or control; and c) articles of foreign manufacture bear a recorded trademark applied under authorization of the U.S. owner. In a 1988 decision, *Kmart Corp. v. Cartier Inc.*, the United States Supreme Court upheld exemptions a) and b) as a legitimate exercise of discretion by the Customs Service, but struck exemption c) as being contrary to the statute and consequently closed one gray market loop hole.

The Court of Appeals in the District of Columbia put further pressure on gray market importers in a 1993 case, *Lever Brothers Company v. United States*. The court held that section 42 of the Lanham Act bars foreign goods with a trademark identical to a valid U.S. trademark when the goods are physically and materially different, even though the trademarks are under common ownership or control.

BENEFITS

Patent and trademark owners who adequately secure their proprietary rights may benefit from either the exclusive manufacture and sale of their products or from the royalties received in licensing their rights or both. The potential profit is enormous, depending on the marketability and utility of the invention and the desirability of and goodwill attached to the trademark. Licensing has become a multibillion dollar business. When IBM licensed its patented computer technology, it spawned the IBM clone market. The "Coke" name now appears on clothing as well as soft drink cans. Licensing requires vigilance and monitoring to ensure quality control and to prevent unauthorized disclosure and unauthorized use. Patent licensing must contend with antitrust laws in the U.S. and in other countries where competition laws restrict exclusive licensing agreements.

IMPLEMENTATION

On both the domestic level and the international level, securing the protections available for proprietary rights in intellectual property requires the use of experts. An error can result in the loss of ownership and exclusive use rights and in the loss of profits and licensing royalties. Decisions must be made on the coordination and timing of the applications for patents or registrations for trademarks and on the countries in which to apply or register. Conflicting laws of the individual countries make the process of multinational registration complex notwithstanding the treaties which attempt to simplify and unify that process. Multinational registration is an expensive process, not only in terms of the registration fees but also in terms of the cost of hiring the specialists to do the registration. Determining how much protection is needed for a particular invention or trademark will depend on the cost of securing protection versus the expected profit from business in that market and the likelihood of royalties generated in that market.

If enforcement of a patent results in unreasonably restraining competition in a market, the patent may be challenged and upset. Care must be taken in drawing up licensing agreements, particularly exclusive licensing agreements, to avoid anticompetitive effects. The Commission of the European Economic Community has issued regulations allowing exemptions for certain types of patent license agreements and that has eliminated some of the uncertainty regarding their enforceability in Europe. The antitrust implications of patents, trademarks and licensing add to the necessity of using a specialist in the field of intellectual property.

EVALUATION

While the focus of this article has been on the ways in which a business may protect its rights in intellectual property, it is essential to keep in mind the other side of the issue, namely, the necessity for business to avoid infringing patents or trademarks owned by others. It is imperative, for example, that a new product name be adequately searched to ensure that it does not infringe on existing trademark rights. Infringement can result in being sued for damages, treble damages under the Lanham Act, being forced to change the name of a successful product, or being forced to buy the name under unfavorable negotiating circumstances.

APPLICATIONS TO SMALL BUSINESS

There are no short-cuts available to small business in protecting intellectual property rights. The same registration procedures apply, both domestically and internationally. The small business must evaluate for itself the cost effectiveness of obtaining a patent in a foreign country or of protecting its trademark in foreign markets. It is essential to evaluate the long term prospects for an invention or trademark. Often the decision to patent an invention or register a trademark must be made before the marketability of the product can be determined. Small business should take advantage of state law and common law protection for its trademarks in the domestic market and explore the possibility of protecting its property rights through the use of laws restricting unfair competition in foreign markets. In some instances, depending on the product or invention, trade secret protection may be an alternative to a patent.

Small business must be as vigilant in avoiding patent and trademark infringements as large multinational firms. A number of companies specialize in conducting patent and trademark searches for business. Such a search should be conducted when introducing a new trademarked product or company logo or slogan, or when introducing a product patterned on non-proprietary technology.

CONCLUSION

The intangible assets evidenced by a patent or trademark are as important to a business as its tangible assets, maybe more so. A business can lose its physical assets and still remain in business based on the goodwill associated with its trademarks or the rights protected by its patents. While physical assets can be replaced, a patent or trademark lost is gone forever. While theft or forces of nature may cause a loss of the tangible, it is inattention, ignorance, carelessness, or miscalculation which causes the loss of intellectual property rights. Avoiding the loss of rights is costly; undertaking patent or trademark rights should be evaluated in light of potential profits and royalties.

SOFTWARE/DATABASES

The two available computerized database research systems for general legal research are LEXIS, owned by Mead Data Central and WESTLAW, a service of the West Publishing Company. Both systems provide access to a broad range of databases including U.S. court decisions on patents and trademarks, the federal and state statutes dealing with patents and trademarks, as well as articles in law journals and other legal periodicals. New databases are continually being added.

Thomson and Thomson, Inc. provides a computerized database TRADEMARKSCAN which accesses the record of issued, pending, abandoned, expired, and cancelled federal and state trademark registrations. Dialog Information Services, Inc. maintains an online database of patent and trademark information including periodical indexes.

Saratoga Associates, Inc. introduced its software PATENT PENDING, a PC based program to assist in preparing patent applications.

The Patent and Trademark Office is in the process of computerizing its records to assist the patent examiner in the search for comparable existing patents as part of the patent review process.

REFERENCES/SOURCES

The majority of references are intended and written for attorneys who either practice intellectual property law on a regular basis or for the general practitioner who needs to be able to recognize patent and trademark issues. Many of these references are in looseleaf form with periodic updates. There are many articles concerning patent and trademark issues, both domestically and internationally, in the major business periodicals and in the publications of specific industries. Two looseleaf services containing primary and secondary sources of law integrated and indexed by topic are: *Patents, Trademark & Copyright Journal* (BNA) and *United States Patents Quarterly* (BNA).

McCarthy, J. Thomas. *Trademarks and Unfair Competition.* 2d ed. Rochester, NY: Lawyers Cooperative Publishing Co., 1984. Treatise on trademark law.

Rosenberg, Peter D. *Patent Law Fundamentals.* 2d ed. New York: Clark Boardman, 1980. Treatise on patent law for both the nonspecialist and active practitioner; annual supplements.

Siedel, Arthur H. *What the General Practitioner Should Know About Patent Law and Practice.* 4th ed. Philadelphia: ALI/ABA, 1984. General introduction to patent law and the patent application process. Written for the nonspecialist.

―――. *What the General Practitioner Should Know About Trademarks and Copyrights* 5th ed. Philadelphia: ALI/ABA, 1986. General discussion of trademark law and the procedure for registering under federal statute. Brief one chapter overview of copyright law. Written for the nonspecialist.

Sinnott, John P. *World Patent Law: Patent Statutes, Regulations and*

Treaties. New York: Matthew Bender, 1974. Multiple volume set with quarterly updates; contains text of foreign patent laws and related treaties.

Diane B. MacDonald
Associate Professor
School of Business
Pacific Lutheran University

Diane MacDonald, MBA, JD, is a practicing attorney and an Associate Professor in the School of Business at Pacific Lutheran University. She has been teaching undergraduates for seven years and has practiced business law for over thirteen years, concentrating on small and mid-size business clients. Professor MacDonald's publications include articles in *Employment Relations Today, Journal of Professional Services Marketing,* and *The Journal of Legal Studies Education.* In addition to academic writing, she has published numerous articles on legal issues affecting small and closely held businesses.

Management Contracts

OVERVIEW

Various types of contracts exist for the management or administration of enterprises, properties or assets. One increasingly familiar type of management or administrative services contract ("management contract") is an arrangement whereby one party agrees to provide defined services either to the other or to a third entity for specified compensation, such as in a joint-venture between the two. In an international joint-venture where the foreign firm's Board of Directors insists on "control" as an essential condition of participation, a management contract may provide the greatest assurance of control, due to its complex provisions of local law and its unique patterns of local business and social culture. Hundreds of U.S. companies operating abroad during the 1960s to 1980s have learned this lesson the hard way.

The management contract has not been common or well known in the United States due to differences between the Anglo-American common law system and the continental or civil law system which prevails in far more countries. The Anglo-American system contains a legal doctrine of "non-delegable duty" whereby the President or chief executive officer is legally obliged to personally direct the administration of the company. Under the civil law system in Europe, for example, the management of a corporation is in the hands of the Board of Directors, and no such historical constraints exist. Thus, organizations exist throughout Europe and in certain "tax havens" around the world whose sole purpose is to administer the affairs of another firm, properties, or assets of individuals, acting as a type of fiduciary. These trust companies are governed by a trust agreement, which is a specialized form of management contract.

EXAMPLES

When an American or European company entered into a joint-venture in the Middle East during the heyday of the oil boom from 1975 to 1983, the foreign partner nearly always entered into a management contract, often at the insistence of the local partner. The latter wanted the American technology while the U.S. firm wanted to enter the markets of the oil-rich countries in the Persian Gulf. In many cases local laws prohibited the foreign company from establishing a wholly owned subsidiary. Consequently, a joint-venture was the chosen vehicle. However, due to long-standing traditions, local cultures and even religious influences in countries like Saudi Arabia, a local managerial class did not exist. Thus, the oil rich countries would insist that the American or European partner administer the joint-venture by means of a management contract.

Conversely, when a firm entered into a joint-venture in Mexico with one of the "Supergroups" during their heyday from 1977 to 1982, the local partner often took a management contract with a fee (usually equal to the technology transfer fee received by the American partner). The local group had all the necessary corporate staff skills and experience which the new joint-venture company could not yet afford to employ on a full-time basis. Thus, in order to take advantage of the skill and expertise available in the local partner's organization, without adding too much overhead to the fledgling company, the local partner entered into a management contract with the joint-venture.

A less well known and certainly less-publicized variety of management contract exists where a bank or other respected organization agrees to act as a fiduciary to administer investments or corporate affairs. Mutual fund or investment advisors are engaged by a type of management or advisory services contract. A variation on this theme is the business trust, well-known in England and former British Commonwealth countries, including America, and in countries like the Netherlands, the Netherlands Antilles, Panama, Liechtenstein and Switzerland. The trustees of these trusts manage properties (real or personal property investments) under the instructions contained in a trust agreement for the benefit of the named beneficiary or beneficiaries. Individual trusts function similarly. When the property to be administered under a trust agreement includes the running of a business, the trustees often engage a services organization under a management contract.

Another common example involves hotel chains. While once wholly owned, many hotels around the world are now locally owned. Episodes of nationalization, destruction and sabotage of these high visibility properties contributed to this trend. The internationally known companies including Sheraton, Holiday Inn, Intercontinental and Hilton, license their names and trademarks and accept obligations to train local employees, reducing their costs substantially. They also contract to provide a range of administrative or management services, from reservations, advertising, promotion and public relations, to complete management.

The most recent examples may involve countries in transition from command or Socialist (Communist) economies to market economies. Although they desperately require education and training of a managerial class, management contracts may be appropriate in the early stages, with a heavy training or mentoring component.

BENEFITS

A management contract has several advantages to each party involved. For the owner, one of the more obvious is obtaining experienced, skilled personnel to administer the affairs of the company or property. At the same time, the expense can be limited to the services obtained and performed, rather than extending to all of the complications of overhead, fringe benefits, contingent liabilities and learning curves involved in recruiting senior executives. Timing is another benefit. Where a management contract is used, the application of experience with similar business becomes important if not critical. Whether it is one of the shareholders in a joint-venture, the trademark licensor, or an individual in a professional services organization, these experts will be familiar with the technology, the timing, services which need to be rendered, the competition and the general parameters of the customer and supplier relationships.

Benefits to the supplier of the management services include immediate entry into the market with minimal investment, and the opportunity to supply goodwill, technology, trademarks, formulas, and other services. In addition, the supplier is able to use the contacts, marketing knowledge and other resources of the local investor to maximize return. Finally, the supplier has the use of an in-place work force recruited by the local investor.

IMPLEMENTATION

The typical management contract in an international joint-venture may contain the following descriptions of services to be provided.

1. Financial administrative support, including the determination and evaluation of working capital and future financing needs of the enterprise; the alternatives for obtaining necessary funds, assistance in arranging lines of credit, loans, letters of credit, or other short- or long-term financing.

Management Contracts

2. Local procurement, including advice and assistance in negotiations to obtain raw materials, supplies, parts, assemblies or sub-assemblies at favorable prices, including possible volume discounts.

3. Accounting and tax advice including development of accounting policies and procedures in accordance with generally accepted accounting standards and principles, assistance with formulation of budgets and financial projections, development and implementation of standards of financial controls to assist management, guidance on inventory and asset valuation, and control and revaluation in order to minimize taxes.

4. Human resource administration including guidance on the selection, recruitment, compensation and evaluation of executives, design and administration of wage and salary systems, coordination, guidance and advice/support in collective bargaining and any negotiations with local unions. Other areas include advice and assistance in interpreting and complying with local laws and regulations relating to social security, medical and hospitalization benefits, training, education, profit sharing and other fringe benefits; techniques for providing physical plant security for offices and employees of the company on premises.

5. Legal assistance, including representation before all authorities and administrative and juridical bodies which may hear and determine matters affecting the interests of the company, its Board of Directors or its shareholders, and advice and guidance in obtaining import and export permits, foreign exchange permission, investment and technology transfer approvals, registration of patents, trademarks, copyrights and other intellectual property, maritime permits or approvals, zoning or property tax abatement rulings, and any other legal or administrative proceeding arising in the normal course of business. This includes legal

advice and preparation of agreements, documents, memoranda, reports or whatever may be necessary to facilitate the conduct of affairs of the company, directly or by means of outside representatives.

6. Public and community relations, including representation before industry and general news publications, chambers of commerce, business and professional organizations, municipal, state and federal authorities; imple-mentation of communication systems and media to inform management and employees of current events, activities and plans which have been approved by the Board of Directors, and generally to maintain a favorable image for the company both inside and outside of the local community.

EVALUATION

Management contracts should be controlled and evaluated like any other contract for services. The objectives of the arrangement should be developed and negotiated between the owner and the provider of services, such that both sides are satisfied with the fairness and feasibility of accomplishment before the agreement is signed. Milestones must be included, particularly relating to the training of management and employees. The services to be provided should be analyzed for technical content or other skills to determine which services are to be assumed gradually by local managers and which may continue to be supplied by a management contract.

Although it is uncommon, one system of evaluation and control involves incentive payments relating to schedules for completion of the milestones jointly defined and agreed upon. Furthermore, systems which are even more sophisticated consider rewards and penalties relating to scheduled completion of training or other milestone items, much like project management systems involving turnkey contracts with cost plus incentive-fee compensation arrangements.

APPLICATIONS TO SMALL BUSINESS

Management contracts act as a device to leverage resources at minimal cost and gain immediate results. Thus, a small business may use the device as a strategy, much as financial leverage may be used. In such a context, however, the small business entrepreneur is well advised to assure himself that a highly skilled and experienced person is administering the management contract, to obtain the desired results with a minimum of burden on the entrepreneur personally.

CONCLUSION

Contracts for management services can be the ideal answer to staffing new international joint-ventures or offshore investment arrangements in tax haven jurisdictions where specialized administrative experience, anonymity and tax advice are essential to accomplish objectives. They can also be well suited to situations where technology, goodwill and other resources, and expertise can be applied to generating attractive returns with little or minimal risk and virtually no investment, such as hotel franchises.

SOFTWARE/DATABASES

Business International. "Investing, Licensing, Trading in . . . [By Country]." Revised periodically. Provides a good discussion of the local investment rules and regulations, by country, information about restrictions placed on foreign companies, and the experience of selected U.S. companies in that country. They contain references to management contracts held by various multinational companies on an irregular basis.

Robert J. Radway

Robert J. Radway, an attorney in New York, has been involved in some 80 international joint-ventures, and a large number of acquisitions, mergers, licensing and distribution arrangements, and turnkey projects. He has concentrated his work in Asia (Japan and the ASEAN countries), and Europe (primarily Finland, Sweden, France, and Germany). His U.S. clients have included SOHIO, General Motors, Westinghouse, General Electric, Ingersoll-Rand, Electrolux, Memorex, American Optical, NeoRx (a small biotech firm), and Combustion Engineering. Radway has published some 40 articles and monographs in professional journal, and is currently working on his second book (on Strategic Global Alliances). During 1989 he taught executive courses in Europe and Asia on International Joint-Ventures, Cross-Cultural Negotiations, Internationalization of the Firm, and related topics.

Foreign Contract Agreements

OVERVIEW

Freedom of contract principles are taken for granted by American business managers. U.S. lawyers have advised American businessmen that for a contract to be binding and enforceable, there must be an offer and acceptance, consideration, definiteness and lawful subject matter. What they have not told their clients is that many foreign governments frequently interfere with business contracts. The rules of the game are different, and these differences do not relate merely to differences in legal systems (i.e., common law, civil law, Islamic law, etc.). Rather, particularly in many developing and communist countries, the host government frequently becomes a third party in the contract negotiations.

When, where and why these nation-states intervene depends on the culture, level of industrial development, political and economic systems in the country, and often the current political winds. When governments change, contracts with the former government may not necessarily be enforceable against successor governments. The concept of what may be consistent with or contrary to the public policy of a host government may depend on current priorities for attracting technology or capital, balance of payments problems, or a hotly contested political election campaign. Foreign companies may serve as convenient scapegoats to be expropriated or nationalized, despite any previous contractual guarantees. Thus, whenever possible, contracts in countries with such histories must be drafted and negotiated by experienced international business managers and lawyers familiar with this history and must anticipate such occurrences by including exit strategies and available commercial leverage.

The end of the Cold War, breakup of the Soviet Union, and consequences of those major developments, along with worldwide recession in the early 1990s has resulted in massive deregulation, privatizations and conversions of controlled to market economies virtually everywhere. This paradigm change should increase the awareness of international business executives in the U.S. and throughout the West to beware of contracts and "deals" wherein the new foreign partners really do not understand the consequences of their agreements. You do not need to be a rocket scientist to predict that many of these new agreements will be renegotiated for "public policy" reasons when they go sour later on.

EXAMPLES

When Fidel Castro's Cuban Revolutionary Government nationalized the Cuban subsidiaries of a host of American companies in the early 1960s, he devised a novel formula for compensation which considered back taxes computed on a totally different basis than the agreements which those companies had negotiated with the Batista regime. This formula was followed in the subsequent expropriations of copper mines in Peru and Chile, iron ore and oil properties in Venezuela and selected manufacturing and banking investments throughout Latin America and other regions in the 1960s and 1970s. Creative calculations under these formulae resulted in foreign multinationals owing considerable sums to the governments which had nationalized their properties.

The Islamic Fundamentalist (Khomeini) revolution in Iran in 1979, which included 52 Americans being held hostage for 444 days, resulted in a freeze of Iranian assets by the U. S. government, and the non-payment of hundreds of claims by American and European companies working in Iran. The special international tribunal established at the Hague to resolve the resulting disputes continued throughout the 1980s. Other nationalizations arose from communist revolutions in the U.S.S.R. in 1917 and China in 1949, Peronist nationalization of banks and public utilities in Argentina in the 1950s, and François Mitterand's election in France in 1983. Many of these are being and have been reversed and privatized in the recent shift toward market economies globally.

Short of outright nationalization, the phrase "creeping expropriation" has been applied to severe limitations on economic activities of foreign firms in certain developing countries. These have included limitations on profit remittances, dividends, royalties or technical assistance fees from local investments or technology arrangements. Multinationals have also suffered discriminatory tariffs and non-tariff barriers with practical effects of keeping out certain producer goods from those countries (almost always including U.S. firms), and discriminatory laws on patents and trademarks. The intellectual property restrictions had the practical effect of eliminating or drastically reducing protection of pharmaceutical substances, compounds or products. Other countries, especially in Asia, ignored intellectual property protection altogether (especially copyright and trademarks), causing billions of dollars worth of losses to computer software, videos and other products.

Other restrictions required international producers and marketers of certain consumer products, especially including bottled beverages, packaged food, cigarettes, cosmetics and toiletries, to invest huge sums of money to repackage all products to link their internationally recognized trademarks with newly devised local trademarks belonging to unaffiliated distributors. In some countries the MNCs were ultimately advised to fade out their international trademarks altogether. These colossal rip-offs were generally renegotiated but not until tedious and enormously expensive lobbying campaigns were mounted by industry associations around the world and by governments of the U.S. and other western industrialized countries.

In spite of contracts and guarantees negotiated in India prior to the enactment of the Foreign Exchange Reserve Act (1974), Johnson & Johnson and all other foreign investors subsequently had to submit to a host of regulations to retain majority equity positions in companies already established. These restrictions included an agreement to limit production to the original product line (no expansion or modifications beyond the original baby products); limitations on importing equipment even when the foreign parent company agreed to donate the equipment to its Indian subsidiary instead of crediting it as a registered capital contribution; limitations on compensation of expatriate executives to the drastically lower level of nationals and sometimes even limits on compensation to Indians; unrealistic export commitments with no regard to competitiveness on global markets; and, strict transfer of technology rules resulting in international companies withholding new technology from their Indian affiliate due to lack of adequate compensation and protection. Many of these rules were later copied in whole or in part by Malaysia, Indonesia, the Philippines, Nigeria, Brazil and many other developing countries. In the late 1980s and 1990s India and other countries began easing those restrictions, in line with worldwide trends.

It was suggested by some observers that Union Carbide's plant disaster in Bhopal, India, was only one of hundreds of potential disasters waiting to happen. The rationale for this relates to the adoption by some Less Developed Country (LDC) governments in the late 1960s and 1970s of such confrontational and inconsistent rules against foreign companies and their contracts. This argument posits that the MNCs were deprived by these rules of rights of private property (constitutionally guaranteed in the U.S.) without due process of law, and simply placed in untenable positions. IBM and Coca Cola pulled out after unsuccessful attempts to negotiate fair deals in India and other LDCs in order to protect their absolute control over their proprietary technology, previously guaranteed by signed contracts. Due to such events, renegotiation of signed contracts at the insistence of LDC governments became commonplace.

BENEFITS

From the examples above, it is clear that the international playing field differs from its domestic counterpart. Contract agreements must, therefore, be prepared and negotiated in a totally different context. To avoid being locked into a commitment that a firm feels obliged to honor, but which is viewed differently by the other party or its government, both internal business factors and external or environmental factors must be carefully considered.

If the firm has properly researched its contract with its local distributor or agent in advance, and the agent does not sell the quota of product established as essential to justify the agent's exclusive rights, the firm may be able to terminate and replace the agent with a better one, or convert the agent's exclusive arrangement to a non-exclusive one. However, in a majority of countries around the world, the laws are such that if firms do not do their homework, they may be stuck with the nonperforming agent and be required to pay him a huge indemnity for trying to protect the firm's own marketing interests in that territory.

Paternalistic labor laws may also interfere with management rights to lay off employees or control the labor force in many countries in Europe, especially Belgium, France, Holland, Germany, and Sweden. Rights that are often taken for granted in the U.S. are limited or altogether denied in these countries, as well as Communist countries and certain LDCs. This can spoil attempts to restructure during periods of high unemployment, and has ruined many acquisitions when elimination of duplicative forces was a key to synergy.

IMPLEMENTATION

A contract in international business is not merely a document setting forth quantity, price and delivery schedule of the products. Instead, it must take into consideration the local legal system and political and currency risks in the country involved. Contracts should detail how and where disputes should be resolved out of court, by whom (arbitrators), in what language, under what rules, and in which currency the award should be denominated. It should also make clear which substantive and procedural laws should be applied to interpret the contract, and where an arbitral award will be enforced. Certain international treaties now apply increasingly common standards to dispute settlement, but you must verify which countries have signed and ratified these treaties.

The possibilities of denial of the firm's essential rights or privileges by the host sovereign must be considered, as well as the rights to terminate the agreement under such conditions. Where termination of certain agreements may be against local public policy, other provisions should be considered, such as payment of fixed sums of (liquidated) damages in the event of a material breach.

Most importantly, however, the commercial objectives of the international manager must always be kept in mind when preparing an agreement in certain countries. An executive of a U.S. company does not want to be a plaintiff in the courts of most foreign countries for a variety of reasons. Thus, as part of a firm's regional strategy, commercial leverage should always be evaluated and incorporated into foreign contract agreements to consider the social and business culture, the company's international reputation, and the drain on corporate resources resulting from litigation in a foreign country.

The warrantees or guarantees that a company offers with its products should be carefully designed and limited to conditions under its control, and not those which can be changed by a local government when political power shifts. With direct foreign investment, the firm's presence is almost always dependant on agreements with the host government on import duties, taxes, export commitments, price controls, availability of hard currency, supply of utilities to the plant, and a plethora of other items. The international manager must carefully identify all of these assumptions and identify alternatives if and when the host government's permission is revoked or invalidated. If the firm is prevented from including such provisions in an agreement, it should structure the transaction to offset its exposure and should develop contingency plans in such event.

EVALUATION

Major distinctions must be made in evaluating foreign contract agreements. The degree of country or environmental risk (including political, currency and project risk) will differ significantly in agreements with Canada and the United Kingdom on one hand, contrasted with Iran, Nicaragua or North Korea on the other.

Certain types of agreements should be made for shorter terms, with clearly defined performance criteria. They can always be extended, but termination of longer agreements without huge penalties may be more difficult than expected, or for that matter impossible. Joint-venture agreements may also be entered into for short durations. When the relationship has deteriorated, face can be saved on both sides by adhering to a predetermined termination schedule, rather than terminating a charter set to run for 99 years.

So called "boilerplate" language should rarely be used in international contracts. Such language was developed for domestic contracts in a cultural and legal system understood by both parties. The indiscriminate transfer of such language has often had unintended and disastrous consequences. Since many of these agreements are translated into the local language, the language employed in the agreement should also be simple and easily translatable, rather than use the jargon or "legalese" which often confuses domestic business agreements.

APPLICATIONS TO SMALL BUSINESS

Small businesses should be particularly concerned about the problems identified above, since they cannot afford expensive litigation or arbitration either in the U.S. or abroad if their international contracts go awry. International managers from small businesses should take greater care to assure that differences and potential problems are addressed, as they have smaller staffs available to rectify relationships which deteriorate due to misunderstandings.

If a small business is to grow larger in international markets, it must make the important investment expense to research differences in culture, religion and business practices which should be incorporated in the international contract agreements. These small firms may have less commercial leverage in a dispute arising abroad than their multinational counterpart.

CONCLUSION

International contract agreements should be prepared and negotiated by experienced professionals who are familiar with and sensitive to historic, cultural, economic and political differences between domestic and international business. The considerable learning curve with such agreements should not be ignored. Language used should be designed to consider long-term business objectives as well as commercial leverage. Specific remedies under often unfriendly circumstances should be resourcefully provided.

SOFTWARE/DATABASES

American Bar Association (ABA) publications provide detailed case studies, especially those of the Sections of International Law and Practice and

Corporation, Banking and Business Law, including, among others: *The International Lawyer*, quarterly journal of the Section of International Law and Practice; *The Business Lawyer*, quarterly journal of the Section of Corporation, Business and Banking Law: American Foreign Law Association, *American Journal of Comparative Law*; and American Society of International Law, *the American Journal of International Law*, Washington, D.C. (quarterly).

Robert J. Radway

Robert J. Radway, an attorney in New York, has been involved in some 80 international joint-ventures, and a large number of acquisitions, mergers, licensing and distribution arrangements, and turnkey projects. He has concentrated his work in Asia (Japan and the ASEAN countries), and Europe (primarily Finland, Sweden, France, and Germany). His U.S. clients have included SOHIO, General Motors, Westinghouse, General Electric, Ingersoll-Rand, Electrolux, Memorex, American Optical, NeoRx (a small biotech firm), and Combustion Engineering. Radway has published some 40 articles and monographs in professional journals, and is currently working on his second book (on Strategic Global Alliances). During 1989 he taught executive courses in Europe and Asia on International Joint-Ventures, Cross-Cultural Negotiations, Internationalization of the Firm, and related topics.

Selecting and Managing Local Lawyers

OVERVIEW

The international business manager needs the predictability and certainty to make and implement decisions on foreign projects. One decision which is vital to the success or failure of a foreign project is the local lawyer chosen. In approaching this task, the manager must realize that at least three significant differences may exist between U.S. lawyers and foreign counsels: contrasting legal systems, totally different approaches to legal education and training, and major variances in the role of lawyers in different cultures. These are in addition to cultural, political, religious and language differences. Thus, selection criteria must go beyond language in considering qualitative factors like response time, particular areas of experience or expertise, political identification, billing practices, backup in the substantive areas needed (e.g., corporate, labor and tax), and backup language capability. In addition, managing that local counsel's services requires refining communication skills very specifically to what is necessary, including the surrounding constraints, limitations and assumptions, all on a cost effective basis.

This exercise may be particularly difficult in countries in transition from Socialist or Communist systems to market oriented systems. The training of lawyers and complete understanding of market concepts and the role of lawyers in Western societies is not well understood by these new generation of lawyers. Many lawyers from Western country law firms have been established in these countries and may be preferable in early years of the transitions. It is questionable how long nationalist or protectionist attitudes will tolerate foreigners raking in high fees in lieu of local professionals, however.

EXAMPLES

Until recently in Japan, lawyers were rarely used by Japanese companies to prepare business agreements, advise on tax matters, assist in negotiation of contracts or projects, assist in the settlement of disputes, and other tasks where American executives routinely use their corporate attorney. When U.S. firms began to go to Japan with their corporate lawyers along, the Japanese generally reacted adversely. More recently in the People's Republic of China (PRC), after its "opening" in the late 1970s, one large U.S. multinational mining company took a huge delegation of executives and "Wall Street lawyers" with them to negotiate a long term mineral development project.

This is a repeat and exacerbation of the mistakes made in Europe in the 1960s, when American business executives "led" with their lawyers, as they were accustomed to do at home. Much to their surprise and dismay, this practice was greeted negatively with antipathy and even hostility, except for England where there is a similar system and tradition. The role of lawyers in business planning and implementation was and remains much more limited in almost every foreign country (except England and English "influence" jurisdictions) than in America. In many countries the public accountant or the banker is much closer to the client than the lawyer, which is often the reverse of the U.S. international company's experience at home.

In France, Italy, Spain, Portugal and the Latin American countries (and virtually all "Civil Law" countries), even when experienced U.S. corporate lawyers ask a simple question like "What are the tax consequences of the proposed project", they frequently get back 15-20 page memoranda on the history of foreign investment, certain legal philosophical and taxation policies. The fact is, such is not a simple question, and is far too open-ended, as are many questions asked of local counsel by inexperienced U.S. corporate lawyers and international business executives. Nearly all of this is irrelevant in the foreign context; and the degree of irrelevancy increases when you go from Western Europe to Japan to communist countries and to Third World or developing countries.

BENEFITS

It is useful to think about specific requirements of a foreign counsel before charging into the selection process, especially if it is being done without the assistance or management of experienced U.S. international counsel. Finding objective, high quality legal advice in a timely manner and for a reasonable cost is the goal. In other words quality, delivery and price are as important in this case as anywhere else. But selecting the right local lawyer can bring far greater benefits in many countries, since if they are well respected in the community, they can both add to the corporation's credibility, and greatly facilitate market entry into an alien culture and marketplace.

Examples abound of U.S. companies charging into countries led by enthusiastic but culturally insensitive marketing executives, where they initially lost lots of money, despite outstanding quality products or technology. The U.S. is the exception, rather than the norm, and most foreign business cultures require a totally different kind of "courtship" before buying a product, taking a license of a certain technology, or entering into a joint-venture. Seasoned local lawyers can be helpful if listened to, which itself is a skill in which U.S. international business managers are often underdeveloped. The more senior partners (often the father in a firm including a generous dose of his children, children-in-law, and nephews) can provide these non-legal benefits while the younger lawyers do the grunt work.

The most important benefit, however, is long-term success in the local business environment. It is essential to engage a network of appropriately skilled local advisors, and a firm's foreign counsel is a vital member of that network. Possibly more than any other local advisor, especially in Third World countries, a good foreign lawyer can help to avoid, forestall or obviate serious problems if the relationship is cultivated properly.

IMPLEMENTATION

Finding the most suitable lawyer and developing a meaningful legal relationship is a time-consuming task. If the project (investment) has significant long term economic impact, it is highly recommended that the corporation's U.S. "in-house" international lawyer manage the selection and supervision task, and even travel to the country to interview potential candidates. Obviously this is not always possible or cost justified, especially if the transaction is nominal and the distance (and trip expense) is great. But as international activity increases, selection and management of the local lawyers becomes a larger and more critical part of the management function, and has a greater impact on profitability of international operations.

The task lends itself well to project planning techniques. Surveys should be done through the counsel's domestic network of international lawyer organizations and groups, such as international committees of local and state bar associations, the American Foreign Law Association, the International Law and Practice section of the American Bar Association (ABA), ad-hoc international lawyers groups (which exist in an increasing number of major cities across the U.S., and contacts in the legal departments of other international corporations (legal departments), banks and public accounting firms, as well as international committees of other professional or trade associations. Contacts at the local level of the bilateral Chamber of Commerce (U.S.-local) can also be valuable.

Once the list is narrowed, criteria should be developed, including the substantive skills and functions which will be required most often. Some corporate General Counsels have developed a memorandum which briefly describes the company's international operations, with an emphasis on the type of legal advice and assistance most frequently needed from foreign counsel—a type of legal prospectus—just for this purpose.

Criteria should include language capability, and backup language skills. Caution is in order here, however. Many U.S. companies have made the identical blunder of selecting a local law firm merely because they met their most polished, English-speaking partner. When it came time for quick response on a critical question, however, he was off in London, and his backup lawyer spoke little English. Distinguish between form and substance, and even though some excellent speakers are also fine lawyers, focus on who will perform the work, how long will it take, and what will it cost. The practice of law and the role of lawyers differ greatly in Europe, Asia, Latin America and the Middle East. Highly competent and "familiar" lawyers are more likely to be found in Canada, the United Kingdom, Australia, Hong Kong, and a few other places (in addition to U.S. firms with foreign offices), but beyond that, there are gross differences in such critical business concepts as: approaching local government agencies, evaluating compliance with deadlines in local foreign investment regulations, disclosing sensitive plans when attempting to obtain interpretations of unclear laws or regulations from local bureaucrats, requesting waivers or extensions from local content rules, or exporting quotas for "extreme circumstances."

EVALUATION

There is little difference in techniques employed to evaluate foreign counsel from the means used to judge outside domestic "special counsel" for litigation, patents and trademarks, or any other legal services. Communication problems are to be expected and they are a part of international business life, but they should be managed like any other risk. It is to be expected that there will be times when foreign counsel needs to be prodded. Different cultures admittedly have different conceptions of time. The important question is whether they respond to the prod. Foreign counsel in small firms may not specialize as much as is common in the U.S., and this should be discussed in advance at the interview stage. If they are not accustomed to providing tax advice, for example, (commonly the case in many countries), the competent local tax partner in one of the reputable public or chartered accountant firms for tax advice should be used. This principle may apply to trademarks and patents and maritime or admiralty advice in particular.

APPLICATIONS TO SMALL BUSINESS

For smaller companies without the staff with appropriate skills or seasoning, the outside U.S. specialist becomes even more critical. Small business (chief) executives themselves must develop some of these skills, and they therefore may want to take a seasoned consultant along on the first or critical foreign negotiations. The consultant can be sent a day or two in advance to do the screening after the stateside preparation, and make appointments for the CEO to meet two or three local lawyers and select the one with the best chemistry. Depending on their experience, some U.S. international business lawyers/consultants can also assist in selecting local bankers, public accountants and occasionally licensees and/or joint-venture partners in countries where they have appropriate contacts and knowledge of the business culture.

CONCLUSION

The task of selecting and managing local lawyers is one that will generally weigh heavily on longer term success or failure in foreign markets. It is thus important to treat the problem as a task, and plan it accordingly. It is equally important that the staff person assigned responsibility for the task is appropriate for the assignment. If such experience and skill is lacking in an organization, however, the task is important enough to merit investment in an outside consultant to help develop a criteria and train the staff, and perhaps to participate in the first and more delicate of these assignments from time to time. A periodic audit of foreign counsel to update the degree of satisfaction and effectiveness they provide is also recommended, with an outside resource bringing more objectivity to such an assignment than the staff person who has been involved with the local relationship for some period of time.

REFERENCES/SOURCES

Lists of local law firms or lawyers are available through U.S. embassies and consulates abroad, but generally these lists are not updated and are quantitative only (i.e., people are "known", but little or nothing may be known about skills, fees or response time.) Local bar associations and law societies exist but, like their U.S. counterparts, do not recommend lawyers for foreign clients.

Reference Manual on Doing Business in Latin America. D. R. Shea, *et al.*, eds., University of Wisconsin Center for Latin America, 1980: 65-70. This concise piece offers considerable insight into the legal process in Latin America, and some observations apply to other regions.

Robert J. Radway

Robert J. Radway, an attorney in New York, has been involved in some 80 international joint-ventures, and a large number of acquisitions, mergers, licensing and distribution arrangements, and turnkey projects. He has concentrated his work in Asia (Japan and other ASEAN countries), and Europe (primarily Finland, Sweden, France, and Germany). His U.S. clients have included SOHIO, General Motors, Westinghouse, General Electric, Ingersoll-Rand, Electrolux, Memorex, American Optical, NeoRx (a small biotech firm), and Combustion Engineering. Radway has published some 40 articles and monographs in professional journals and is currently working on his second book (on Strategic Global Alliances). During 1989 he taught executive courses in Europe and Asia on International Joint Ventures, Cross-Cultural Negotiations, Internationalization of the Firm, and related topics.

10.

Global Alliances

The Impact of GATT on the Global Business Environment

OVERVIEW

Although the ambitious and lengthy negotiations of the Uruguay Round of the General Agreement on Tariffs and Trade (GATT) achieved less than had been hoped for by some participants and observers, the accords are nonetheless significant in both an economic and political sense. In deepening and broadening the multilateral process regulating global trade, the Uruguay Round will help to create a more stable environment for the conduct of international business. While slow in coming, the accords are especially notable accomplishments in light of the ongoing upheavals in political and economic conditions around the world.

The signing, on April 15, 1994 in Marrakesh, Morocco, of the GATT accords represents the culmination of seven years of difficult negotiations. Inaugurated in September 1986 in the resort of Punta del Este and begun officially in January 1987, the Uruguay Round was concluded on December 15, 1993, much to the relief of its 117 participants. Set to take effect in 1995, and actually a package of twenty-eight separate agreements, it was by far the most ambitious of the several rounds of negotiations undertaken since the creation of GATT in 1947.[1] Indeed, the Uruguay Round will be the last within the existing framework; GATT is to be incorporated into a new World Trade Organization (WTO), which embraces the service and intellectual property agreements of the accord. While still to be based in Geneva as was its predecessor, the WTO will seek to play an even broader role in shaping the future of international trade.[2]

EXAMPLES

Since it includes provisions on a number of economic sectors previously omitted from GATT negotiations, the present agreement represents an important extension and strengthening of the multi-lateral framework governing international trade. The major provisions of the Uruguay Round are described and analyzed below, followed by an assessment of the accord's current significance and future import for international business.

Industrial Goods

As in past GATT rounds, the current accord provides that tariff rates on industrial goods will continue to fall, even to zero in some cases, and are to be cut by 1/3 overall.[3] While these measures will bring tariffs down to an average of 4% for industrialized countries, the impact in developing nations, where rates have been prohibitive to imports in some sectors, will be even more dramatic. International trade in industrial goods should therefore be stimulated, with producers in developed countries gaining access to markets from which they had been excluded.

Textiles

In taking on trade in textiles and clothing, GATT negotiators addressed a crucial sector that had been governed under a "temporary" regime in place since 1974, the Multi Fiber Arrangement (MFA). Implemented by the industrialized nations to restrict their volume of textile imports from developing countries, this complex and cumbersome system of quotas will be phased out entirely over ten years beginning in 1995, and tariffs in the sector will be cut substantially, though not completely eliminated.

By reducing restrictions and simplifying trade regulations, these measures should increase activity in a sector whose trading activity is already valued at $250 billion (1992). Given the labor-intensive nature of the industry, producers in countries with low wage rates should continue to gain market share under the new agreement, as consumers enjoy a wider selection of products and intensified price competition.

Agricultural Products

By including trade in agricultural products, the Uruguay Round brought under consideration for multi-lateral regulation perhaps the most heavily subsidized and politically volatile sector in the global economy. Predictably, negotiations were contentious from beginning to end, with the United States and the European Community (since January 1, 1994 the European Union or EU) hammering out last-minute modifications to the year-old Blair House Accord that allowed the placation of vociferous French farmers concerning price support payments.

Not surprisingly, the new agreement achieves less than had been hoped for by some (including the United States and the Cairns Group of major food exporters), but nonetheless is quite important in placing limits on both the volume and value of agricultural products that can be subsidized for export. Using as a base for calculation figures from 1986-1990, the signatories agreed to reduce over a six-year period the volume of subsidized agricultural exports by 21%, while their value must fall by 36%.

In addition, a variety of restrictions on trade in food products will be converted into tariffs and then progressively reduced, by 36% over six years for advanced nations, and by 24% over ten years for developing nations.[4] So while cuts in subsidies may initially cause a reduction in the volume of some agricultural products on the international market and a concomitant price rise, over the long run consumers worldwide should benefit from increased access to the output of more efficient producers.

Services

By addressing services (the fastest growing component of global trade and currently estimated at least $900 billion a year) in the Uruguay round, GATT negotiators again entertained initial ambitions that exceeded actual results. Since restrictions on the international exchange of services are more difficult to identify explicitly than those involving industrial goods or agricultural products, the parties agreed to general provisions for "liberalization" and "non-discrimination" in the sector, and promised to conduct future negotiations within these guidelines.

Notably absent were concrete measures on shipping, financial services or telecommunications. Also, the audio-visual market emerged as a major bone of US-EU contention, with France insisting that the sub-sector be dropped from consideration for liberalization because of fears of US "cultural imperialism," especially in film-making. Finally, the perennial question of subsidies to builders of civil aircraft was left out of the accord, again with the US and EU merely agreeing to disagree.[5]

Yet despite these shortcomings, the mere fact that trade in services was broached in the GATT forum, and indeed a substantial convergence of views was realized is quite significant. Those firms prepared to offer services to overseas clients should find an improving international climate in future, as the sector promises to benefit from continued liberalization.

Intellectual Property Rights and Patents

Industrialized nations had long demanded inclusion in the GATT negotiations protection for proprietary designs and trademarks, including computer chips and software, databases, films and recordings. Important specific provisions were written into the final accord, including the extension of copyright for fifty years and the legal protection of trade secrets.

However, the most significant aspect of the negotiations is the explicit recognition by all signatories, especially the developing nations, that the proper use of intellectual property constitutes a legitimate area of multilateral regulation. While the GATT agreement will not mean an end to the piracy of proprietary information, governments will now have a new forum through which to pursue legal remedies. Finally, according to new dispute resolution provisions (described more fully below), countries may introduce punitive measures in one area for damages incurred in another, meaning that failure to respect the intellectual property accords might have repercussions in the industrial, agricultural, or services sectors.

Subsidies, Anti-dumping, and Dispute Resolution

Since the conclusion of the prior GATT agreement (the Tokyo Round 1973-1979), so-called "unfair competitive practices" have caused serious disputes among signatories, and frustration with procedures to resolve them has threatened the entire multi-lateral framework. Therefore, Uruguay Round negotiators invested substantial time and energy in clarifying the criteria to be used in determining precisely when government subsidies for or aggressive pricing of internationally traded products constitutes an unacceptable injury to competitors. Also, all complaints concerning such practices will be subject to a single dispute resolution procedure, with a much streamlined and more binding arbitration and appeals mechanism. By providing a more transparent and responsive means of adjudication, these measures should dampen recent trends toward unilateral retaliation for perceived trade injustices.

BENEFITS

In taking on anew a number of complex economic sectors as subjects of multilateral trade regulation, the Uruguay Round exposed the GATT framework and process to a potentially devastating loss of credibility.[6] Failure to meet highly publicized deadlines exhausted the patience of the participants and bred cynicism in the public.[7] But the accord signed in the end was of both economic and political significance, and promises to shape the global business environment for years to come.

On the economic front, if ratified by the respective governments and implemented in full, it has been estimated that the current GATT agreement could raise global GDP by up to $270 billion by the year 2002.[8] Given its apparently auspicious timing, it could well be that the Uruguay Round will be viewed in retrospect as a catalyst of global economic growth.[9] But whatever the precise magnitude of the ultimate effect, the continued liberalization of the rules and practices governing the exchange of industrial goods, and now agricultural products and services as well, will serve to reinforce the accelerating pace of global economic integration.[10]

IMPLEMENTATION

Coming as it does during a time of extreme fluidity in international politics, the GATT accord introduces an important element of stability (if not predictability) into transnational economic relations. As many countries turn inward to confront divisive social problems and centrifugal political forces, tendencies to blame outside elements for domestic problems can easily degenerate into mutually damaging and self-perpetuating conflict over foreign economic relations. By providing a framework of both increasing scope and specificity for the regulation of international trade, the successful conclusion of the Uruguay Round should provide a much less volatile environment for global business than might well exist in its absence.

EVALUATION

In order to realize its full promise in contributing to a stable and open global economic system, the GATT process and framework must continue to widen and include more of international economic life. Obviously, the continued absence from the organization of two of the world's most important nations, China and Russia, is not compatible with this expanded role.[11] But the conclusion of the arduous Uruguay Round and the creation of the WTO provides both a strengthened regulatory structure and an improved political context conducive to the eventual integration of these powers into a viable multilateral framework.

APPLICATIONS TO SMALL BUSINESS

While certainly an ambitious undertaking, the potential gains from the GATT accords for globally-oriented enterprises outweigh the associated costs. For smaller firms in particular, the agreement should reduce the uncertainty inherent in the international business environment, while opening up opportunities in new sectors to those enterprises well-positioned to provide products and especially services previously denied foreign customers. Therefore, in their present as well as future efforts, trade negotiators need and deserve the support of the international business community.

CONCLUSION

As the last session of international trade negotiations held under the auspices of GATT, the Uruguay Round was both the most difficult and most important. Not only does it continue the important momentum established in past rounds, the new accords open up vital new sectors to increased exchange and competition. Moreover, the new WTO is being established at a crucial juncture in history, and promises to provide a robust framework for the orderly regulation of a potentially divisive area in international relations.

REFERENCES/SOURCES

Business Week. Various Issues.

Cable, Vincent. "GATT and After." *The World Today* (February 1994):26-28.

The Economist. Various Issues.

Facts on File. Various Editions.

Far Eastern Economic Review. Various Issues.

Financial Times. Various Issues.

OECD. *Assessing the Effects of the Uruguay Round.* Paris: OECD, 1993.

The New York Times. Various Issues.

The Wall Street Journal. Various Issues.

ENDNOTES

1. For a concise yet thorough analysis of this and past GATT negotiations and accords, see *Financial Times* (December 16, 1993): 4-7.

2. In addition to the article footnoted above, for analysis of the future workings of the WTO, see *Financial Times* (Thursday, April 7, 1994): 6

3. Industries in which tariffs will eventually cut to zero include: construction and medical equipment, steel, pharmaceuticals, paper, and alcohol. See *Facts on File* (1993): 930-931.

4. The practice of "tariffication;" the conversion of quantitative (quotas) and qualitative (licensing requirements, health or purity standards) restrictions on the exchange of designated items into specific monetary charges, has proven in past GATT negotiations an effective tactic in first standardizing and then reducing barriers to trade. But it is not always easy, as seen in the special conditions that were granted Japan and Korea regarding their agreement to convert traditional and socially sensitive restrictions on rice imports into tariffs.

5. The dispute between the American airframe manufacturers and the Airbus Industrie consortium has intensified as Airbus gained market share in the late-1980s, and remains a major source of transatlantic political tensions.

6. One observer argues "The main achievement of the negotiators was negative: they avoided a disaster." See Vincent Cable, "GATT and After." *The World Today* (February 1994:26-28).

7. It has been noted that the presence of new negotiators for the EU (Sir Leon Brittan) and the US (Mickey Kantor), along with the appointment of a Peter Sutherland to replace Arthur Dunkel as GATT Director-General, gave important impetus to talks that were badly in the doldrums. See *Financial Times* (Thursday, December 16, 1993): 4-7.

8. See *Assessing the Effects of the Uruguay Round.* Paris: OECD, 1993. Although prepared prior to the conclusion of the negotiations and signing of the accord, this study is a valuable attempt to estimate the economic impact of the agreement. Its authors note that because many of the accord's most important elements apply to sectors whose output is inherently difficult to quantify (services, intellectual property rights), the various models used in all probability underestimate the overall impact on the global trade picture.

9. The nature of the relationship between trade agreements and economic growth is problematic, but it was recently observed that "seven rounds of GATT negotiations since 1948 have reduced the average worldwide tariffs on manufactured goods from 45% to 5%, and each round has been followed by a period of robust global growth." See "Finally, GATT May Fly" *Business Week* (December 20, 1993): 36-37.

10. In presenting an overview of the accords to Congress, United States Trade Representative (USTR) Mickey Kantor was quite positive in his assessment of their likely impact on the US economy. See his testimony 23 March 1994 to the Subcommittee on Commerce, Consumer Protection, and Competitiveness.

11. Intensive negotiations have already begun concerning Chinese membership; both the US and EU have sent high-level trade missions to Beijing, and Chinese

officials were in Geneva 15-19 March 1994 for consultations with the GATT Secretariat. For analysis of these talks, see Far *Eastern Economic Review* (March 17, 1994:42-43), and *Financial Times* (Wednesday, March 16, 1994): 6.

Dr. David W. Thornton
Director of Government Studies
Campbell University

Dr. David W. Thornton holds an M.A. in European History from the University of North Carolina at Greensboro, and a Ph.D. in International Relations from the University of South Carolina. In addition to issues of international trade, his research interests include the impact of geopolitical conflict on economic and industrial competitiveness, relating especially to the global aeronautics industry.

Strategies for the European Union

OVERVIEW

Events in Europe continue to have a pervasive impact on firms' planning and strategies as U.S. executives evaluate the evolving opportunities and threats posed by the continent's economic and political initiatives. Beginning with the European Commission's White Paper, *Completing the Internal Market* in 1985, the Single European Act and its 282 directives (originally known as EC92 in the U.S.) have produced a "Europe without frontiers." The tide of activities not only swept forward the 12 members of the European Union (EU, formerly the European Community, EC); Austria, Finland, Norway, and Sweden were scheduled to vote on joining the EC in late 1994/1995. In addition, recent agreements with the remaining members of the European Free Trade Association (EFTA) have extended trading rules of the Single European Act throughout a region to be called the European Economic Area. By 1995, the stage is set for a market of 380 million consumers from 18 countries, accounting for more than 40% of the world's trade (Eurecom, December, 1993). Furthermore, queuing up for "association agreements" with the EU are the former Eastern European countries which may lead to additional unified markets within a 10 year transition period. Clearly, Europe in the mid to late 1990s will offer an era of unprecedented opportunities for many U.S. and other international firms.

However, because of the very same immense opportunities represented by a European Single Market, Europe is also poised to become the battleground of the major international business firms. In addition, even for those companies who are not doing business in Europe (nor plan to do business), European integration will have major consequences as the "winners" of the European Single Market competition will become even more formidable competitors that can compete back in the U.S. or other non-European markets. Thus, the evaluation of the many economic, political and regulatory issues of the new European Union become critical to the long-term success of many international and domestic firms.

While the notion of an integrated European market captures the imagination of ambitious corporate leaders, the evolving process by which the market is being united presents many elements of uncertainty for international executives. This article poses four key strategic questions of extreme importance to firms doing business or intending to do business in Europe in the near future. Three of these issues are a direct result of the EU regulatory process and include directive reciprocity, directive harmonization, and directive ambiguity. The fourth is the inherent globalization (or lack) of the firm's customer markets. In the sections that follow, a decision tree will be built to guide the executive in examining these critical issues; then, alternative strategies will be offered to take advantage of the newly integrated Europe.

EXAMPLES

Key Questions

1. EU Reciprocity

Does your company's home market or the sourcing country where your products are manufactured have restrictions on EU products for your industry?

The 282 directives *are* the governing legislation by which the various internal trade barriers are to be broken down by the Single European Act. Originating by law in the European Economic Commission (EEC), these directives specify not only EU market integration rules, but policies in regard to trade access to firms located outside the EU. These formal external trade policies are known as *reciprocity,* and they vary among industries affected by the Single European Act.

The EEC has adopted a general policy of reciprocity with non-EC members concerning trade in goods and services. The directives give some specifics to the nature of reciprocity that is expected in regard to individual policies concerning access to the home markets of non-European trading partners. For example, the directive on the automobile industry establishes an EU-wide ceiling of 10% of the market on Japanese cars, provides a target of EU cars to Japan of an equivalent amount, and mandates a minimum local requirement of 70% for cars built by the Japanese companies in Europe.

The actual type of reciprocity may take on several forms, such as the one above which could be described as "trade opening" reciprocity. Other more likely forms are considered to "identical" or "equivalent." Identical reciprocity means that if you want the treatment offered by EEC rules, your own country must give the EU competitors the *exact same treatment as offered in the EC,* so that they can offer the same products and services they offer in the EC. In most non-EC countries this would require revising their own regulations.

A second form, equivalent reciprocity, means that non-EC competitors would have access to the EU markets if, and only if, EU businesses are treated similarly to national firms in their non-EU markets. Any form of "double standards" for EU firms competing in that non-EC market would preclude that country's firms from competing in the EU. While the EEC suggests privately that the reciprocity measures are generally directed toward Japan and the Asian tigers, the majority of the directives are not explicit.

Another issue to be resolved is an international firm's world-wide sourcing activities. For example, it is unclear if the Japanese automobiles produced in the U.S. will be considered Japanese cars, and subject to import constraints and local content requirements, or as U.S. cars with less stringent reciprocity requirements. A worse case scenario for many international firms is for the EU to take a very hard line on reciprocity—that is, if either your home country (non-EU) *or* your source country (also non-EU) have restrictions on EU imports, your firm will face the highest level of reciprocity requirements in the directives affecting your industry and firm.

The general implication for non-EU firms facing high reciprocity requirements is that a strategy of *only exporting* products to the EU will be largely precluded. In order to do business in the EU, the firm will either have to move production to a country with low reciprocity hurdles with respect to the EU, or set up a production presence as a joint venture with an EU firm and use substantial European content in its products.

2. EU Harmonization

Has the EU adopted a directive(s) that has unified specifications for your industry's products and services rather than following mutual recognition of EU member states' specifications?

As a general rule, the directives will supersede national laws within the community members, and may force the re-writing of those laws, particularly when the directive has required unification of standards across Europe. This unification or "harmonization," a favorite "Euro-word," is the agreement within a directive concerning the accepted norms of standardization required for the product, service, industry and/or sector in question. Included are issues of product safety, labelling rules, testing requirements, broadcasting standards, and agricultural inspections. It is to be expected, and confirmed in many directives, that European business and industrial practice will serve as the basis for these standards—giving firms currently operating in Europe (both home country companies and established foreign multinationals) some competitive advantages over new entrants.

For example, the Hystra Co., a maker and exporter of forklifts to Europe since 1952, ran afoul of the directive from the EEC concerning forklifts. In order to meet the unified harmonization requirement, they made fifteen design changes, revised their shipping pattern, and changed to a European vendor on some parts because current American suppliers could not make the required certification tests. Although Hystra was able to successfully meet the directives regulations, the final result was that their costs went up, making them less competitive.

Initially, the EEC drafted single specification harmonizing rules with the aid of various European testing and certification groups and industry associations. This policy procedure worked well in areas where there existed broad agreement or reasonable compromises among EC member countries, but became extremely slow or impossible where major disagreements occurred. In order to avoid some of this conflict and to speed up the legislative process later, directives have taken on the form of "mutual recognition." Mutual recognition means that EU member countries maintain their own rules and regulations for the product or service specified in the directive while explicitly agreeing that other members' rules and regulations are equivalent.

The relative impact of a mutual recognition rather than harmonization can be shown by reviewing the Hystra Company case cited above. The EU country within which Hystra had previously been competing had approved their product for sale within that country since Hystra met their standards. Had the forklift directive been "mutual recognition," Hystra would *not* have had to make the changes, and they would have been able to sell their current product line throughout the EU. Thus, U.S. firms currently doing business within the EC would be little affected by mutual recognition. Additionally, firms intending to do business in Europe could select among national "mutually recognized" standards that would pose the fewest problems for their products or services.

3. Directive Ambiguity

Are there high levels of directive ambiguity for your company posed by haziness in the directive, translation to national law, public procurement directives, and/or potential invocation of national welfare rulings to protect consumers (or national champions)?

Uncertainty concerning the specific impact of some of the directives will exist even after they are successfully passed by the EEC, the Council and Parliament. This uncertainty is derived from three sources—ambiguity in the directives, the EU member country's right to protect national welfare, and the EU member country's latent desire to protect national champions. The potential for this uncertainty to be increased derives from the requirement that the 282 directives must be transposed into national law for each of the member states after they are passed by the EEC institutions.

In the case of some directives, it should not be surprising that some of the rules remain vague or hazy. In order to wind its way through a regulatory-political process, some issues cannot be addressed explicitly because the voting rules allow interested minorities in the Council to halt progress of the directives. For example, the public procurement directive may allow member country procuring agencies to throw out bids from non-EU firms with less than 50% EU content (or keep the bid under consideration if they desire), or where the non-EU firm meets the 50% EC content, may require the non-EU firm's price to be 3% lower than EU competitors to be accepted (or, on the other hand they may accept equal bids). Thus, for a product or service that has a strong national champion from that country bidding, a U.S. firm should expect that the most stringent rules facing non-EU companies would be exercised. Given that public procurement ranges up to 60% of GDP in some EU country economies (because so many companies are owned by government), many U.S. companies, particularly those in telecommunications, may have to set up production in Europe, even if U.S. markets are open to European competitors, because of heavy government ownership patterns in the EU.

The second issue, national welfare contingencies, is uncertainty caused by the basic charter of the European Union's founding laws. Section 100A, of the original Treaty of Rome, maintains that a country may still ignore the EEC law when it can establish a claim to be acting for its citizens' protection. This need for protection can be argued under cases of health, competitive trade, or fiscal responsibility. It is conceivable that EU countries losing a vote in the Council on some directive they deem critical to their competitive success, will "try" again by continuing to operate according to transposed national law which may be partially inconsistent with the EEC directive, and justify the difference under some national welfare issue according to the Treaty of Rome.

Concerning the third source of ambiguity, the protection of national champions, while European business firms initially embraced the Single European Act, some firms are beginning to become more aware of the difficulties to be imposed by increased competition in their markets and may be beginning to have second thoughts. The specter of the deregulated U.S. airline industry's competitive rivalry and low profitability tends to offer an experiment of the kind to be brought about by European integration, but on a grander scale. Various EC member states' national champions are sure to make member governments aware of such issues as jobs, taxes, or increase/decrease in prestige. It is anticipated that "national welfare" and consumer protection arguments could be used in initial efforts to aid national champions, particularly when faced with competition from non-EU firms. Therefore, when competing in an EU country against its threatened national champion, one might expect either subtle forms of discrimination or overt national welfare rulings.

The element of uncertainty cited above will only be resolved on a case by case basis, company by company, industry by industry, by legal arguments in the European Court of Justice. The Court is the final arbiter of EU law, and their precedent sets the standard for national law as well. Thus, if the EU directive(s) that applies to your industry is "hazy" or there is the expectation of "national welfare" claims concerning some parts of the directive's regulations, or that these welfare claims may in fact just be protectionism for the national champion, then it may well be the late 1990s before some measure of certainty exists in the EU for your company's European operations. In addition, as the firm which is harmed by the "haziness" or a "national welfare protection" action must generally bring the suit to the European Court of Justice, there remains the business problem of the long term impact of suing a potential customer. U.S. firms facing competition with the national champion of an EU country, particularly in industries with large public procurement, may prefer a cooperative strategy rather than one of confrontation. IBM's joint venture with Groupe Bull, the French computer national champion (owned by the French government) seems a good example of this approach.

Strategies for the European Union

4. Industry Globalization

Is the inherent nature of the firm's products/services largely national rather than global?

The general nature of a company's product or service with regard to its global usage is the last factor to be considered when assessing the opportunities presented by the Single European Act. Many authors have argued that products and services could be categorized as being either *global* or *national*. Characteristics of products/services that should be manufactured, distributed, and sold "nationally" (e.g. by country or region) include cultural or economic differences that result in differentiated customer needs, heavy customer involvement in post sale activities, small minimum efficient scale requirements, differing distribution channels, and perhaps local commitment to national companies. Global products or services, on the other hand, are manufactured, distributed, sold, and used in essentially the same manner everywhere. In addition, scale economies are typically large, and there exist some major benefits from large market share (e.g., experience and/or learning curve effects). Generally, as one's business moves closer to the final consumer, there is the tendency for greater "national" factors being in evidence; on the other hand, the closer the firm is to raw material extraction, more global factors will apply. Additionally, some products or services will have characteristics of both. For example, while the distribution, packaging, and marketing of detergents may pose country specific strategies (thus, "national" products), the production of detergents can be pan-European from a single site (thus, "global). It seems apparent then, that careful analysis of all phases of business operation must be analyzed in regard to the globalization issue.

The analysis of whether the firm's products/services are essentially global, national, or perhaps a mix, is no mere academic exercise. It is expected that in the European industries that are global in nature, European integration will have some very dramatic effects, while there will be lesser impact on national products/services—those being limited to lower factor of production costs from global industries which supply them such as the transportation sector. Thus the potential profitability of a company's European strategy may depend in large measure on the inherent globalization of its products. For example, in banking, which has both global and national segments, Citibank has had major success in pan-European corporate banking (global segment), but many failures, and in consumer retail banking in individual countries—the national segment of banking.

IMPLEMENTATION

The proposed decision tree framework shown in Figure 1, shows an implementation plan by linking strategic alternatives for the European markets with the four key questions on reciprocity, harmonization, directive ambiguity, and globalization. To determine an appropriate alternative, the manager must answer each of the questions posed previously which appear as nodes of the decision tree. While general strategic implications were discussed for each question earlier, the 16 branches of the decision tree offer alternatives which satisfy the general implications and the interaction among the answers to the questions. Thus, the decision tree provides a preferred alternative(s) for each scenario that the firm may face with respect to the impact of reciprocity, harmonization, ambiguity, and globalization.

The alternatives shown in Figure 1 were developed primarily from the perspective of the U.S. firm with limited investments in the EU. Either an *export only* strategy from the U.S. (or other non-EU sourcing countries) or no current sales in the EU would be consistent with the position. If the reader is

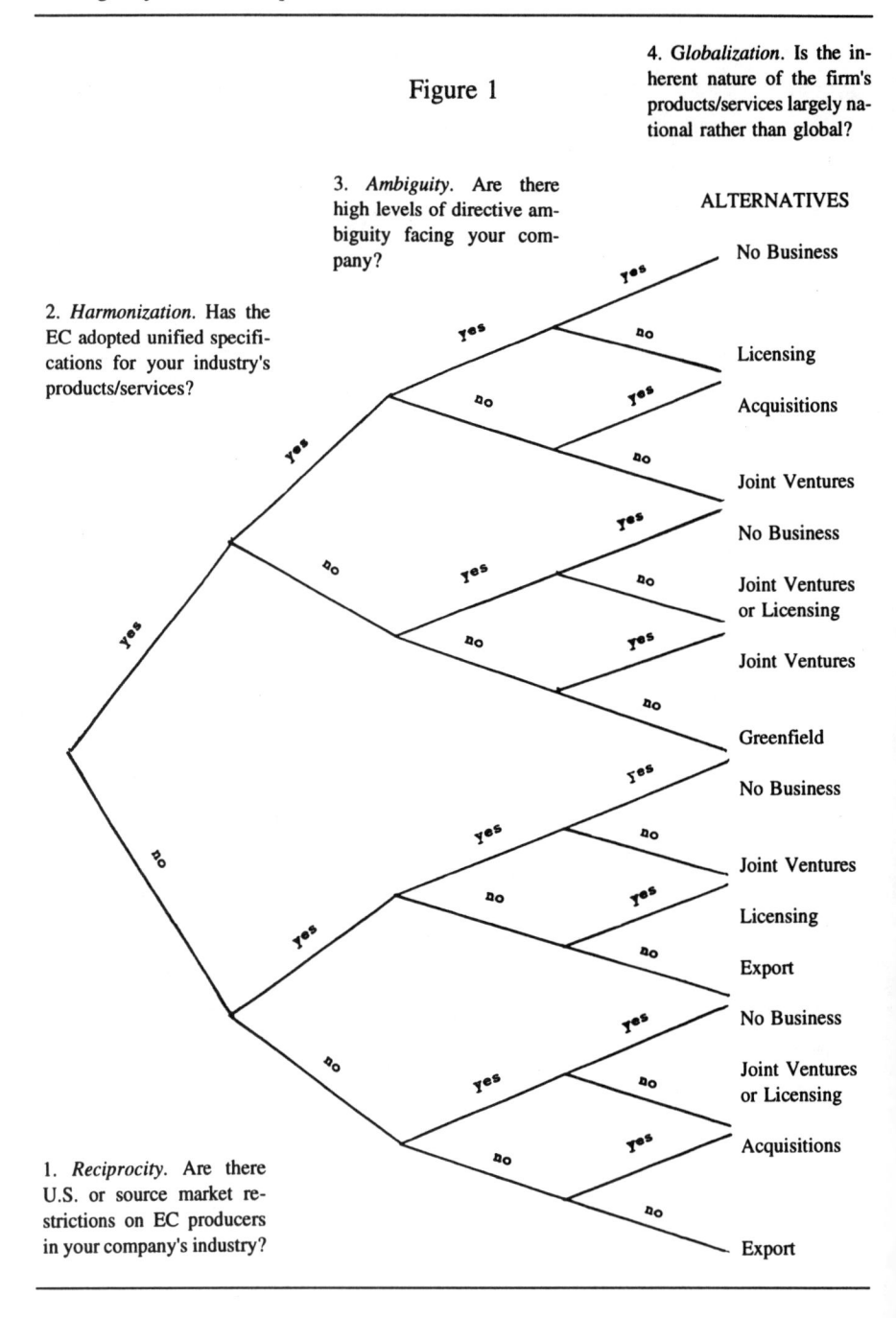

Strategies for the European Union

Figure 1

2. Harmonization. Has the EC adopted unified specifications for your industry's products/services?

3. Ambiguity. Are there high levels of directive ambiguity facing your company?

4. Globalization. Is the inherent nature of the firm's products/services largely national rather than global?

ALTERNATIVES

- No Business
- Licensing
- Acquisitions
- Joint Ventures
- No Business
- Joint Ventures or Licensing
- Joint Ventures
- Greenfield
- No Business
- Joint Ventures
- Licensing
- Export
- No Business
- Joint Ventures or Licensing
- Acquisitions
- Export

1. Reciprocity. Are there U.S. or source market restrictions on EC producers in your company's industry?

a non-U.S. based firm, the only modification would be to Question 1, where the reciprocity evaluation should be of home market of the non-U.S. (and also non-EC) firm and its sourcing markets. If the corporation already had local EU production by the end of 1992, and local EU procurement for its sales in Europe, then the firm is already considered to be "European" for the application of Questions 1 and 2. Additional insights may be offered in Figure 1 concerning issues related to national champions and public procurement (Question 3) and the inherent globalization of the firm's products and services (Question 4), and a consistency check with the firm's current investment position. Given the above perspectives and assumptions the following six alternatives are shown as end points of the decision tree:

1. *Export:* The conditions under which your company/industry will operate in Europe indicate that an export strategy is most feasible. The firm may wish to set up a sales and marketing subsidiary in Europe, or use an EU sales representative with strong pan-European distribution.

2. *Licensing:* Finding an EU firm which can make use of either your production process or product itself may be the best approach to the EU. Care, of course, should be taken to protect the firm's competitive position back in the U.S. or other non-EU markets.

3. *Joint Ventures:* Conditions suggest that finding an EU partner currently competing in your industry in the EU offers the most advantageous strategy to your firm. In some cases the venture partner will provide market knowledge of different European customers (national products), and in other situations the venture partner may be the national champion of a major EU country (high directive ambiguity).

4. *Acquisition:* The answers to the key questions indicate that your best approach to the EU markets is the acquisition of an EU firm which has a good strategic position. U.S. investment banks are extremely active in Europe (applying the analytical skills developed in the U.S. merger/LBO heyday of the 1980s) and would serve as useful sources of candidates.

5. *Greenfield:* Opportunities and requirements suggest that your firm success in Europe is best served by a greenfield operation. That is, you would take your entire business concept to Europe, do a new business start up, and become a "European" firm. Currently, greenfield operations must be established in EFTA countries, because the deadline has already passed (December 31, 1992) for setting up operations in the EU and achieving "European status."

6. *No Business:* Answering the four key questions will help to determine business opportunities for the firm or suggest that no business be transacted in the EC. In all cases in Figure 1, the "no business" options occurs in situations of high directive ambiguity and national products. Where a strategy of acquiring an EC competitor might seem a reasonable alternative, European discrimination against the British computer firm ICL (a national champion) after its purchase by Fujitsu argues against an acquisition recommendation.

In the final analysis, Figure 1 must be interpreted in conjunction with the strategic capabilities and positioning of the firm. For example, the licensing and joint venture strategies of IBM in Europe are supported by the fact that they have key technologies to license and excellent distribution channels to share with joint venture partners. Furthermore, firms totally lacking any international experience may wish to avoid greenfield operations initially (despite the fact that the answers to their questions in Figure 1 suggests it is the best) and seek a partner which aids them in developing their European expertise. The evaluation of all other strategic contingencies that may moderate the alternatives shown in Figure 1 are beyond the scope of this article.

EVALUATION

It seems obvious that the evaluation of the four key questions of reciprocity, harmonization, ambiguity, and globalization requires substantial information gathering activities on the part of company managers. Copies of the EU directives after they have been adopted may be obtained from the Single Internal Market 1992 Information Service at the Department of Commerce. In addition, the major trade associations (e.g., National Association of Manufacturers, Health Industry Manufacturer's Association, Electronic Industry Association, U.S. Chamber of Commerce, etc.) generally have monitored the reciprocity and harmonization issues on behalf of their members and most have prepared briefing documents on the Single European Act (SEA or known as EC92 in the Department of Commerce). European perspectives on trade barriers (and a good indication of reciprocity problems facing your industry) in the U.S. and other countries (which may be used by your firm in foreign sourcing) may be obtained from the Directorate General for External Relations at the European Commission in Brussels (last document on the U.S. was the *Report on the United States Trade Barriers and Unfair Practices,* 1991). Information sources suggested above should give the firm reliable information concerning EU reciprocity and harmonization.

Determination of the level of directive ambiguity is less straightforward than reciprocity and harmonization. First, the key factor of public procurement levels varies by country in the EC. For example, public procurement as a percent of GDP is 59% in Belgium and 43% in the U.K. (*Research on the Cost of Non-Europe,* Volume 5: The Cost of "Non-Europe in Public Sector

Procurement, 1988). As was suggested earlier, historically, these large public sector procurements have been used to shield home country firms from other EU and non-EU competitors. While one of the major thrusts of the SEA was to open up this large sector to intra-EU trade, non-EU competitors should expect substantial use of the ambiguous barriers to trade if you attempt to compete in a country and industry with high levels of public procurement. Information concerning public procurement levels may be obtained through the European Community Information Services Office or through WS Atkins Management Consultants (authors of *The Cost of Non-Europe* in the Public Sector).

In addition, directive ambiguity is affected by both the existence of home country national champions (sometimes government owned) and past history of discrimination against non-home country trade. Discussions with the other U.S. Government offices listed in the Reference section (below) and your industry association may provide valuable information concerning these issues. In general, you will find that countries in southern Europe (e.g., France, Italy, and Greece) will pose higher levels of directive ambiguity than northern Europe (e.g., Denmark, Germany and the Netherlands). This implies that if the directive ambiguity levels are dramatically different for your industry/company between northern and southern Europe, you will have to perform the analysis suggested by Figure 1 separately for each region which will yield two alternatives. Unfortunately, synthesizing these two alternatives requires other situation-specific information about your firm and industry and cannot be generalized in this article.

Initial estimates of the last major factor, industry globalization, may be obtained by rough proxies that are currently being used in research in this area. Earlier in this article, it was suggested that the existence of international competitors was a sign of globalization. If these same competitors can viably use export strategies, and cross border intra-industry trade increases, this is evidence of globalization of an industry. Currently, a measure of 50% of "traded" goods to total sales is used as a determination of a "global" industry in some current academic research. International trade statistics for manufacturing firms are available from the U.S. International Trade Commission.

However, ascertaining critical information about globalization will require additional search activities beyond just the review of secondary sources. The rough proxies suggested above do not provide sufficient information to make the determination of industry globalization with confidence. Given the importance of this factor, industry globalization can only be estimated after many visits to Europe personally—focusing your attention on getting first hand information on the underlying industry factors that contribute to globalization.

In review, the above knowledge sources should provide a basis for business judgements with regard to the key questions posed in Figure 1. The review of this information will remain a highly qualitative and individualistic exercise. The magnitude of the phenomena, the virtual re-writing of the business rules for an entire continent, suggests that managers must continue their information gathering activities over time, as one may expect the "answers" to the questions to change (e.g., increasing globalization, decreasing directive ambiguity, etc.). Thus, the analysis of the firm's strategies for the EU remain, for the foreseeable future, largely management "art," not "science."

APPLICATIONS TO SMALL BUSINESS

The situation presented by the newly integrated European Union to small businesses, primarily exporters, is what *Business Week* described as "a strategic dilemma of the first order." Unless a small business has set up a manufacturing activity in Europe by the end of 1992, most of their business opportunities will be subject to the reciprocity rulings that are established in the directives. In the ebb and flow of trade relations between the U.S. and the EU, small business may be rightfully reluctant to commit resources to markets that may be suddenly closed.

The second consideration, harmonization, is that the new standards for products and services may likely have a strong bias toward the major European firms' practices. A small business' best hope is that the harmonization of their product is one of mutual recognition, and that there is one EU country whose national standards are close to the small business' current product designs, or are easily achievable.

In conclusion, the best strategy for small businesses may be to rely on the resources of a trading company or distributor with good pan-EU experience. Care should be taken to insure that the agent has good distribution channels throughout Europe to take advantage of open access to all EU and EFTA members. Difficulty in obtaining the services of quality European agents may be an early signal that the firm's products and services are not well suited to the unified markets of the European Union.

CONCLUSION

In summary, while it can be argued that the EU offers a market opportunity of unparalleled size, it also poses threats and uncertainties to businesses around the world. It is probable that reciprocity, harmonization and directive ambiguity may put non-EU companies at a competitive disadvantage and that the exact nature of those disadvantages await their thorough resolution before the European Court of Justice; finally new European entrants must remember that although the regulations may be harmonized, Europe is still a continent of different languages, cultures, and media—continuing to make some markets significantly less unified than one might hope.

Whether the firm's analysis leads to aggressive approaches to the EU such as joint ventures and/or acquisition strategies, or redeployment of assets to less "harmonized" business environs, depends on the individual firm's strategic positioning and the directives' specific impacts as shown in the variety of alternatives in Figure 1. One must also be aware that the EU market unification is a dynamic process, remaining to be completed well into the 21st century. Efforts undertaken today will await years of competitive action and reaction before bottom-line results can be determined. However, experts seem to agree that actions concerning EU should be taken as soon as possible.

In conclusion, there remains little doubt that the EU of the 1990s presents managers with one of the most exciting, yet uncertain, business challenges of this century, and next. The diversity and breadth of the events present management dilemmas whose resolution must be both creative and situation specific. The situational characteristics that were developed in this article included the issues of harmonization, directive ambiguity, reciprocity, and the globalization of markets. Only after careful analysis of these factors relative to the strategic capabilities of the business can, or should, executive actions be attempted to take advantage of opportunities presented by the new European Union.

REFERENCES

The U.S. Department of Commerce has established a special office to deal with the 1992 market integration. For information on the 1992 Internal Market program, contact:

Single Internal Market: 1992 Information Service
Office of European Community Affairs
U.S. Department of Commerce, Room 3036
14th and Constitution Ave., N.W.
Washington, D.C. 20230
Telephone: (202) 377-5276.

Copies of the Single Internal Market regulations, background information on the European Community, and assistance on specific opportunities and/or potential problems can be obtained from this office. A particularly relevant publication is *EC 1992: A Commerce Department Analysis of European Community Directives,* Volumes 1-3. Trade Development industry experts for several industries have been assigned to the 1992 program. Write the U.S. Department of Commerce, or call the offices listed below for further information:

Textiles and Apparel, Office of Textiles and Apparel, Room 3119. Tel. (202) 377-2043.

Service Industries, Office of Service Industries, Room 1128. Tel. (202) 377-3575.

Information Technology, Instrumentation and Electronics, Office of Telecommunications, Room 1001A. Tel. (202) 377-4466.

Chemicals, Construction Industry Products, and Basic Industries, Office of Basic Industries, Room 4045. Tel. (202) 377-0614.

Autos and Consumer Goods, Office of Automotive Affairs and Consumer Goods, Room 4324. Tel. (202) 377-2762.

Construction Projects and Industrial Machinery, Office of the DAS for Capital Goods and International Construction, Room 2001B. Tel. (202) 377-2474.

Aerospace, Office of Aerospace Policy and Analysis, Room 6877. Tel. (202) 377-8228.

Information about exporting to the European Community can be obtained from the International Trade Administration District Offices located in most state capitals. The National Bureau of Standards has additional information about European standards; these can be obtained by contacting:

GATT Inquiry Point/ Technical Office
Office of Standards Code and Information
National Bureau of Standards
Administration Building, Room A629
Gaithersburg, MD. 20899
Tel. (301) 975-4040
(GATT Hotline: (301) 975-4041).

Additional U.S. government contacts are

U.S. Department of State
Europe/Regional, Political and Economic Affairs, Room 6519
Washington, DC 20520

DAUSTR for Europe and Mediterranean
600 17th St., N.W.
Washington, DC 20506
Tel. (202) 395-3320

The European Community Information Service (2100 M St., N.W.-7th floor, Washington DC 20037) has a collection of studies published in 1987 and 1988 that discuss the potential impact of the 1992 market integration. These titles are available (for a fee) from their office:

The Economics of 1992
Creation of a European Financial Area
The Social Dimension of the Internal Market

Transport and European Integration
Lawyers in the European Community
Telecommunications in Europe
Common Standards for Enterprises
Individual Choice and Higher Growth: The Task of European Consumer Policy
Europe in Figures

Concerning U.S. reciprocity issues of the E.C., copies of the *Report on United States Trade Barriers and Unfair Practices: 1991, Problems of Doing Business with the U.S.*, and *Services of the Commission of the European Commission, 1991,* are available from

Directorate General for External Relations
Unit I.B.1
B-1049 Brussels
Tel. 32 2 235 58 861
FAX 32 2 235 97 23

Joel W. Cook
George Washington University

Deborah Smith Cook
University of Baltimore

Dr. Joel W. Cook is an Associate Professor of Strategic Management and Public Policy in the School of Business and Public Management at The George Washington University. His publications and research interests are in the area of global strategic management and strategic decision making. He has held administrative positions in product management and as director of a university research center.

Dr. Deborah Smith-Cook is an Associate Professor of Management and Director of the Change Management Group in the Merrick School of Business at the University of Baltimore. Her publications, research and consulting have been in the area of change management, cross-cultural management, and strategy implementation. Her writings have appeared in the *Academy of Management Review, Human Resource Management,* and *Entrepreneurship Theory and Practice.*

North American Free Trade Agreement [1]

OVERVIEW

On June 30, 1993 the Canadian Parliament approved the North American Free Trade Agreement. It was approved by the Congress of the United States on November 18, 1993 and by the Mexican Congress on November 22, 1993.

EXAMPLES

To contextualize NAFTA, one must go back eight years to the beginning of free trade talks and negotiations between the United States and Canada. This chronology is brief and much work, debate and struggle took place between the highlighted dates.

CHRONOLOGY OF FREE TRADE AGREEMENT (FTA) AND NORTH AMERICAN FREE TRADE AGREEMENT (NAFTA)

The Beginning: Canada and the United States

March 1985
President Ronald Reagan and Canadian Prime Minister Brian Mulroney meet and agree to explore the possibilities for reducing and eliminating trade barriers.

September 1985
President Reagan and Prime Minister Mulroney exchange letters of resolution to negotiate a Free Trade Agreement (FTA).

October 1987
U.S. and Canadian negotiators sign a draft of the Agreement.

January 1989
The FTA between the United States and Canada goes into effect.

April 1990
The Mexican Senate establishes a forum for consultations on the FTA.

June 1990
The United States Senate opens hearings on a "fast track" bill that would allow President George Bush to negotiate directly with President Carlos Salinas and the two Presidents issue a joint communiqué announcing their intention to negotiate a FTA.

September 1990
Canada, the United States and Mexico agree to negotiate a free trade agreement.

June 1991
Trilateral negotiations between Canada, Mexico and the United States open in Toronto, Canada.

December 17, 1992
President Bush, President Salinas and Prime Minister Mulroney sign the NAFTA

January 1, 1994
NAFTA implemented.

BENEFITS

Like most issues that have an emotional edge, the passage of NAFTA was debated by many Americans, Mexicans and Canadians. Many doomsayers vehemently argued their impassioned positions, citing the fear of job loss and low wages, more damage to struggling U.S. and Canadian economies and the continued deterioration of the environment among reasons to not support the agreement. Billionaire H. Ross Perot and Vice President Al Gore took to the airwaves to crystalize public opinion and add fuel for the fray.

Conversely, big business in Mexico, Canada and the United States, hopeful of expanded opportunities for increased trade and the growth and development of possible manufacturing sites, supported the forthcoming ratification of NAFTA. Business spent large amounts of money to lobby for the passage of NAFTA. *The New York Times* estimated that pro-NAFTA forces spent between $5 million and $30 million. This is understandable when 86% of *Fortune* magazine's top 500 manufacturers have operations in Mexico.

IMPLEMENTATION[2]

The North American Free Trade Agreement is unique. It is the first trade agreement entered into between industrial countries and a developing nation, and the first trade agreement that includes intellectual property, labor rights and the environment. A trade agreement is an agreement that permits the nations who are signatories to decrease tariffs or custom duties on trade between or among themselves within a reasonable period of time. Such agreements are possible with the present rules regarding international trade, provided that the member nations do not raise existing tariffs for non-member nations. Free trade agreements do not create common markets for they do not permit the free movement of people. Historically, free trade agreements have allowed for the free trade of goods.

The Canada—U.S. Free Trade Agreement (FTA), the precursor for NAFTA, became operational January 1, 1989. That agreement broke new ground by including services and providing new mechanisms for dispute resolution. With the several years of experience that Canada and the United States had in implementing their agreement, areas that needed to be fine-tuned in NAFTA, such as how to determine whether a good was indeed of Canadian, Mexican or U.S. origin, or the procedures to be followed if there were a trade dispute, were more adequately covered in NAFTA. Having a framework in place enabled the negotiators to proceed quickly to discuss substantive matters and achieve consensus.

The NAFTA agreement is a very complex document. When Perot challenged his critics by asking whether they had read the agreement, he was asking the wrong question. The better question should have been whether having read it, they understood what was written.

Some claim that NAFTA is a misnomer. It is not really a free trade agreement but rather an investment agreement. It establishes the principle of "national treatment" not only for trade, but guarantees that service providers will also have the right to invest and provide services in the other nations, as if they were nationals, although there is a phase-in period. Investors are also protected by the principles of non-discriminatory treatment; free transfer of capital for investment purposes, freedom from performance requirements (for example in the automotive sector, previously Mexico demanded a percentage of export before sales were permitted in the domestic market); limited exercise of the sovereign right of expropriation, i.e. taking of property, which must be conducted in conformity with established international legal principles; and finally, the use of international arbitration rather than a nation's courts to settle trade disputes if violation of the Agreement is alleged.

Tariffs

All internal tariffs will be reduced to zero at the end of fifteen years for trade between the United States, Canada and Mexico. Based on the Canada—U.S. Free Trade Agreement (FTA), all tariffs on goods moving between those two countries will end in 1998. As relates to trade with Mexico, those items that require a longer adjustment period, primarily agricultural goods, tariffs will remain in place for approximately fifteen years.

Goods have been classified into general categories: the "A" category in which tariffs were removed entirely as of January 1, 1994. These include computers, telecommunications, aerospace equipment and medical products. In the "B" category, tariffs diminish at the rate of 20% a year for five years, and in the "C" category they diminish by 10% a year for ten years. The "C+" category is comprised of goods that will have tariffs diminished for the next fifteen years in equal annual reductions, including glassware, orange juice, peanuts, sugar and watches. It is believed that 65% of U.S. goods entering Mexico will be at zero tariff within five years. It should be noted that prior to the passage of NAFTA, the average U.S. tariff was 4% for goods being imported from Mexico, whereas the average Mexican tariff was 10%. There are provisions in the Agreement that provide for the accelerated reduction of tariffs on a number of goods including flat glass.

There were reservations or exceptions made by each of the three nations to protect sensitive sectors. Mexico would not negotiate regarding investment in petroleum and basic petrochemicals based on its constitutional provisions that declare petroleum as belonging to the State. Canada, concerned about protecting cultural identity, retained the right to ban materials/services that would infringe on Canadian identity, such as objectionable radio and television programs, movies and print media. The United States protected farmers by demanding the right to maintain price supports.

EVALUATION

Mexico, in the past, has been a bastion of nationalist pride. Harvard-educated President Carlos Salinas de Gotari has endeavored along with his appointees to modify and change these traditional ideas and to encourage economic development, increase trade and remove trade barriers. Economic stability and reduced inflation followed the signing of the GATT in 1986, which dramatically reduced tariffs, and the ratification of El Pacto in 1988, which created an alliance between Mexican labor and government.

With the passage of NAFTA in November 1993, many hopes for the sustained growth of the economy of Mexico are given another shove in the direction of economic fulfillment and realization. At this point in time, it is too soon to delineate and categorize the overwhelming positives of the NAFTA. The media has given us a cursory view of some of the immediate positive results of the treaty.

APPLICATION TO SMALL BUSINESS

Small business, particularly in Mexico, must benefit from NAFTA or the potential for social unrest in that country will significantly increase and undermine the goals of the agreement. In Canada and the United States, it will be much easier for small business to benefit if the resources and contacts identified are utilized.

North American Free Trade Agreement

CONCLUSION

With the enactment of the North American Free Trade Agreement the continued economic and cultural integration in North America is inevitable. The long-term benefits of NAFTA will unfold with time, but at the end of the first year, trade and business opportunities between the U.S. and Mexico far exceeded expectations. Laredo, Texas, for example, which was considered the second poorest city in America, is now one of the most prosperous. Critics argue that these are short-term gains and that eventually Ross Perot's predictions will come true. Certainly, the political instability in Mexico and the secessionist movement in Quebec, Canada, combined with NAFTA opposition in the U.S., will play important roles in determining NAFTA's future.

RESOURCES

To further assist small businesses in pursuing opportunities in Mexico, Canada and the United States, a few sources are listed that may prove helpful in seeking information regarding NAFTA, trade, or questions regarding business in the three countries.

Mexico City
United States Embassy
Reforma 305
Col Cuahuatemos
06500 Mexico, D.F.
Tel. (525) 211-0042, 207-5307

American Chamber of Commerce
Lucerna 78

Col. Juarez
06600 Mexico, D.F.
Tel. (525) 724-3800
Fax (525) 701-3908

Monterrey
American Consulate General
Commercial Attache
Ave. Constitucion, 411 Pte.

64000 Monterrey, N.L.
Tel (528) 345-2120, 340-9705
Fax (528) 342-0177

Canadian Consulate
Zaragoza 1300 Sur, Desp. ten8
Edificio Kalos
64000 Monterrey, N.L.
Tel (528) 344-3200

American Chamber of Commerce
Pichachos 760, Desp. 4
Col Obispado
64060 Monterrey, N.L.
Tel (528) 348-0414, 348-7141
Fax (528) 358-5574

Guadalajara
American Consulate General
Progreso 175
44160 Guadalajara, Jal.
Tel (523) 625-2700, 625-2998

American Chamber of Commerce
Av. Moctezuma No. 442
Col Jardines del Sol
45050 Zapopan, Jal.
Tel (523) 634-6606
Fax (528) 634-7374

SECOFI
Av. Mariano Otero 3431
1 Y 2 Piso
Col. Valle Verde
44550 Guadalajara, Jal.
Tel (523) 621-0694, 621-1642

Canadian Government Departments and Services in Canada

Department of Foreign Affairs and International Trade (Ottawa) is the Canadian federal government department most directly responsible for trade development. The InfoEx Centre is the first contact point for advice on how to start exporting; it provides information on export-related programs and services; helps find fast answers to export problems; acts as the entry point to DFAIT's trade information network; and can provide interested companies with copies of specialized export publications.

InfoEx Centre
Tel 1-800-267-8376 or (613) 994-4000
Fax (613) 996-9709

Latin America and Caribbean Trade Division promotes trade with Mexico. There are several trade commissioners at the Embassy of Canada in Mexico City, and there is a satellite office in Monterrey. Trade Commissioners can provide a range of services including introducing Canadian companies to potential customers in Mexico, advising on marketing channels, assisting those wishing to participate in trade fairs, helping identify suitable Mexican firms to act as agents, and compiling credit and business information on potential foreign customers.

Latin America and Caribbean Trade Division (LGT)
Department of Foreign Affairs and International Trade
Lester B. Pearson Building
125 Sussex Drive
Ottawa, Ontario K1A 0G2

United States Government Resources:

NAFTA Facts: 24 Hour Automated Information System providing information on NAFTA Implementation, Tariff Rates, Rules of Origin and Doing Business in Canada and Mexico. Telephone (202) 482-4464. After you obtain the menu, you may select materials, which will be faxed to you within 12 hours. NAFTA Facts: Canada (202) 482-3101

National Trade Data Bank: CD-Rom database updated monthly. Subscription fee. (202) 482-1986

Trade Information Center of the U.S. Government provides general information to companies interested in exporting to Mexico and Canada. Advises companies on services available from the government and on documentation necessary to export to Mexico and Canada. Telephone: 1-800-USA-TRADE.

REFERENCES/SOURCES

Adler, Nancy J. *International Dimensions of Organizational Behavior.* Boston: PWS-Kent Publishing, 1991.

Barrett, John K. *American Competitiveness in Mexico Under the North American Free Trade Agreement.* Cambridge, MA: Harvard University, 1993.

Elashmawi, Farid and Philip R. Harris. *Multicultural Management, New Skills for Global Success.* Houston, Gulf Publishing, 1993.

Kennedy, Paul. *Preparing for the Twenty-First Century.* New York: Random House, 1993.

Ohmae, Kenichi. *The Borderless World.* New York: HarperCollins Publishers, 1990.

Orme, William A., Jr. *Continental Shift: Free Trade & the New North America.* Washington, D.C.: The Washington Post Company, 1993.

Reich, Robert B. *The Work of Nations.* New York: Vintage Books, 1992.

Thurow, Lester. *Head to Head.* New York: Warner Books, 1993.

ENDNOTES

1. Much of this material is taken from NAFTA: Managing the Cultural Differences. Gulf Publishing, Houston, TX, 1994.

2. From Chapter 1, *NAFTA: Managing the Cultural Differences*, researched and written by Dr. Shoshana B. Tancer, Professor of International Studies and Director of the NAFTA Center at American Graduate School of International Management, Glendale, Arizona. Dr. Tancer is also Of Counsel to the law firm of O'Connor, Cavanagh, Anderson, Westover, Killingswoth & Beshears.

Dr. Robert T. Moran
American Graduate School of International Management

Jeffrey D. Abbott
Euromonitor Research Consultancy

Dr. Robert T. Moran is an Organizational Management Consultant in cross-cultural training, organizational development, and international resource management. He is Director of the Program in Cross-Cultural Communication, and Professor of International Studies at the American School of International Management. As an international consultant, he has designed and conducted seminars for Aramco, Arthur Andersen & Co., AT&T, General Motors, Honeywell, Intel, Miles, Exxon, Volvo Truck and Singapore Airlines.

Jeffrey D. Abbott is an international management consultant specializing in U.S. and Mexican market analysis and strategy. During 1993-1994, he was Visiting Foreign Professor of International Management at the Instituto Technologico y de Estudios Superiores de Monterrey, Mexico, where he initiated programs in marketing and consumer behavior in Mexico, intercultural communications, negotiations, and U.S.-Mexican business relationships.

Legal Standards Imposed by International Organizations

OVERVIEW

Regulating trade and employment relations with international legislation has been a hotly debated topic since the 19th century. The International Labour Organization (ILO) was the first intergovernmental organization to adopt laws to regulate employment conditions throughout its member countries. In the 1920s, the ILO adopted its first set of laws, which are referred to as the international labor standards. International regulation of trade and employment, however, became a topic of interest particularly in the last few decades. The increasing power of the multinational corporations (MNCs) in developing countries drew intergovernmental organizations' (IGOs) attention to the MNCs behavior in those countries.

In response to the demands of developing countries, as well as international and national labor unions and some nongovernmental groups, the IGOs, such as the United Nations Commission on Transnational Corporations (U.N.CTC), the United Nations Conference on Trade and Development (U.N.CTAD), the ILO, the Organization for Economic Co-operation and Development (OECD), and the European Community (EC), formulated or are negotiating to formulate codes of conduct for MNCs. These codes cover a multitude of issues from corporate disclosure and taxation, to industrial relations. The emphasis of this article is on the regulations in the field of labor and industrial relations.

Sources of international labor laws are mainly found in the international regulations of the United Nations (U.N.) and the ILO, regional instruments, and bilateral treaties. The legal obligations of such laws on the ratified countries vary from binding rules to voluntary guidelines. The constitution of the ILO and its standards are the primary sources of international labor law.

The two major instruments of the U.N., namely the 1948 Universal Declaration of Human Rights and the International Covenants on Human Rights, cover the general scope of basic human rights.

The EC has developed Company Law and Social Affairs Directives to harmonize employment conditions as well as economic, social, and trade standards within the community. The 1975 Directive on Collective Redundancies and the 1977 Directive on Acquired Rights of Workers on Transfers of Undertakings, adopted to protect labor, are more progressive than American labor laws. In addition, the proposed European Company Statute will regulate company law issues as well as worker participation and related industrial relations issues.

American, Middle Eastern, and African regional organizations have also adopted instruments to deal with labor and employment matters. Among these, the 1969 Convention on Human Rights, adopted by the Organization of American States, the 1967 Arab Convention on Labor Standards, adopted by the League of Arab States, and the 1971 Conventions on Labor Matters, adopted by the Arab Labour Organization, particularly deal with labor and employment conditions. Apart from these, a number of bilateral treaties in the field of labor are legally binding on the parties.

The U.N. agencies have also formulated or are developing codes to regulate the activities of the MNCs in developing countries. The two principal agreements are the U.N.CTAD's Code on Restrictive Business Practices, adopted in 1981, to set the guidelines for multinational businesses in developing countries, and the ILO Tripartite Declaration of Principles Concerning Multinational Enterprises and Social Policy (ILO Declaration), adopted in 1977 to regulate employment behavior of the MNCs.

The OECD guidelines for Multinational Enterprises (the OECD Guidelines), adopted in 1976, have been mostly effective at the European level. They were originally adopted with the hope of transposing them into a code at the U.N. level. The guidelines contain various business related issues. Among these, however, the section on employment and industrial relations has been in the forefront of public discussions.

EXAMPLES

The adoption of the OECD Guidelines provided areas of confrontation that were not present in the earlier life of the organization. They are constantly challenged by the international and European trade unions. While acknowledging the voluntary nature of the OECD Guidelines, the unions see them as a step toward binding international regulations governing the behavior of MNCs. In 1976 and 1977, two cases, one involving the Badger (Belgium) N.V. Company and the other involving the Hertz Corporation in Copanhagen, Denmark created the first challenges to the guidelines.

In the first case, the Badger Company, a subsidiary of the U.S. based Raytheon Company, decided to close down its office in Antwerp, Belgium in 1977, affecting approximately 250 employees. The Belgian government and the unions claimed that in its decision the company failed to observe the guidelines, which in their judgment required informing employees prior to the closure decision. The case was resolved after an agreement was reached between the parties. The case encouraged the European and international unions' and some governments' belief that the OECD guidelines are more regulatory than voluntary.

The next important case involved a strike in Hertz, Denmark, in 1976. After the strike the company brought in several employees from its subsidiaries in the United Kingdom, Italy, and France to operate its facilities in Denmark. At the end of the strike, Hertz reorganized its operations in Denmark and reduced its work force in that country. The unions, through their representatives at the OECD, challenged the legitimacy of the multinational transfer of employees in order to maintain operations at a strike facility. The case resulted in a textual change in the OECD guidelines.

A second example of legal controls involves the ILO standards. The ILO standards, which if ratified will have to be incorporated into the national legislation, have caused more controversy within the ILO circles than the ILO Declaration had. For example, nonimplementation of the basic ILO principles regarding freedom of association by ILO members has been a topic of debate and an issue of criticism since the 1960s. The countries also criticized by the ILO supervisory bodies range from developed market economy countries (such as Canada and Japan) to developing countries of Europe (such as Turkey, Greece, and Spain), and Latin America (such as Chile and Uruguay). Even the socialist bloc countries (such as Poland) have been criticized for not fulfilling their obligations under the ILO constitution and standards.

BENEFITS

The ILO standards' most important contribution to the international legal environment is that they provide the internationally accepted minimum standards on employment relations for all the countries in the world without differentiating among them according to their political structure or economic development level.

The benefits of various codes of conduct for MNCs are, however, controversial. Unions, particularly the ones from continental Europe, consider the impact of the codes as a positive development for closely monitoring MNCs' behavior by the IGOs. The MNCs, on the other hand, acknowledge the need for international standards to regulate international trade and employment, but prefer voluntary guidelines as opposed to compulsory regulation. For example, the U.S. Council on International Business, a spokesgroup for MNCs originating in the U.S.A., demands less regulation on labor matters at the international level.

IMPLEMENTATION

According to the U.N. Declaration, the International Covenants and the ILO standards, all organizations are required to recognize freedom of association, the right to work, and an adequate standard of living as basic rights for all employees. The laws include provisions against discrimination in employment, the right to inform and join unions, the right to strike, and the right to be covered by a social security program. Protection of economic, social, and political rights is also included in these laws. The U.N. Declaration and the International Covenants are voluntary regulations. The ILO standards, however, are binding upon a country when they are ratified. After ratification, the government must enact laws that enforce the standards.

The EC Directives are similar to the ILO standards in terms of the legal obligations. When a Directive is adopted, it then becomes a law affecting all member governments and MNCs operating in the EC countries. Therefore, a MNC operating in a country which is a member of the EC should be aware of the existing laws on investments, accounting procedures, social security, trade, and employment, and should apply those laws in practice. For example, in mergers or takeovers, involved MNCs have to consult the representatives of labor. In some cases, they may have to regularly provide information to union and non-union employees on company plans or they may have to appoint an employee representative to the Board of Governors.

Furthermore, MNCs operating in OECD countries should keep two key elements of the "investment package" in mind. First they should observe the voluntary OECD guidelines, and second, they should demand and receive equal treatment as domestic firms.

Prior to ratifying (or adopting a standard into national law), a country debates at the national level whether to adopt the specific standard. After ratification, the ILO evaluates its member compliance through a regular supervision mechanism. In addition, a special mechanism is established to supervise the implementation of the freedom of association standards.

At the MNC level, the evaluation of regulations, codes and/or laws varies depending on the institution it is administered by. Complaints regarding OECD Guidelines are supervised by the Committee on International Investment and Multinational Enterprises (CIME). Business interests are represented before the CIME by the Business and Industry Advisory Committee, and employees' interests are represented by the Trade Union Advisory Committee.

EVALUATION

In order to evaluate the effectiveness of the OECD Guidelines, one has to look at the rationale behind its adoption. The OECD Guidelines were adopted as a reaction to the negative publicity given to the alleged malpractices of some MNCs in the early 1970s. Furthermore, the OECD wanted to develop the first set of guidelines (before the ILO and the U.N.) to protect business interests as much as possible. The resulting guidelines do not have the force of law, but prescribe voluntary regulations for MNCs that have been agreed upon by member governments. The guidelines are less detailed than the ILO Declaration and more protective of business than labor.

The application of the ILO Declaration is monitored by the tripartite Committee on Multinational Enterprises (CME) which was established in 1980. Since there have not been any complaints to the CME, it is difficult to comment on its effectiveness. On the contrary, the EC is quite effective in supervising the implementation of the Directives by domestic companies and MNCs. When the EC was established in 1957, the Treaty of Rome (the constitution of the EC) vested legislative power in the Council of Ministers and judicial power in the Court of Justice. In practice, however, the European Commission, the executive of the EC, is also the decisive organ of the EC with regard to regulating MNCs activities.

APPLICATIONS TO SMALL BUSINESS

The standards of the ILO should be of interest to small business management because, when ratified, they become national law governing all businesses. The U.S. government, however, has ratified only a few standards, and almost all pertain to seafarers. Small businesses should follow MNC regulations regarding the general guidelines of investment, taxation, accounting principles, and international employment principles if they plan to invest in another country.

CONCLUSION

Legislation on international employment and trade issues has been in existence since the beginning of the century. The recession of the 1970s, however, made developed and developing countries and national unions more sensitive to economic interdependence and related internal economic, political, and social regulation of MNCs through voluntary or binding codes of conduct. Regulating the activities of MNCs may be appropriate since they have enormous financial power to influence the social, political, and economic development in many countries. Controversy surrounds the legal obligations of MNCs under international regulations or laws; business prefers voluntary and flexible guidelines, while unions insist on binding regulations to harmonize employment conditions throughout the world. Some governments, from among European and developing countries, prefer binding rules on MNCs to protect their sovereignty and economic and social structure, while governments from countries where most MNCs originate, prefer minimum restrictions on international trade and business. The debate on the necessity and appropriateness of multinational legislation or regulation will continue as MNCs increase in number and in importance throughout the world.

SOFTWARE/DATABASES

The U.N., ILO, OECD, and EC have departments that provide information on organization activities as well as data on member countries. Managers planning to operate in an OECD or in an EC member country should consult these organizations for data. The U.N.CTC maintains a good database of investment regulations in developing countries. The ILO can provide information in the field of labor and employment relations. Data obtained from these organizations are either free or provided at the cost of computing the data. In 1986, the EC adopted the European Economic Interest Group, which can provide service to all companies in advertising, processing, and data distribution.

REFERENCES/SOURCES

Campbell, Duncan C. and Richard L. Rowan. *Multinational Corporations and the OECD Industrial Relations Guidelines*. Multinational Industrial Relations Series, No. 11. Philadelphia: Industrial Research Unit, the Wharton School, University of Pennsylvania, 1983. Presents cases on the application of the OECD guidelines and how those problem cases were resolved.

Feld, Werner J. *Multinational Corporations and the U.N. Politics: The Quest for Codes of Conduct.* New York: Pergamon Press, 1980. Discusses the issues and controversies in the development of U.N. Codes of Conduct for MNCs, the power of MNCs, and third world concerns.

International Organizations Monitoring Service. *The International Organizations Regulatory Guidebook.* New York: Annual. Presents a review of international regulatory development influencing international business.

Latta, Geoffrey W. and Janice R. Bellace. "Making the Corporation Transparent: Prelude to Multinational Bargaining." *Columbia Journal of World Business* 18,2 (Summer 1983): 73-80. Argues that the legislative development within the European Community may be setting the stage for future development for multinational collective bargaining.

Long, Frank. *Restrictive Business Practices, Transnational Corporations and Development: A Survey.* Boston: Martinus Nijhoff, 1981. Examines business practices of MNCs in developing countries.

Northrup, Herbert R. and Richard L. Rowan. *Multinational Collective Bargaining Attempts.* Multinational Research Unit, the Wharton School, University of Pennsylvania, 1979. A study of collective bargaining attempts at the international level. Provides information on international unions and organizations.

Northrup, Herbert R., Duncan L. Campbell, and Betty J. Slowinski. "Multinational Union-Management Consultation in Europe: Resurgence in the 1980s?" *International Labour Review* 77,5 (1988): 525-543. Discusses new initiatives toward multinational union-management consultation in the 1980s, and the prospects for the future.

Ruth, David A. *Corporate Handbook to the International Labour Organization and the International Organization of Employers.* New York: United States Council for International Business, 1982. Provides introductory information on the ILO and the International Organization of Employees.

Valticos, N. "International Labor Law." In *International Encyclopedia for Labour Law and Industrial Relations.* Roger Blanpain, ed. Vol. I: 1-262. Deventer, Netherlands: Kluwer, 1979. Describes the history and development of international labor law with an emphasis on ILO standards.

Zeytinoglu, Isik Urla. "The Impact of the ILO's Freedom of Association Standards on African Labor Laws." *Comparative Labor Law Journal* 8,1 (Fall 1986): 48-87. Analyzes the application of the most important ILO standards. Appendix includes the full text of two freedom of association conventions, Nos. 87 and 98.

Isik Urla Zeytinoglu
Associate Professor of Industrial Relations
McMaster University
Ontario, Canada

11.

Global Differences in Labor and Management Issues

European Labor Relations and Industrial Democracy

OVERVIEW

The differences between labor relations in the United States and in Western Europe are as wide as the Atlantic. Expatriate American managers who overlook these differences may experience difficulties that range from a poorly motivated work force to a lengthy battle in a labor court. Even within Western Europe, important differences exist. One of the most distinctive features of European labor relations is the practice of industrial democracy which refers to the rights of employees in relation to the rights of owners/managers within the work place. Industrial democracy takes different forms in different countries but the most common forms are works of councils, codetermination, information sharing and quality of work life programs. The form of industrial democracy may be determined by law or by collective bargaining. European industrial democracy has some similarities with American practices of participatory management and quality circles. However, its impact is more pervasive and it more clearly assigns rights to employees vis-a-vis management.

European labor law plays an important role in determining labor relations and is generally very protective of employees. Laying off or firing employees may be a lengthy and expensive process. The law also grants employees extensive social security coverage and vacation rights. These legal protections mean that managers must be very careful when taking on new employees. Managers also need to be aware that laws on health and safety are becoming more stringent and uniform among the twelve countries that belong to the

European Community.

A distinctive feature of labor relations in northern Europe is the constructive relationship between labor unions and employers. The adversary relationship which characterizes American labor relations is much less noticeable in Germany, Sweden or Norway. Labor unions are powerful and confident participants in the economic life of these countries. They have won high living standards for their members but they have also given employers a productive and peaceful work force. The labor relations system works because both employees and managers respect quality and expertise. Managers in northern Europe need to be leaders and facilitators rather than commanders.

Tension is more characteristic of labor relations in southern Europe where the rhetoric of class warfare may still color the language of labor unions and employers associations. However, ideological divisions are gradually diminishing. A new generation of managers and labor leaders is building a more workable relationship. Foreign investment is attracted to southern Europe today, in part, because investors expect to find a plentiful supply of inexpensive labor and steadily improving productivity rates. They also expect to find a better climate for labor relations than the one that characterized the region in the past.

Labor relations in the United Kingdom does not fit either of the continental patterns. Despite new legislation, labor relations are still governed by old traditions of a we/they attitude between labor unions and managers. The labor union movement remains fragmented among competing unions. British managers have experimented with participatory management and quality circles but the British government opposes laws mandating industrial democracy. In general, British employees are more dependent on labor unions to bargain for their protections and benefits than are other European employees who have more extensive legal protections and benefits.

The European Community is in the process of establishing a number of policies which will affect labor relations in the twelve member states. One of the most important topics to be addressed by the European Community is industrial democracy. Managers operating in one of the member states of the European Community should anticipate a European norm for a form or forms of industrial democracy.

1. Works Councils

Most countries in Western Europe have a law that requires employers to establish a council inside the work place composed of elected representatives of the employees. The employer must provide a place for the council to meet and allow meetings to be held periodically. The powers of the council, the range of topics with which they may deal, and their relationship with management will usually be defined by law. To a certain extent the works councils fill a space occupied by shop stewards of other labor union representatives in the United States. Although labor unions are active and powerful in Western Europe, they traditionally have not been active inside the work place. The works councils, therefore, serve as a channel for communications and sometimes for problem solving. Managers need to be aware of their legal responsibilities to the works councils in the country where they are operating. Usually managers will routinely have to transmit to the works council information that deals with personnel matters.

Works councils in Belgium provide a useful illustration. Works Councils were established by law in 1948. Their powers were increased significantly in 1973. Today the law applies to any private sector enterprise or non-profit organization that has at least 150 employees. The size of the works council varies from four to twenty-two depending on the number of employees. Its members are elected once every four years by all non-managerial employees; the head of the enterprise, or his representative, chairs the meetings. The powers of the works council are to be informed, to be consulted, and to codetermine. Since 1973 the right to be informed includes full disclosure on the economic and financial position of the enterprise. The works council must be consulted regarding any matters affecting the organization of work. Topics such as work rules and job evaluations must be codetermined with the works council.

2. Codetermination

Codetermination most generally is associated with the Federal Republic of Germany but variations of it are practiced in other countries such as the Netherlands and Sweden. Quite literally, managers must co-determine with representatives of the employees a wide range of business decisions. Two different structures are involved in German codetermination. One is the selected works council, which must be informed on any plans concerning:

a. jobs
b. the operation of work
c. changes in technology
d. the construction or alteration of the business premises or manufacturing plant

On many of the above issues, managers must not only inform their works council, but they must also actively consult with them. On issues that have to do directly with the work day, managers must find a mutually satisfactory solution. German works councils are the most powerful in Western Europe. They are usually very professional and well organized.

The second part of codetermination is more well known but is probably less significant in practice. German corporations have a two-tier board structure. Members of the larger board (supervisory board) are elected by the shareholders while members of the smaller board are elected by the employees. The proportion varies depending on the size of the corporation and the sector of the economy in which it operates. For large corporations the proportions are almost fifty-fifty with a slight edge given to the shareholders. The primary task of the supervisory board is to select the board of managers. It also oversees the operation of the board of managers and sets broad policy.

German codetermination laws apply to the subsidiaries of American corporations operating in the Federal Republic of Germany. Adjustment to the practice of German codetermination requires significant changes in American management practices but does not appear to be harmful to either productivity or the successful operation of a business. German productivity rates are among the highest in the world.

Codetermination in other countries does not entail as large a sharing of managerial power as it does in Germany. The powers of the workers councils are weaker and the representation of employees on the corporate board is much smaller.

3. Information Sharing

The demand for information sharing is second only to the demand for jobs among labor unions in Western Europe today. Traditionally firms in Western Europe have not had to disclose as much information as have American firms. This situation changed dramatically in the 1970s, however, when laws requiring information sharing—especially with the firm's own employees—were put on the books throughout Western Europe. Today it is normal that employers must routinely give to representatives of their employees information that is quite comparable to the information that American firms must provide to their shareholders. In addition, they must inform the representatives, in advance, of plans to cut the work force or to close an operation.

European law differs greatly from American law on this point. The importance of knowing the requirement of the law of the country in which you are operating cannot be over-emphasized. Many American firms have been in difficulty when they have moved quickly to streamline a work force without prior notification.

The European Community (EC) has enacted two directives on information sharing and is considering others. These directives mean that all twelve member states of the EC must have laws requiring information sharing (The twelve are France, Italy, the United Kingdom, The Federal Republic of Germany, Ireland, the Netherlands, Belgium, Luxembourg, Denmark, Greece, Portugal, and Spain). The first directive deals with collective redundancies. All member states must provide a law that requires that employees receive written notification and have an opportunity to consult with their employer in advance of a layoff. Member states have some scope in defining when the law must apply. For example, they can stipulate that the procedure must be followed only if the layoff affects at least 10% of the workforce. The second directive deals with situations in which, as a result of a merger or a closure, employees obtain a new employer. The existing rights and obligations of the employees must be respected by the new owner. In addition, the employees must be informed and consulted regarding the reasons for the transfer and the expected consequences of the transfer. The EC has also been considering for some time another directive that would require routine information sharing with employees by multinational corporations operating in the EC concerning their worldwide operations.

4. Quality of Work Life

"Work humanization", "work redesign," "quality of work life" are familiar themes in Western Europe today—especially in the Scandinavian countries.

Highly skilled and highly paid Scandinavian employees have demanded a better work place. Scandinavian employers, facing high absentee rates and highly protected employees, have acceded to the demand. Work places in Norway, Sweden, and Denmark have been redesigned to provide job enlargement, team assembly and the delegation of managerial responsibility to groups of employees. These experiments have generally paid off in decreased absenteeism and improved quality. Interest in these programs is not limited to the Scandinavian countries although the interest is most developed there. The German government has funded important efforts in this regard and the Italian labor unions have made serious studies of the subject.

Quality of work life is a form of industrial democracy because it involves a sharing of traditional prerogatives with employees. The employees are actively involved in planning the work place. They frequently assume, as a team, many of the traditional responsibilities and duties of foremen and inspectors. The distance between shop floor and upper management is correspondingly diminished.

EXAMPLES

Probably the most famous example of a successful quality of work life program is the Volvo factory at Kalmar, Sweden. Volvo has many factories in Sweden and abroad but in 1972 the board of directors of Kalmar decided to build a plant specifically designed for team work. The Kalmar plant has no assembly line. It is arranged so the 25 teams of workers each operate as a small factory. The car that is being manufactured by a team is moved around on a mobile carrier that can be stopped at different sites for varying amounts of time. Most of the workers rotate their jobs and there are fewer supervisors since the teams share responsibilities. Although the Kalmar plant cost more to build, the head of Volvo believes that the costs have been recovered through lower turnover and absenteeism and increased employee satisfaction.

Most of preceding types of industrial democracy are to be found throughout Western Europe. The United Kingdom is the major exception, possibly due to the traditional adversarial relationship between labor and management in that country. The wide practice of industrial democracy in Western Europe, however, does not include many examples of financial participation, which is common in the United States. Neither employees nor their labor unions have shown a great deal of interest in profit sharing or stock option plans. Sweden does have a unique system by which a portion of the profits of firms are placed in regional funds under the control of an appointed committee. Some interest in the Swedish policy has been noted in other countries but it is still too early to tell if the practice will spread.

BENEFITS

It is widely recognized today that good employee relations must take into consideration the culture expectations of the employees. Today, in Western Europe, employees expect to be involved in decisions and to assume responsibilities that formerly were assigned only to managers and owners. Managers must make changes in their style of operation but the benefits may be worth the effort.

Many arguments can be made in support of industrial democracy, but only three will be noted here:

1. Workers in northern Europe tend to be very well trained and responsible. Their suggestions can be of real value to managers who take the time to consult them.

2. The parts of Europe which have the most industrial democracy have

also the highest productivity rates and a solid reputation for the quality of their products.

3. Industrial democracy may result in lower manpower costs in the long run due to decreased need for lower level managers, less turnover, and decreased absenteeism.

IMPLEMENTATION

All Western European countries have national employers' associations which bring together the associations of employers for each sector of the economy. Firms in Western Europe generally belong to these associations and depend on them for information and even to conduct their labor negotiations. Small American firms that are not familiar with European practices should consider membership in the appropriate association. The Washington D.C. embassy of the country where a firm plans to locate will be able to direct inquiries to the appropriate association.

EVALUATION

The three concrete measures which a manager can use in order to evaluate industrial democracy are productivity, turnover, and absenteeism. These have to be balanced against the costs of a slower decision-making process and greater constraints on managerial flexibility. Where industrial democracy is mandated by law, of course, evaluation can only be made on the basis of the advantages of the location in that country measured against the difficulty in adapting to the system.

APPLICATIONS TO SMALL BUSINESS

Small businesses are exempt from many of the laws regarding industrial democracy. However, laws requiring works councils may apply to any businesses having as few as five employees (the minimum number varies according to national law). While the law may not require industrial democracy, small firms should still consider implementing some aspects of it. Small firms are particularly conducive for industrial democracy. A nonhierarchical, working relationship is easier to establish in a small firm than in a large one. Since industrial democracy is a widely accepted value in Western Europe, firms that practice it can anticipate better worker morale and a better public image.

CONCLUSION

Labor relations in Western Europe differs significantly from the practice in the United States. Managers going to Western Europe need to adjust their practices and expectations. They need to be aware of differences in labor law as well as the growing impact of EC policies. Finally they need to be sensitive to the meaning of industrial democracy.

Industrial democracy, in its various forms, is a fact of life in Western Europe today. The future is likely only to bring further extensions of it and a greater uniformity in the practice of industrial democracy in the countries belonging to the EC. It has been successful in northern Europe where the education level of employees is high and where there is a tradition of cooperative relations between employers and employees. Industrial democracy may be more difficult to implement in parts of Europe where traditional employer/employee relations have been more adversarial.

Managers who take over an operation where some form of industrial democracy is in place will need to adjust their style of management. Managers who have been trained in American participatory management or who have worked with quality circles will find that the adjustment is not great. However, managers who believe firmly that traditional styles of management are essential for business success will experience a high level of frustration. They should remember, however, that a decision has two stages—the making stage and the implementing stage. Industrial democracy probably will slow the first stage but it may also greatly facilitate the implementing stage.

Managers taking over an operation using industrial democracy should have particular concern for their middle level managers and foremen if these are being transferred from traditional operations. Numerous case studies show that these two groups find the greatest difficulty in adjusting to the new system. Foremen realize that their position is threatened by the increased responsibility of lower level employees. Both foremen and middle level managers need to be trained in new skills as communicators and facilitators rather than order givers. Moreover, both are likely to experience some anger at what they perceive to be a loss of status.

REFERENCES/SOURCES

Devos, Tom. *U.S. Multinationals and Worker Participation in Management.* Westport, CT: Quorum Books, 1981. A useful general introduction written for the American to explain the European experience.

Roberts, B. C., ed. *Industrial Relations in Europe.* Dover, NH: Greenwood, 1985. A study commissioned by the Swedish employers' association. It has separate chapters on nine Western European countries as well as two chapters on general trends.

1992: The Social Dimension. A 1989 publication of the European Community on the pending changes in labor policy. It is available from UNIPUB, 4611-F Assembly Drive, Lanham, MD 20706-4391.

Dr. Beverly J. Springer
International Studies Department
American Graduate School
Of International Management

Dr. Beverly Springer is a professor of International Studies at the American Graduate School of International Management. She is a specialist on labor issues in Western Europe and social policy in the European Community. She is a member of the Industrial Relation Research Association, the European Community Studies Association, and the Council for European Studies. She is on the editorial board of the *International Journal of Human Research Management.*

Japanese Management by Consensus

OVERVIEW

The Japanese management style that has been most popularized in the business literature is consensus management. The two contrasting roots of this approach are Western organizational behavior principles and ancient Japanese cultural traditions. Organizational behavior research indicates that concern for people increases productivity, so that job enrichment programs balance the more quantitative styles of Management by Objectives (MBO). Concurrently, Japanese cultural traditions are rooted in agricultural village life, a central characteristic of traditional Japan, wherein everyone was required to cooperate and work together for the survival of the whole village. Thus the Japanese concept of *wa*, or harmony, has become a central tenant of Japanese management.

EXAMPLES

Consensus management stems from a series of concepts that are deeply rooted in Japanese culture. Fundamental to everything in this tradition is the primacy of the group over the individual. It is not too strong to say that individualism, as commonly understood in the West (especially the United States) is not a positive or "good" value in Japan. Rather, individualism is seen in Japan as containing selfish, unstable, unreliable, rash, risky, and other negative personality characteristics. The only thing that is worse than being individualistic is being "different." Both negative concepts (from a Japanese cultural perspective) are drawn from the importance of the group in any Japanese setting.

The necessity for consensus impacts on all forms of decision-making. First, and most important, decisions are made in a group setting, not individually. This forces the entire relevant group to both participate and share in the responsibility for any decision. Also, the hierarchical nature of the Japanese society in general requires that a senior leader preside over such deliberations, but he alone cannot make a decision; rather he may be bound by the decision of his group.

Thus it is very difficult to assign individual responsibility for decision-making. Individuals are not held responsible in the limited sense for their own ideas, but are a part of a group process. This creates a vagueness which makes cross-cultural negotiations and business transactions between Japanese and non-Japanese companies difficult.

Further, there is a definite cultural bias in favor of face to face (oral) communications rather than written memos. Memos are used in the Japanese setting to document decisions after the fact; i.e., after a decision has been reached, rather than as a document to stake out an individual position for which the initiator is responsible. Thus, decisions are often slow in coming with consensus decision-making because a superior cannot simply write a memo and initiate action without consulting others.

The memo or written document associated with consensus decision-making in Japan is the *ringisho*, a document central to the "ringi" system. The ringisho is a written plan which is first submitted horizontally to one's peers within the middle management structure of a large Japanese organization. It also must cross departmental lines and be examined by other relevant departments. Thus, all impacted personnel must either accept, suggest modifications, or reject the document. With all relevant personnel involved, once a decision is made implementation is rapid and complete—the "NIH" Syndrome (Not Invented

Here) is precluded by definition.

The *ringi* system gives junior managers a chance to gain visibility as well as experience. This feature encourages managers to become generalists rather than specialists. Managers from different parts of the company interact and become familiar with one another. Since consensus decision-making requires extensive interpersonal skills in top management, negotiating various changes in a *ringisho* is excellent training for future company leaders.

By the time senior management receives the document, it has been accepted by a large number of lower-level personnel. Through informal conversation, "bar talk," and after-hours socializing, top management informally guides the process under review. Thus, this form of participative management is viewed as having many advantages from a Japanese perspective.

Yet there are some drawbacks: decision-making is slow; less talented personnel may hide within the consensus and be carried along like dead-wood; individual responsibility is hidden by design; and good ideas are not attributed to their authors, as individual credit is discouraged in favor of group achievement. Ultimately this makes rewarding superior individuals difficult, a key issue in high technology and rapidly changing knowledge-intensive fields.

BENEFITS

The Japanese system has been credited with many benefits, some of which have already been discussed above. Another result of the ringi system is paperwork reduction. As much of the decision-making process takes place in a face to face environment, the legal and bureaucratic aspects of management are reduced. This forces a company to limit staff activity and documentation and work toward action and implementation.

Further, many more individuals are made aware of and responsible for the future of the company. The entire process transforms people from "employees" to "participants." Because the circle of those consulted is large, more people are included in the destiny of the company. Departmental and specialist boundaries are broken down, allowing matrix management and cross-training, which are viewed by many as valuable management techniques in today's rapidly changing business environment.

Another key element in Japanese consensus management is lifetime employment, or a "no layoff" policy. The relationship stems from the idea that as lifetime employees, there is more incentive to work together for the long term development of the company, rather than struggling to position oneself for "the next job."

Lifetime employment allows for the gradual and non-specific evaluation of managerial talent over a long period of time, often with regard to how effectively a manager works within the consensus decision-making system. This requires leaders with high inspirational qualities. The technical competence of an individual manager is not an over-riding requirement in consensus decision-making, as technical input is provided by many sources. But leaders have to have a high moral stature and be able to command the loyalty and dedication of subordinates. Seniority is valued because an "older" person is presumed to have experience and judgement, and thus be more effective as a leader.

Another aspect is compensation based upon group performance, rather than on a strict individual merit basis. In the Japanese context, bonuses are awarded twice a year, solely in relation to the overall performance (profitability) of the firm. Rewards are deferred until the "results are in" and are then distributed to all who participated in the firm's activities.

The gap between executive salaries and those of line workers is less than in the U.S. Much has been made about the salaries of top executives in U.S. corporations as compared with their Japanese counterparts. The purpose of the Japanese approach is to demonstrate the unity of everyone within the firm, and to discourage tensions and conditions within the organization that would make consensus in the future difficult to achieve.

In the area of manufacturing production, consensus management is represented by the now famous concept of Quality Control (QC) circles. In QC circles, line workers practice consensus management within their areas of manufacturing. QC circles first require interpersonal interaction. Workers must talk to each other, not just "show up for their shift." Also, the focus of QC circles is production improvement, thus requiring worker involvement in the production process. This violates the fundamental principles of Taylorism, in which a manger is supposed to determine the "one best way" and order the workers to follow it.

In QC circles emphasis is on involvement rather than tangible or explicit results evolving from specific suggestions and they are expected to produce specific improvements in the way a manufacturing process is accomplished. But most important is the identification of the worker with his job such that he will take great responsibility in his work. However, total quality control and zero defect, objectives of Japanese industrial management, would be impossible to achieve using only QC methods. But, by requiring workers to become involved, through consensus, in decision making and the total work flow, higher quality is achieved from the resulting increase in worker dedication.

In U.S. corporations several efforts at forms of consensus management have been suggested. "Management by Walking Around," a contemporary management term, is an attempt to create more direct interaction between management and workers. Additionally, paperwork reduction campaigns have been directed toward reducing the flood of memo writing which has clogged communication lines, and in production, suggestion campaigns are being implemented to encourage input and involvement in management decisions from line workers.

Currently, American corporations are following the lead of the Japanese in employee recruiting and development. American firms are learning that spending more time on training and career development gives employees a greater sense of belonging to the company and a greater sense of the corporation's goals and objectives. This makes them more prepared and motivated to contribute positively to group decision making.

IMPLEMENTATION

It is possible that consensus management may not work well for all international corporations. Certain fundamental national characteristics in Japan are considered to be a major factor in the success of consensus management. Japan is a crowded, culturally homogeneous nation that fosters collectivism over individualism. Conversely, the United States is a nation of differing racial and cultural traditions, with a greater ratio of land to people and whose entire social and legal structure is dedicated to individualism. However, ignoring the benefits of consensus management could prevent a firm from being competitive domestically as well as internationally. Implementation of techniques such as Management by Objectives (MBO) and job enrichment and job enlargement, in the spirit of consensus management, may work better initially for non-Japanese corporations.

Also, drastic implementation of a new corporate culture, from an autocratic, centralized management style to a democratic, decentralized style may create stress and confusion within an organization. Older managers may be particularly adverse to change and may actually work to subvert new procedures.

An understanding of the nature of corporate culture is critical to effective implementation. A corporation may find the assistance of a consulting firm necessary to help analyze a corporation's potential adaptability to consensus management.

EVALUATION

Non-Japanese corporations can learn much from consensus management, but managers must understand that the uniqueness of Japanese society may contribute much toward the success of the system. Additionally, top managers should monitor the reactions to change at all levels within the corporation. Continued training and development of managers, as well as employees, will make changes smoother and less disruptive and will make the effectiveness of changes greater.

APPLICATIONS TO SMALL BUSINESS

Small businesses (i.e., those with less than 100 employees) should benefit most from consensus decision making, because the span of communications and control is greatly reduced. Further, small businesses are characterized by the domination of their leader/founder, who projects an image similar to the mythical Japanese leader/teacher. Thus the social characteristics of small business offer a setting more conducive to an open consensus-management style.

The severe limitation upon small business rests in the need to accomplish all functions in a short time frame with limited resources. This can divert the attention of the leader/founder from personnel management motivational concerns, and also force the firm to take a short-run orientation in order to survive. Additionally, the firm's shortage of capital (both working and long term), a general problem in small businesses, may force the company to adopt a variable cost approach to employees, dismissing them when short-term fluctuations in business reduce revenues. This could inhibit attracting well qualified, creative people who would otherwise be receptive to consensus management.

CONCLUSION

Consensus management has contributed greatly to the rapid rise of Japan from a small, war-torn country to a major global economic power. It has sublimated traditional management-labor frictions resulting in greater productivity and profitability, as well as unequaled intracorporate harmony and employee devotion. But the success of strict consensus management in non-Japanese firms may be difficult to achieve due to different cultural situations. However, non-Japanese firms can benefit greatly by adopting the spirit, if not the strict practice, of consensus management. Corporations wishing to compete domestically as well as internationally will have to start incorporating consensus management theories into their organizations if they want to be competitive now and in the future.

REFERENCES/SOURCES

Alston, Jon. *The American Samurai: Blending American and Japanese Managerial Practices*. New York: Walter De Gruyter, 1986. Cross cultural managerial comparisons.

Clark, Rodney. *The Japanese Company*. New Haven: Yale University Press, 1979. A study of firm specialization and its relationship to consensus.

Drucker, Peter F. "Japan's Choices." *Foreign Affairs* 65,5 (Summer 1987): 923-941. Issues of societal/managerial consensus in a global context.

Fields, George. *From Bonsai to Levi's: When East Meets West, An Insider's Surprising Account of How the Japanese Live*. New York: New American Library, 1985. A popular account of Japanese society and group consensus.

Gerlack, Michael. "Business Alliances and the Strategy of the Japanese Firm." *California Management Review* 30,1 (Fall 1987): 126-142.

Gould, William B. *Japan's Reshaping of American Labor Law*. Cambridge, MA: MIT Press, 1984. The implications of Consensus on the U.S. legal framework of management.

Harris, Philip R. and Robert T. Moran. *Managing Cultural Differences*. 2d ed. Houston: Gulf Publishing Company, 1987.

Kawashima, Y. and T. Tachibanaki. "The Effect of Discrimination and of Industry Segmentation of Wage Differentials in Relation to Education." *International Journal of Industrial Organization* 4,1 (1986): 43-68. Wage differences and their impact on consensus.

Kujawa, Duane. *Japanese Multinationals in the United States: Case Studies*. New York: Praeger, 1986. Cases of U.S. subsidiaries of Japanese firms and their management experiences.

McMillian, Charles. *The Japanese Industrial System*. New York: Walter De Gruyter, 1984. Contains chapters on "Samurai Management," which focus on consensus.

Moran, Robert T. *Getting Your Yen's Worth: How to Negotiate With Japan Inc*. Houston: Gulf Publishing Company, 1985. The relationship of cross-cultural negotiations to consensus management.

Ohmae, Kenichi. *Beyond National Borders: Reflections on Japan and the World*. Homewood, IL: Dow-Jones-Irwin, 1987. How a tribal "groupism" fosters consensus but hinders Japanese internationalism.

Peck, Merton J. "Is Japan Really a Share Economy?" *Journal of Comparative Economics*. Vol. 10, No. 4 (December 1986): 427-432. Economic analysis of Japanese salary bonuses as disguised wage payments, yet they promote group consensus.

Pempel, T. J. *Japan: The Dilemmas of Success*. New York: Foreign Policy Association, 1986. An analysis of Japan's economy and society today.

Sasaki, Naoto. *Management and Industrial Structure in Japan*. New York: Pergamon Press, 1981. Culture and consensus integrated into a Japanese production model.

Snowdon, Mark. "The Japanese Approach to Productivity and Quality—A European's View." *International Journal of Technology Management* 1,3-4 (1986): 411-424. Examines Austin Rover's adoption of Japanese consensus management.

Sours, Martin H. "The Influence of Japanese Culture on the Japanese Management System." In Lee, Sang M. and Gary Schwendiman, eds. *Japanese Management: Cultural and Environmental Consideration*. New York: Praeger, 1982: 27-39.

Suzawa, Soichi. "How the Japanese Achieve Excellence." *Training and Development Journal* 30, 5 (May 1985): 110-118. Consensus as a motivator within the Japanese business context.

Martin H. Sours
International Studies Department
American Graduate School
of International Management

Management Infrastructure in the Third World

OVERVIEW

At the end of World War II, Europe lay in devastation and ruin, its physical plant and equipment bombed and destroyed. The economy was in shambles, governments had fallen or had been overthrown, and much of the population displaced. After a long and protracted war, roads and bridges were destroyed, harbors mined, and rail transportation seriously disrupted. The production, communication, and transportation infrastructure had been destroyed.

In less than a generation Europe recovered and began its post-war prosperity. The single most important component of this rapid recovery was not the great influx of capital and assistance, but the fact that Europe had a strong managerial infrastructure. While its physical infrastructure lay in ruin, its managerial resources did not.

This management infrastructure is the foundation upon which a society builds its economic strength. Its foundation is made up of the following six basic infrastructural components.

1. *Management Information/Communication Systems and Skills*: The ability to develop and move needed information in a timely and accurate fashion. The skills and technologies essential to build this foundation for effective organization range from interpersonal competencies to telecommunications capacities. Cultural conditions effect the ways this can best be achieved in a collective setting.

2. *Decision-Making and Action Taking Capabilities*: As information movement is institutionalized, effective decision-making skills are required. These decision methods must then be built into action-taking capabilities using the resources of the organization as efficiently as possible and building on the values of the culture.

3. *Project Planning, Organizing, and Systems Integration*: Planners must look to the future while coordinating the development of the organization. Designing plans for an idealized future state requires building a sophisticated, flexible organization that can change as the state matures.

4. *Systems Evaluation and Internal Control*: As the organization emerges, systems of control must be established. The control system either emerges out of a cultural context or is imposed on it. Imposing it sacrifices long term development of the human self-control capacity for short term compliance.

5. *Leadership, Motivational, and Reward Systems*: The managerial responsibility is to initiate plans, set forces in action and develop systems that drive themselves because of the rewards built into the tasks and the environment. In doing this, managers become the role models and examples for building the work capacity into the organization. With these activities the organizational culture begins to develop.

6. *Selection, Placement and Development of People*: As management builds the infrastructure, the most critical decision point is choosing and/or developing the people who will make it all happen. Diligence and care at this point determines more than anything else whether the organization will produce what it is being asked to.

These six management building blocks, it is argued, existed in the immediate post-war Europe.

If this economic recovery is compared to the developing world, the absence of a sophisticated managerial infrastructure in the Third World emerges as the key factor in its struggle. The question is how developing countries can be aided to create a management infrastructure that will give them a greater capacity for economic growth. This issue has been given only limited attention in part because management infrastructure is not only difficult to measure but its form takes on different meanings depending on cultural context.

IMPLEMENTATION

There are three essential areas which a developing country must examine in order to build its management infrastructure: First, to improve the basic understanding and build a knowledge base regarding the process whereby developing countries can develop their managerial infrastructure; second, to achieve some predictability about the problems, needs, and challenges being faced in this third world management development process; and third, to develop means and methods for helping a country develop a management infrastructure that reflects both social and economic values.

In order to evaluate third world management development, analysts must examine the country's historical and cultural dimensions including: overall world view, child rearing and family practices, motivational forces, organizational relationships, political environment, spiritual and religious beliefs, technology, economic systems/resource allocations, and international/global relationships (see figure 1). There is a lively methodological debate in the anthropological and sociological disciplines about how to interpret data, but it is best to keep in mind that a study of the management infrastructure is as much an art as a science.

Management Infrastructure in the Third World

The cultural analysis approach takes the primary management infrastructure building blocks and analyzes each according to the history and cultural conditions in the country being examined. To illustrate, we can look at the Information/Communication Systems and Skills section and analyze it in terms of the cultural effects. The consensus is that culture will both directly and indirectly affect the communication systems that a manager uses. Third World countries tend to divide beliefs about life based on the assumption that either man or nature is the dominant force, or that they work harmoniously. Also important is whether the people regard time as immediate, linear, or circular. Egypt stands as an example of how a new economic system radically changed cultural sensibilities. For thousands of years Egyptians depended on the flooding of the Nile river for its food supply, and as a result developed beliefs based on the dominance of nature. But the advanced technology that produced the Aswan High Dam—which suggests that man may control some of his environment—caused great disparities among Aswan Dam staff, and has ultimately altered managerial communication patterns and assumptions about life. The impact of technology on Third World culture may not be easily observable, but it does influence how managers and workers behave.

At the present time there is a transition—perhaps more correctly, a turbulent change—in the way managers communicate and use information. Skills based on face-to-face negotiation and social interaction must now be supplemented with technical and mechanical communications systems, which both speed up and disseminate information to a larger audience. Another fundamental transition or change in the culture is having an impact on the temporal dimension. Taking another example, the historic Islamic belief that "Allah determines all" is being replaced by a more western understanding of cause-and-effect relationships. Developing societies are beginning to understand that, in a managerial context, communication has immediate consequences. The traditional pattern of communication was much more personal and not always directly related to cause-effect assumptions and linear action. Managers now realize that if they do not communicate appropriately, work or task completion will be hindered. Because the future, as far as developing management capacity is concerned, demands even more task orientation, more impersonal and mechanically aided communication must take place. If the management of information is to improve, new styles of managerial behavior will be necessary. This change in behavior is ultimately linked to one's assumptions about the world. These changes have consequences for both the way work is done as well as the social relationships found at work.

EVALUATION

In addition to the list of internal historical and cultural dimensions, the following external factors are necessary to consider:

1. Geo-political dynamics of a highly polarized world—not only Western versus Eastern bloc, but the complicated non-aligned nations and the North-South splits.

2. The unique colonial or trade history as it was in the past and as it now influences the culture, politics, and economics of the country. For example, the ties of the French and English with their ex-colonies and the people-to- people relationships that though not often seen, exert strong influence.

3. Changes and disruptions in world resource markets, such as oil, coffee and copper.

4. Transportation, telecommunications, and tourism changes that bring the 20th century world into a Global Village age and move people and ideas around the world at a speed never before imagined.

Management Infrastructure in the Third World

MANAGEMENT CULTURE ANALYSIS MATRIX: A PREPARATION GUIDE

	Overall World View (Man Nature | Time Sense)	Child Rearing & Family (Childhood | Adult Life)	Motivational General Themes* (N ACH, N AFF, N POW)	Organ'l Relationships (Organization / Work Group)	Social Relationships (Community)	Political Environment	Spiritual & Religious Beliefs (Ethics & Values)	Technology Relationships Man/Tool	Economic Systems Resource Allocation	International/ Global Relationships
				Factors Affecting Cultural Conditions & Conditioning						
MANAGEMENT INFRASTRUCTURAL COMPONENTS (The Basics)										
Information/Communication Systems & Skills										
Decision Making & Action-Taking Capabilities										
Project Planning and Organizing Skills (Systems Integration)										
Systems Evaluation and Internal Control Capacity										
Selection, Placement, and Development of People										
Leadership, Motivation, and Reward Systems										

*Using David McClelland's Motivation Theory where N ACH = Need for Achievement
N AFF = Need for Affiliation
N POW = Need for Power

Looking inside a country's historical and cultural conditions, as well as its external influences, can help us understand how a country developed its particular management infrastructure. What is also required in this examination process is a careful and systematic analysis of the present managerial infrastructure. This entails a management audit or analysis. As difficult as an audit is to do for a large organization, it becomes a special challenge when looking at a whole country.

This management analysis builds on an understanding of the external environment or context (see figure 2) combined with a cultural analysis as shown in the management matrix (see figure 1). This analytical process can be complemented with an additional activity of developing accurate case studies of actual managerial situations. These studies then provide not only rich data to help better understand local management but, as they expose the successful management practices found in the culture, they can aid management development within and even in other cultures facing similar managerial challenges.

In brief form, the following are the steps performed to complete a management cultural analysis:

1. Conscious and systematic study of the history and culture of the country through both primary and secondary data sources.
2. Living in and observing a wide range of management activity in the culture.
3. Building the management culture analysis matrix process using local informants and experts.
4. Preparing a systematic internal and external environmental factor analysis.
5. Developing successful practice case studies.

These studies can lead to the formation of a better understanding of the development of the local management infrastructure, as well as set the groundwork for

6. Management Capacity Assessment.

This assessment of the local managerial results should be compared to other similar management activities.

CONCLUSION

It is safe to say that, in the past, concerns for developing country management infrastructure capacity has been very limited. With the exception of those companies that constantly complain about why "those" people can't manage, there is very little, if any, literature that exists either in case studies of successes or in comparative analysis of managerial capacity.

Beyond these first six steps of the management infrastructure analysis comes a seventh step of significant importance, known as "Management Needs Analysis." This analysis, like the first six, must grow from a cultural context that builds a process that is both appropriate and relevant to the culture under study. This becomes a very touchy issue because if outsiders assume that they know what a given country needs in management skills, they are then assuming they know what the culture's development goals are. When there is a lack of certainty or a high political volatility surrounding the country's development goals, it is imperative that the management needs analysis be conducted carefully with regard to the cultural values and differences. As with the earlier capacity assessment, this needs analysis process should be built around a clear statement of goals as developed by the local culture itself. Where this is not possible, the outside analysis group must make its goals and intent very clear.

FIGURE 2
THE EXTERNAL AND INTERNAL VIEW

Geo-Political Dynamic
World Political Change

World Resource	Transportation
Market Changes	Telecommunications
(including capital markets)	and Tourism Changes

EXTERNAL
INTERNAL

OVERALL WORLD VIEW

CHILD REARING & FAMILY PRACTICE

MOTIVATIONAL GENERAL THEMES

ORGANIZATIONAL RELATIONSHIPS

POLITICAL ENVIRONMENT

SPIRITUAL AND RELIGIOUS BELIEFS

TECHNOLOGY

ECONOMIC SYSTEMS/RESOURCE ALLOCATIONS

INTERNAL/GLOBAL RELATIONS

Colonial or Trade	Additional External Ties
History plus Personal	Global Factors
across national borders	Village Effect

A typical problem associated with either performing a capacity assessment or a needs analysis is as follows: If a country desires that its rural development activities take precedence over its industrial development goals, the management infrastructure development process is strongly influenced by the implicit values in emphasizing rural development. There are other important cultural considerations. For example, one style of management, authoritarian, produces a number of by-products like alienation or citizen apathy, in Chile a more participative style equates to a slower pace of development. What this basically says is that the management infrastructure development has potential impact not only on the economic factors but on the social and cultural factors as well. As a result, management development has a significant influence on a country's quality of life; the effect of management is not limited to economic progress; there can be serious implications for how all people will experience their lives.

The quality of life may be positively or negatively affected by the pace of development, whereas cultural value of family and religion, for example, will be changed by a more efficient infrastructure.

The Third World does not share with the West a history of modern organization or industrial life; thus it must be viewed in terms of what its organizational history has been. At that point, management development requires a planned strategic change program built on valid and relevant information about the current conditions. An analysis of management capacity and needs should precede actions to change or develop the infrastructure.

Management in developing countries should not be viewed as desperate or incompetent. The first principle of assistance should be mutual respect based on the understanding that both parties have something to offer each other. Though it hasn't been taken advantage of, it seems clear that the Third World has much to offer the industrial West besides cheap resources. The high level of both family and religious systems offers lessons to any society seriously trying to improve its quality of life. Though these systems may not have a direct economic impact, they definitely serve a strong supporting function for the individual, and that single lesson is worth serious consideration in light of the devastating social problems confronting managers in the West. There is much to be gained in a global free market in addition to the economic benefits. Socio-economic development puts all countries on equal footing, and developed nations can learn much by studying Third World infrastructure.

REFERENCES/SOURCES

Berger, Peter L. *Pyramids of Sacrifice: Political Ethics and Social Change.* New York: Basic Books, 1974. A critical review of both capitalism and Marxism in terms of their abilities to promote socio-economic development.

Boyatzis, Richard E. *The Competent Manager: A Model for Effective Performance.* New York: Wiley-Interscience, 1982. A focused look at specific skills managers need to build effective organizations.

Esman, Milton J., and John D. Montgomery. "Systems Approaches to Technical Cooperation: The Role of Development Administration." *Public Administration Review* 29 (September/October 1969): 507-539. An early review on the importance of management in the public sector primarily.

Farmer, R. N., and B. M. Richman. *Comparative Management and Economic Progress.* Homewood, IL: Richard D. Irwin, 1965.

Haire, M., E. E. Ghisellis and L. W. Porter. *Managerial Thinking: An International Study.* New York: Wiley, 1966. One of the first cultural studies of management.

Hofstede, Geert. *Culture's Consequences: International Differences in Work*

Related Values. Beverly Hills, CA: Sage Publications, 1980. Reports of a 100,000 plus sampling of respondents working in a large U.S. multinational corporation regarding the cultural impact on attitudes.

Jantsch, Erich. *Design for Evolution: Self-Organization and Planning in the Life of Human Systems.* New York: George Braziller, 1975. A creative primer on models for more participative organizational structures and philosophies.

Murrell, Kenneth L. "A Cultural Analysis of the Egyptian Management Environment," in Philip R. Harris and Gerald H. Malin, eds. *Innovation in Global Consultation.* Annual Conference Proceedings, Copenhagen, Denmark, 1979: 2. The first published report of the use of cultural analysis model in a specific setting.

———. "Organization Development in the Third World: Lessons and Reasons Why." *O.D. Journal* 2, 2 (Summer 1984). A description of how and why an organization development methodology can be useful in international development work.

Nath, R. "A Methodological Review of Cross-cultural Management Research." In J. Boddewyn ed. *Comparative Management and Marketing.* Glenview, IL: Scott, Foresman, 1969. An early work on the critical nature of culture in understanding other countries' management and business.

Taylor, Max. *Coverdale on Management.* London: Wm. Heinemann, 1979. A description of the "successful practices" approach to helping developing countries improve their management.

Trist, Eric. "Planning the First Steps Toward Quality of Working Life in a Developing Country." In Louis E. Davis & Albert B. Cherns, eds. *The Quality of Working Life*, Vol. 1. New York: Free Press, 1975. The source for the concept of "century skip" where developing countries can learn significant lessons from the west in order to manage their socio-economic development better.

Dr. Kenneth L. Murrell
Department of Management
College of Business
University of West Florida

Dr. Kenneth Murrell is a management consultant working, both independently and with the United Nations and the U.S. government, in Somalia, Kenya, Tanzania and Yugoslavia. The author of several books on human resource management, Dr. Murrell has consulted with domestic companies as well, including G.D. Searle pharmaceutical and General Foods. He holds an M.B.A. from The George Washington University and a Ph.D. from The American University.

Nepotism in International Management

OVERVIEW

Nepotism is a management topic that has created much debate. The term, derived from the Latin word "nepos" for nephew, is loosely defined as the employment of the relatives of top management and employees in the company. The largely negative connotation of the word dates back to the tendency of the medieval popes to find high level clerical offices for their nephews regardless of their qualifications. Its effect on the efficiency of the church and the morale of the non-nephew priests seemed quite similar to misconceptions about nepotistic management practices today. Thus, the topic represents one of the most difficult and deep-rooted problems faced by human organizations.

Because of the generally negative perception, many large and even medium-sized companies have adopted anti-nepotism policies at least in their company manuals. While there are no accurate statistics on how many executives hire their relatives in their own companies, sociologists and economists estimate that approximately 96% of American corporations are family owned or dominated in the sense that these businesses could not be taken over without the acquiescence of a particular clan. It is reported that 35% of the Fortune 500 companies are family dominated, or at least have had successive generations of the same family somewhere in top management. In Japan, nepotism is widespread. James C. Abegglen and Hiroshi Mannari found that over half of the sons of major executives of large companies in Japan were in the same organizations as their fathers. In Germany, the country whose industrial achievement since World War II is often ranked first among European nations, nepotism is also prevalent. In developing countries and newly industrialized economies, nepotism is sometimes considered as an honorable obligation.

Discussion on nepotism is related to three parties involved—the company, nepots, and other employees. The discussion from the viewpoint of the organization involved is usually centered on questions of advantages and disadvantages of nepotism to the company's performance. The generally perceived advantages can be grouped: desirability of working in a warm family type atmosphere, improved communications, consistency of policy, smoothness of executive transition, and acceptance of a family-led organization by customers and the community. Problems associated with nepotism are generally perceived as follows: negative impact on morale, inability to hire more competent executives from outside, tendency of family affairs to get mixed up with business decisions, and problems shared by nepots and other employees who can never know for sure if someone was hired, promoted or given a raise on the basis of actual performance or kinship.

From the standpoint of nepots involved, the psychological problem that most commonly bedevils the nepot is a nagging need, in some cases lifelong, to establish themselves as a competent, worthwhile person in their own right. Nepots often suffer from a "prince-pauper syndrome"—material desires are satisfied but emotional needs are not met.

The generally perceived standpoint of non-nepot employees can be summarized as follows: nepotism is a great danger; it makes superiors afraid of subordinates who happen to be related to company heads; it makes subordinates fear their actions will be reported directly to top management by nepots; and it makes peers of the nepot fear the specter of unfair competition for promotion.

Critics and management scientists generally tend to look at the question of nepotism from a societal point of view and often on an abstract basis; they tend to allege that nepotism is outmoded and unprofessional. Based on a few large scale surveys, however, they seem to have arrived at a set of broad conclusions.

1. When executives consider nepotism as a general principle, a majority are against it (except in the case of family businesses).

2. They are impressed by certain disadvantages of nepotism, especially its tendency to discourage outsiders from seeking employment in the company and to stir up jealousy and resentment among non-nepot employees.

3. When executives get down to specific problems and situations, a strong majority often accept nepotism despite its shortcomings.

4. By dealing with nepotism objectively, analytically, and knowledgeably on a case-by-case basis, executives feel that they can draw on potential advantages while minimizing disadvantages.

IMPLEMENTATION

Some management specialists have come to view the issue of nepotism within a broader framework of "management succession." "Planned nepotism" has become an integral part of management succession planning. Since all nations have unique business cultures, U.S. companies wishing to expand business abroad will greatly benefit from understanding the subtle nature and degrees of nepotism still prevalent in many countries.

According to Japanese opinion in the Report on Korea-Japan Joint Research on the Korean Economy, as of 1964-65 the most outstanding characteristic of Korean enterprises was a family-dominated management structure. Jongtae

Choi conducted a sample survey of Korean companies located in the province of Kyungsang-bukdo during a period of two years, 1964-65. Choi reports that 82% of the companies practiced nepotism; a strong nepotistic tendency was observed in 60% of them. Among them, several companies were experiencing serious difficulties and they claimed nepotism was the major cause. Tamio Hattori and Hiroshi Uyama report the findings of their 1977 survey of Korean Chaebols (conglomerates). According to them, 70% of the companies were under management by either their founders or the second generation. Among them, 60% have already transferred management to sons or brothers. Hence, many large Korean enterprises are called "clan enterprises." Hattori and Uyama predicted nepotism would continue in the Korean business community.

In 1987, the authors of this piece conducted a sample survey of Korean companies—the 50 largest companies in Korea—focusing specifically on nepotism. Among the 50 companies, about 75% (38 out of 50) continue to support nepotism. These companies have already hired a large number of their relatives as chairmen, presidents, and vice-presidents. Differences in performance, measured in terms of profit rate and growth rate of sales between those companies practicing nepotism and those minimizing the practice, were minimal.

BENEFITS

Albert Rees has shown that hiring one's family members, relatives and/or friends provides direct pecuniary gains or savings to an employer. Recruits feel added pressure to succeed, hence increasing productivity. Kinship and/or friendship also provides a reliable and relatively inexpensive source of information about job applicants; current employees do not wish to anger their employer by recommending relatives and/or friends who are unqualified. Reliable friends' recommendations can be substitutes for other potentially more costly and impersonal sources of information, including recommendations from previous employers or teachers, academic records, and previous work history.

Management literature also supports nepotism as an excellent way to attract and retain a relatively cheap, loyal, dedicated, and committed work force. Many executives agree that there are some circumstances under which nepotism is especially advantageous. A salesman who bears the same name as the company owner has a better chance of making a sale. Outsiders, such as financial analysts, stockholders, and newspapermen, will attach more importance to the words and actions of an executive related to the company's owners.

Small companies may need to take advantage of family trees in recruiting managerial manpower in order to survive. Closely held family corporations may feel that the family has the right to retain management in the family. Further, according to Ewing's survey, many businessmen seem to agree that if a family has produced leaders and executives for several generations, it probably will continue to do so.

EVALUATION

Whether or not to implement a nepotistic policy is a tough question; it is an oversimplification to categorically condemn nepotism as "bad." If the practice of nepotism can bring a net benefit to the whole group of participants—the enterprise, the family and nepots, and the non-nepot employees, it may be considered "good" or "not bad" at least under certain circumstances.

Until a hundred years ago, the family business was by far the dominant force in the United States. Numerically, it remains dominant. Only recently have problems of the family business been overshadowed by those of professional managers in publicly held firms. Nepotism is a viable option if one wishes to pass on a thriving family corporation. Continuity and growth are also viable reasons for implementing nepotism as a policy.

In implementing nepotism, business literacy is a necessary attribute for the successful nepot. As Leon A. Danco says, the nepot must understand and be responsive to the "ebb and flow of information from the accounting system." A potential successor of a company must not become a "nepot" too soon. Instead, he should be trained, and should learn modern management techniques from competent professional managers before assuming the reigns of power.

As a family dominated company succeeds and grows, its board of directors should adapt to the ever changing business environment. The real function of the board is to provide continuity and growth. It has a basic educational commitment to assist the "nepot" after the founder-manager retires. In short, a constant flow of new ideas into the organization and a smooth adaptation to the changing business environment must be assured; shortcomings inherent in family-managed enterprises should turn into positive aspects.

Methods for evaluating the impacts of nepotism on the general performance of an organization are as follows. First, overall performance indicators such as profit rates and growth rates of sales can be compared between nepotistic firms and non-nepotistic organizations, holding all other factors comparable between the two groups as much as possible. Second, literature suggests that motivation research techniques can be employed for analyzing differences in the impacts of nepotism on employees' motivation between the two groups in companies. Third, sociometric techniques are also suggested to evaluate differences in employee interactions in the two groups of companies. Finally, interviews with people who are directly and indirectly affected by personnel changes should be conducted. If possible, these interviews should be conducted both prior to and after the personnel change.

Popular perception has it that when family and business are interrelated, a less efficient business enterprise generally results. A close examination of the subject suggests that this belief may be unfounded.

CONCLUSION

A majority of executives often accept nepotism under specific, concrete situations. Despite adverse historical connotations of nepotism and abuses of the practice, there are as many arguments for nepotism as there are against. Managers should understand the contribution nepots can make to a firm's long-term strength; they should analyze the weaknesses involved; and they should implement organizational restraints to control foreseeable problems.

As international business becomes more global, multinational managers must be aware of nepotistic practices; they are practiced worldwide and are more prevalent in countries whose culture, management thought, and practices are significantly different from those in the U.S. Before the multinational manager begins dealing with foreign counterparts, it is desirable that he have a general knowledge about the extent and degrees of nepotistic management structures of major companies in the foreign markets.

APPLICATIONS TO SMALL BUSINESS

Many retiring presidents of small corporations are the founders of their companies. Their average length of tenure is longer than that of nonfounders and of larger companies. Lack of planning for succession of any organization tends to be followed by a post-succession period of lower organizational performance; this relationship is especially crucial for small firms where lowered performance can threaten their survival.

A plan for succession consists of three elements, all of which must antedate the actual successions:

1. The designation of the successor by the president or an appropriate higher authority.

2. A period of effective training of the successor-designate in the top management tasks of the particular firm.

3. Acceptance of the planned succession by the successor-designate himself and by other major power figures who could later successfully dispute the succession.

In many small companies, however, there exist numerous inhibitors of successful succession planning. They include:

1. Size of management group—the smaller a firm is in size, the more difficult it is to support a successor-designate.

2. Growth conducive to planning for succession—where growth is absent, planning is less likely.

3. Ownership—smaller firms are more likely to be family owned and managed; planning for succession is difficult if there is no available successor within the family.

4. The manager of a small firm is likely to be concerned largely with the problem of day-to-day operations; he may not have the time or ability to train a successor.

5. Small firms are less likely to have access to outside counsel that might encourage planning for succession.

6. Managers of small firms frequently refuse to retire; hence, planning for succession is either likely to be postponed or a successor-designate may become impatient and leave.

7. Managers of small firms often have the attitude that "time will produce a successor."

These inhibitors often lead to high costs resulting from the search for a successor-designate. These high costs can be detrimental to the continued success of the small business.

Whether the management succession is achieved through "planned nepotism," through a selection of a competent candidate from inside the business or through a search for a candidate outside the business, the management selection requires a serious and systematic planning for success and growth of the small business.

REFERENCES/SOURCES

Nepotism in General: Opportunities, Problems, Solutions

Copeland, Lennie. "Cross-Cultural Training: The Competitive Edge." *Training* (July 1985): 49-53. Purports that every country has a distinctive business culture, and intercultural relationships are fragile and liable to fail; it is important to provide international managers with cross-cultural understanding. For example, in the Middle East, one's primary responsibility is to family; what Americans reject as nepotism is an honorable obligation to Arabs.

Dailey, Robert C. and Thomas E. Reuschling. "Human Resource Management in the Family Owned Company." *Journal of General Management* (Spring 1980): 49-56. The authors compare strengths and weaknesses in American family enterprises with respect to hiring, evaluation and promotion, termination and retirement, and managerial training and development.

Davis, Peter. "Realizing the Potential of the Family Business." *Organizational Dynamics* (Summer 1983): 47-56. This article has examined the family business as a joint system and has attempted to outline the elements of a change technology on the basis of a systems perspective.

Donaldson, Thomas. "Multinational Decision-Making: Reconciling International Norms." *Journal of Business Ethics* 4 (1985): 357-366. Managers of multinational corporations (MNC) are often faced with the problem of reconciling conflicts between their home country moral traditions and the ones common in the host country. This study constructs and defends an ethical algorism for MNC managers to use in the reconciliation of such international normative conflicts; its application is illustrated in a number of situations, including pollution and nepotism.

Flarsheim, Henry. "Nepotism and Family-run Company." *Business Management* (June 1970): 23-24, 36. The author brings many examples of companies practicing nepotism in varying degrees to answer a continuing and controversial problem: Does nepotism hurt a company? After a full circle, he concludes that the "answer would seem to depend on the individual talents, characteristics and harmonious working relationships relatives can bring to a business."

Ford, Robert and Frank McLaughlin. "Nepotism." *Personnel Journal* (September 1985): 57-60. The authors conclude that whether nepotism is good or bad often depends upon the size and ownership pattern of a company. Prohibiting nepotism can adversely affect female employees who marry other employees or dual-career couples not allowed to work for the same company.

Greenberg, Jonathan. "All in the Family." *Forbes* (April 25, 1983): 147. This is a case study of a company which plans to diversify through friendly acquisitions of other family-owned businesses; the company will offer an alternative to public companies, and it plans to be an alternative that will allow nepotism to flourish.

Holland, Phyllis G. and William R. Boulton. "Balancing the 'Family' and the 'Business' in Family Business." *Business Horizons* (March-April 1984): 16-21. The authors claim that family businesses may be large, growing, small, national, or international in scope, but they do have certain characteristics, unique problems, and challenges for the strategist. In the family business, an important component of the general management task is the management of family and professional relationships on a personal and business level.

Kiechel, Walter, III. "How to Relate to Nepotism." *Fortune* (February 6, 1984): 143-144. Problems and opportunities of family owned and/or dominated companies are discussed. The author thinks potential nepots would do well to prove themselves in an outside concern first.

Lansberg, Ivan S. "Managing Human Resources in Family Firms: The Problem of Institutional Overlap." *Organizational Dynamics* (Summer 1983): 39-46. Contradictions between (1) the norms and principles that operate in the family and (2) those that operate in business, frequently interfere with the effective management of human resources in family firms. The author offers mechanisms to cope with these conflicting institutional prescriptions.

Levinson, Harry. "Consulting with Family Businesses: What to Look for, What to Look out for." *Organizational Dynamics* (Summer 1983): 71-80. The author summarizes fearsome and unexpected pitfalls for those consulting with family businesses.

Nadler, Paul S. "Nepotism in Banking." *Bankers Monthly* (October 1983):

5-6, 22. In many banks, particularly community banks, it is traditional for successive generations of the owning family to work in the bank. The author discusses problems related with nepotism in banking, especially serious for the children of the banking family; the author suggests to have them trained in a program run by a correspondent bank.

Poe, Randall. "The SOB's." *Across Board* (May 1980): 23-27. The author estimates that only 30% of all family businesses survive into the second generation, and he reports three central reasons for the succession quandary. Business owners are too busy keeping their business alive to plan their own exit; don't have any real confidence in their offspring even though many do expect their sons to replace them; and do not see family perpetuity as a major concern.

Rutigliano, Anthony J. "Some Would Call It Paternalism." *Management Review* (July 1986): 34-37. A case study of a business owned by members of three families; the company achieves tremendous productivity and encourages nepotism among workers.

Schein, Edgar H. "The Role of the Founder in Creating Organizational Culture." *Organizational Dynamics* (Summer 1983): 13-28. The author examines what organizational culture is, how the founder creates and embeds cultural elements, why it is likely that first-generation companies develop distinctive cultures, and what the implications are in making the transition from founders or owning families to professional managers.

Surveys and Quantitative Analyses

Donnelley, Robert G. "The Family Business." *Harvard Business Review*

(July-August 1964): 93-104. This article is based on a study of 15 successful family companies, supported by personal interviews with family managers and other interested businessmen and executives. The author observes weakness in the family firm if nepotism is unchecked by objective standards of meritorious managerial performance.

Ewing, David W. "Is Nepotism So Bad?" *Harvard Business Review* (January-February 1965): 22-40, 156-160. This is the report on an HBR's survey of the attitudes of over 2,700 managers about nepotism. According to the findings of this special study, nepotism can be good or bad, depending on how it is practiced.

Ford, Robert and Frank McLaughlin. "Nepotism: Boon or Bane." *Personnel Administrator* (November 1986): 78-89. A survey of 252 members of the American Society for Personnel Administration to compare nepotism policies by type of organization and to determine resource managers' attitudes toward the advantages and disadvantages of nepotism.

Management Succession

Barnes, Louis and Simon A. Hershon. "Transferring Power in the Family Business." *Harvard Business Review* (July-August 1976): 105-114. Should a family business stay in the family? This question is really academic, since families appear to be in business to stay. But, when the management moves from one generation to the next, the transition is often far from orderly. According to these authors, family and company transition will be more productive when they are simultaneous.

Beckhard, Richard and W. Gibb Dyer, Jr. "Managing Continuity in the

Family Owned Business." *Organizational Dynamics* (Summer 1983): 5-12. The authors offer a careful plan for managing continuity in the family owned business; the planning involves the founder, the family, and the firm's key professionals.

Christensen, C. Roland. *Management Succession in Small and Growing Enterprises*. Boston: Division of Research, Harvard University, School of Business Administration. 1953. The author offers a general framework and examples of management succession of small businesses.

Danco, Leon A. "Why Nepotism Should Be Saved." *Industry Week* (May 8, 1970): 40-43. The author sees that the most serious weakness of nepotism lies not with the heir or the incompetence of the "nepot" but with the incompetence of the "teacher." The author offers a "guide to planned nepotism."

Tashakori, Maryam. *Management Succession: From the Owner-Founder to the Professional President*. New York: Praeger, 1980. This is the author's doctoral dissertation based on a survey of family owned companies with respect to their management succession from the founder to the professional manager.

Nepotism in Other Countries

Abegglen, James C. and Hiroshi Mannari. "Leaders of Modern Japan: Social Origins and Mobility." *Economic Development and Cultural Change* (October 1960). The authors trace social origins of Japanese business leaders back to the time of Meiji Restoration. In this, they point out that the business leaders and their sons work in the same companies in Japan.

Choi, Jongtae. "A Study on Nepotism in Korean Business Management." *Korean Economic Review* (1967): 146-167. A sample survey of companies in a province in Korea; nepotism was prevalent among the companies and some experienced serious problems due to nepotistic personnel practices.

Copeman, George. *The Chief Executive and Business Growth: A Comparative Study in the United States, Britain and Germany.* New York: Leviathan House. 1971. A survey of successful executives in the three countries with special emphasis on their personal qualities and their visions.

Hattori, Tamio and Hiroshi Uyama. "Management Thought of Korean Chaebol Owners." *Asian Economy,* Japan (July 1978): 60-81. The authors studied management thought, styles and practices of founders-owners of large companies in Korea; they found nepotism was one of outstanding characteristics in Korea.

Joseph, Jonathan. "In Search of Theory K." *International Management* (UK). (September 1986): 107-110. Management styles and practices unique to Korean conglomerates are presented; aspects of management succession are also discussed.

Liggett, Donald R. *Small Industry Development Organization.* Ford Foundation, 1959. A study on industrial development in Southeast Asian countries; the author discussed about nepotism prevalent in the region.

Mannari, Hiroshi. *The Japanese Business Leaders.* Tokyo: University of Tokyo Press. 1974. A book on the social characteristics, career profiles, and mobility of Japanese business leaders during 1880s through 1960, the most critical stages of Japan's modernization.

Yoo, Sangjin and Sang M. Lee. "Management Style and Practice of Korean Chaebols." *California Management Review* (Summer 1987): 95-110. The authors discuss major characteristics of management thought and practices of Korean business leaders; they discuss some aspects of management succession in large Korean companies.

Economics of Nepotism

Becker, Gary S. *The Economics of Discrimination*. Chicago: The University of Chicago Press, 1957, 1971. Nepotism is treated as a kind of economic discrimination within a broad economic framework.

Kaufman, Roger T. "Nepotism and Minimum Wage." *Journal of Labor Research* (Winter 1983): 81-89. The hypothesis that an increase in the minimum wage or minimum wage coverage leads to an increase in the incidence of nepotism is empirically tested using 1972 data on job-seeking methods used by American workers. The author has found the hypothesis is supported by the data.

Rees, Albert. "Information Network in Labor Markets." *American Economic Review* (May 1966): 559-566. The author discusses cost saving aspects involved in hiring relatives and/or friends of existing employees in the same company.

Dual Career and Nepotism

Gilmore, Carol B. and William R. Fannin. "The Dual Career Couple: A Challenge to Personnel in the Eighties." *Business Horizons* (May-June 1982):

36-41. A new personnel problem in the 1980s when female work force increases and the 16-24 male work force is declining; especially, in case a female worker is married to a male worker in the same company.

Kopelman, Richard E., Lyn Rosenweig and Laura H. Lally. "Dual—Career Couples: The Organizational Response." *Personnel Administration* (September 1982): 73-78. This new issue in the personnel field becomes increasingly important; some lawsuits have been brought and the management must respond intelligently.

Dr. Youngho Lee
Dr. Joe W. Lee
Howard University

Dr. Youngho Lee obtained his B.A. and M.B.A. degrees from Seoul National University and D.B.A. from the George Washington University. His research and consulting activities are in the areas of comparative management practice with particular focus on China, Japan and Korea, and of financial market developments in China and Caribbean nations.

Dr. Joe W. Lee is Associate Professor of Business Economics at the School of Business, Howard University. He obtained his D.B.A. degree from Indiana University in 1962. His research and consulting activities include management thought and practice, and he has written extensively in the field.

Cultural and Legal Advantages to Decentralizing Human Resources Management

OVERVIEW

Human resources management involves attracting, hiring, training, developing and maintaining personnel. The many challenges faced by a domestic organization in performing these functions acquire a new dimension when the organization expands to include other nations and cultures. Cultural background affects how people see and respond to statements, representations and actions of the business organization. Government policies and actions are also interpreted in deference to cultural differences. Because law and regulation are derived from institutions representing the people, and because human resources management activities involve the citizens of a country, it is likely that many legal influences will be brought to bear on this aspect of international management.

Cultural and legal influences may assist the organization in its objectives for managing human resources. Or, they may impede the process. Managers must look for ways to enhance the positive aspects of these influences and to minimize the negative aspects.

EXAMPLES

The public accounting firm of Arthur Andersen & Co. is an organization of

46,000 people working in more than 45 countries. A number of cultural influences affect the human resources management functions. For example, the style and approach used for recruiting new employees into this worldwide organization must match the cultural environments in which the recruiting effort takes place.

This implies the need for benefits which are appropriate within the cultures represented, as well as training and development approaches which meet the individual's needs *as defined by the culture involved.* This aspect is particularly challenging. For example, the emphasis on career growth, important to those from the United States, is less important to the Japanese, where the emphasis is more on relationship development between the individual and the employer.

Cultural considerations also influence the flexibility of the organization in assigning its personnel according to the needs of the organization. For example, the expertise of an individual may be required within an office in another culture—and it could very well be that the individual would undergo highly desirable self-development by relocating. However, such a relocation may be hampered by cultural considerations or immigration restrictions.

Immigration regulations represent only one aspect of the legal influences on human resources management within an organization like Arthur Andersen. One of the most significant impacts of legal restrictions has been local country requirements that audit work be limited to personnel who are citizens of the host country. These restrictions can reduce a firm's flexibility in relocating people to where they are most needed or can experience the greatest self-development. To overcome these restrictions, Arthur Andersen & Co. implemented a legal restructuring of the firm into an organization of member firms, each nationally owned and operated, with worldwide coordination provided by a Swiss Société Coopérative, of which each local partner is also a member.

Other legal influences include the variations in national laws and regulations concerning benefits for employees, tax considerations affecting compensation structures, and legal limitations on the termination of employees for unacceptable performance. The difficulty created by these differences comes from the firm's desire to accommodate local requirements while simultaneously achieving its worldwide objective of providing incentives for the best and brightest to join the organization and to remain with it, without giving rise to accusations of inequitability between employees of various member firms.

The Arthur Andersen approach to the challenge of cultural and legal influences is to embrace them to the greatest extent possible. Firm management has long operated under the philosophy that resistance to these challenges is, in the long term, not in the best interest of the organization. Even if it is not snubbed by the potential employees and clients it seeks, it could lose its permit to practice in one or more countries.

The approach used to accommodate these differences is to operate through the member firms. The member firms, owned by national citizen partners, also operate according to the culture and laws of the local environments. The worldwide organization influence in human resources issues is limited to establishing broad policies and guidelines to govern activities on a global scale. For example, it is worldwide policy that a common career path be used for employees within the practices. This uniformity is required to permit the economies of scale (and uniformity of quality) available in centrally-delivered training. Common career paths permit the more effective design of training to support those career paths. A universal career path approach also encourages the interchangeability of personnel, when cultural and legal considerations permit.

BENEFITS

One benefit of a policy which tolerates cultural and legal variations within the location of organization operations is the obvious one: an organization is more successful in attracting and retaining the quality of personnel it desires.

Cultural conflict is removed as a potential disincentive to spend one's career with the organization. A second benefit is that an organization is more likely to be welcomed and valued within the country or countries of operations. The harmony of organization and cultural and legal structures can go far to encourage the long-term success of a firm within the local environment. A third benefit is the reduction of stress among a firm's management personnel. Time and energy not spent in finding methods for defeating or escaping local cultural and legal influences is time and energy available for developing strategies to enhance the human resources management activities. One major improvement resulting from the use of locally owned and operated entities is both the pride of national ownership and the absence of resentment that is sometimes associated with foreign ownership.

IMPLEMENTATION

The approach used for maximizing the benefits of cultural and legal influences and minimizing their negative impact requires an organizational philosophy which places control of operations at the local level. It is not compatible with a centralized decision-making policy directed by a central world headquarters. Implementing this approach can be done with a series of steps.

First, the legal structure of the organization may require modification to accept the notion of local control. This will depend on the organization and regulatory environment in which it operates. For Arthur Andersen, this was necessary because of its partnership form and because of regulatory requirements in many countries for locally owned accounting firms.

Next, the individuals responsible for worldwide human resources management should identify the overall objectives and policies which should transcend cultural and legal considerations. These are the philosophies and policies believed to be directly significant to the long-term success of the organization on a worldwide basis. They are the policies over which the organization would be willing to separate from a nationally-owned member firm if unresolvable conflict over the policies were to arise.

The policies should be communicated in meaningful terms to the local operating entities, along with well-thought structures for the local entities to use in communicating back their compliance with those policies.

Procedures for compliance should be left to the local entities. However, communication between the entities and the worldwide organization should be encouraged, to permit the synergy of different cultural approaches to the common policy objectives.

It is especially important that the process of developing an approach like the one described be undertaken with a sincere desire to accept and embrace local cultural and legal influences—not with a desire to "get around" these factors. The attitudes with which such a process is pursued will be evident to all concerned; any attitude that is less than receptive to local considerations is destined to encourage failure of compliance and hence, failure of the effort.

The worldwide organization must be flexible in its approach to the inevitable conflicts arising from operating in more than one culture and country. The objective is to attract, develop and retain the people so vital to success. This is the paramount objective, transcending ego, personal cultural background, and quests for personal power. The question demanding the *least* flexibility is the need to operate within the laws of the nations involved. In extreme cases, compliance with local law may require separation of the local firm from the worldwide organization. That action may seem extreme but is preferable to the risks of operating outside the law.

EVALUATION

The effectiveness of any approach to maximize the values of cultural and legal influences and to minimize their potential for disruption of the human resources management functions can be evaluated by reviewing the frequency and nature of the disruptions which do occur.

Objective measurement of the success of such an approach would be difficult to achieve. Subjective criteria could include the frequency and intensity of complaints about recruiting challenges in various countries, as well as similar complaints concerning retention of personnel who are valued and termination of personnel who are not valued. The frequency or absence of legal or civil action taken against the organization could represent some measure of success.

In the longer run, however, the truest measure of the approach used may well be (in the case of labor-intensive organizations) the success of the organization in achieving its human resources management needs. Obviously, other factors will affect the degree of success as well, including labor market demographics, general economic climate, and local management styles and decision-making.

APPLICATIONS TO SMALL BUSINESS

To the extent that a small business may operate in more than one country, the approach and philosophy described above is equally applicable. The desire to view cultural and legal influences as potential benefits, and to treat them as such, is justified for a business of any size.

CONCLUSION

It would be difficult to argue in favor of organizational disregard and subordination of cultural and legal influences on human resources management activities. Yet, there have been many instances of business arrogance, based on the assumption that local economic desperation may justify such disregard and subordination. Compliance and compatibility with local cultural and legal influences may not always bring with it long-term success in coping with these influences. But the use of approaches similar to the one described above may increase the chances for success in not only the labor markets but product markets as well. With a desire to accommodate such influences, rather than to subordinate them, it is possible to find ways to do so. The result cannot help but be beneficial to the firm.

REFERENCES/SOURCES

Gorlin, Harriet. *Innovations in Managing Human Resources.* New York: Conference Board, 1984.

Kim, W. Chan, and R. A. Mauborgne. "Cross-Cultural Strategies." *Journal of Business Strategy* 7, 4 (Spring 1987): 2,835. Discusses factors relevant to international human resources management.

Laurent, Andre. "The Cross-Cultural Puzzle of International Human Resource Management." *Human Resource Management* 25,1 (Spring 1986): 91-102. Discusses steps required for effective international human resources policy.

Mendenhall, Mark, and Gary Oddou. "Cross-Cultural Training Programs." *Columbia Journal of World Business* 21,4 (Winter 1986): 73-79. Describes types of potential expatriates and predicts how each will succeed in acculturation.

John O. Bigelow
Arthur Andersen & Co.

John O. Bigelow is Director—Human Resource Development for Practice Management and Services personnel at Arthur Andersen & Co, S.C. His responsibilities include the planning and coordination of training and development programs for all personnel within the organization who support those providing client service. He received a B.A. in Broadcasting and Film from Boston University in 1964, an M.A. in International Relations in 1972 and an M.A. in Law and Diplomacy in 1973 from the Fletcher School of Law and Diplomacy, Tufts University.

The Global Reach: Headquarters and Foreign Subsidiary Communication

OVERVIEW

Parent companies across the globe are opening foreign subsidiaries and establishing joint ventures in record numbers with over 6,000 foreign subsidiaries in the United States alone. The rise in joint ventures and foreign owned companies is producing unique communication problems that surface during electronic, print, and face-to-face communication between headquarters and a foreign subsidiary. Many of these communication issues can be traced to a collision of corporate cultures: neither parent nor subsidiary sufficiently understands one another's corporate communication patterns.

These patterns structure the ebb and flow of information in an organization, determining who sends a message to whom, how often, and via what medium. They also regulate how decisions are made, the communication style of managers and employees, interdepartmental contacts, the marketing approaches, and protocols of the chain of command. Communication between the headquarters and a foreign subsidiary can be significantly improved by Systematic Pattern Analysis (SPA). SPA is a framework for identifying key organizational patterns within a corporate culture.

EXAMPLES

Since many Europeans and Japanese firms don't adequately understand the patterns of American corporate culture, they are often unprepared to deal with the personnel and management struggles in a U.S. subsidiary. For example, one of Sweden's largest multinational companies decided to structure an American subsidiary like a Swedish firm—flattening the company's chain of command, compressing reporting relationships and eliminating positions and titles. When this happened, it caused corporate rebellion because the Swedish hierarchy reduced the American managers' prospects for promotion and managerial status and power. These are grave issues in U.S. companies, but not in Swedish organizations, where managers function as team coordinators, not bosses, and promotion is not a critical personnel issue.

American corporate life revolves around managers; they tend to zealously guard turf and title in a fairly rigid chain of command in which the accepted pattern is that employees should not go over their boss's head. This system poses problems for Scandinavian companies since they generally place employees in essential positions and consider managers as facilitators, not bosses.

For example, Norwegians and Swedes transferred to the U.S. are often angered by the American manager's request that all upward communication be approved by them before anyone else is contacted. From a Scandinavian perspective, this corporate pattern is inefficient and irrational: an employee should be able to talk to anyone, including the president, without managerial approval. it expedites the solution of a problem. The patterns of superior/subordinate communication and departmental interfacing are generally more flexible in a Scandinavian company in order to facilitate problem analysis and solution.

The Japanese also have problems with American managers, particularly when they train managers to be consensus decision-makers and encourage them to listen to all employees before making decisions. While American corporate patterns require middle managers to include top managers in substantive decisions, American managers are not used to drawing subordinates into decision-making on a regular basis—a common pattern with Japanese subsidiaries in the U.S.

The traditional U.S. corporate culture tends to emphasize individualism, achievement, and recognition. These values are often incompatible with more team-oriented European and Japanese companies. A transferred Norwegian vice president could not understand how concerned American managers are about personal survival and that individual needs are clearly paramount to company interests. As a result, few American managers will risk upsetting a vice president by making a substantive decision without consulting top management first.

The American employees' concern for occupational survival and individual success can convert them into careful corporate communicators—guarded, deferential, and conflict avoidant, particularly in large companies. This pattern of communication is viewed with suspicion by European managers who work regularly with Americans, particularly straight-shooting Germans, British, Swedes, and Norwegians who believe in communicating directly and to the point (particularly with criticism). In fact, European managers complain that American personnel frequently tell a manager what they think he wants to hear and conceal their real opinions. One German president of an American subsidiary was so annoyed by this that he purposely expressed a position contrary to his own just to find out what his American employees actually thought. It didn't work. The Americans soon realized what he was up to and avoided him at all costs.

Europeans and Japanese companies often do not realize that many of their employee policies are alien to Americans and potentially threatening. For example, a French company was surprised to learn that American personnel were angry about the relocation benefits the French received when they transferred to the United States for three years. To the French company, relocation benefits, such as purchasing employees' major appliances or paying for vacations, were reasonable incentives to attract French personnel to the

United States. The American employees who had no prior experience with international personnel thought the benefits were outrageous and discriminatory. To make matters worse, the Americans heard about the relocation package through the grapevine, not senior management, and the benefits were inflated each time they were described. This fueled the cultural fires.

Personnel tensions in the U.S. subsidiaries are also influenced by the number of managerial positions that are filled by Europeans, Japanese, or other non-Americans. No matter how skilled these managers are, American employees usually view them as obstacles to their own promotion.

In one Japanese firm, the Americans nearly revolted because most management positions were filled by Japanese transferred to the United States for three to five years. To remedy the promotion problem, the company created job titles like Assistant to the Vice President, Section Leader and Work Leader and promoted Americans to these positions. At work, the Americans wanted authority, not just titles. The Japanese management was not about to give that up.

Whenever a European or Japanese manager replaces an American executive, cultural sparks are sure to fly. This happened in a Swedish company when a 55-year-old American president was replaced by a 35-year-old Swede. To the Americans, this replacement was a signal that the subsidiary was going to be run by Swedes, not Americans, and the prospects for company promotion were considered dim.

To complicate matters, the Americans were appalled that a senior American executive was replaced by a 35-year-old who, in their view, was inexperienced—a corporate teenager as some Americans referred to him. Of course, by Swedish standards, the new president was not too young to run the company; on the contrary, the 55-year-old was considered too old for the job.

Certainly, American companies operating subsidiaries abroad have their share of communication problems. Communication can be particularly troublesome with standard American polite expressions like "I would appreciate" and "at your earliest convenience" which are often misinterpreted by European and Asian subsidiaries as requests that do not require immediate attention. However, European and Asian companies are generally used to receiving time bound messages—"blue boxes needed by March 21"—and are confused by Americans' polite expressions. In fact, even when American personnel discover Europeans or Asians prefer time bound requests, they are reluctant to dispense with polite expressions because they fear appearing too commanding or demanding.

Americans are also insensitive to the management and marketing cultures of their foreign subsidiaries. This insensitivity can create havoc. For example, a mid-western business delegation wishing to give Chinese officials an American product as a gift on the eve of a new joint venture, gave the Chinese wheels of cheddar cheese. What the Americans did not realize is that the Chinese consider cheese to be barely edible. Moreover, Chinese officials like to display gifts from foreigners as a mark of pride, and the perishable product defeats the purpose.

The same company experienced marketing problems when it relocated an American marketing manager to China in order to head up the company's marketing efforts. As a marketing specialist, and not an engineer, one executive was prepared with only general information about product design and operation of the company's vast product line, and with even less knowledge of the intricacies of competitive equipment. The Chinese, who openly admit that their ultimate goal is self-sufficiency, traditionally ask questions in such detail to allow them to practically duplicate the product themselves. In addition, they rely heavily on comparative buying strategies and often ask questions that require in-depth knowledge of the competitor's product which was unfamiliar terrain for the American marketing executive.

U.S. companies make the mistake of imposing their management and marketing cultures on their foreign subsidiaries. Take sales forecasts, for example. Traditionally, American firms require long-range sales forecasts of two to four years and often require their foreign subsidiaries to conduct them as well, often without realizing that long-range forecasts are virtually nonexistent in Asia, Latin America, and Africa. In East Asia, particularly Taiwan and Korea, sales-forecasting beyond several months is considered unusual—three to five years is viewed as impossible. The same is true in Africa and Latin America where sales forecasting has no tradition.

Invariably, American headquarters will impose a sales forecasting requirement on their foreign subsidiaries only to find that the forecast is not completed at all or is done inadequately. This is often interpreted by the senior vice president as any number of things, including corporate irresponsibility, stupidity, or manipulation and game playing. The obvious is often not considered—that sales forecasting is an anathema to a subsidiary's corporate culture.

BENEFITS

To rectify communication problems in parent/subsidiary transactions, it is necessary to systematically identify possible organizational areas where corporate culture collisions might occur. This can be done through Systematic Pattern Analysis (SPA).

SPA consists of a series of questions about communication within organizations, referred to as operational communications, and communication between parent companies and subsidiaries, which is referred to as extra-organizational communication. By asking these questions, parent companies and their subsidiaries can identify areas of difference in their corporate communication which can produce misunderstandings.

SPA can help parent companies and their subsidiaries to identify potential problem areas in operational and extra-organizational communication. Take vertical communication for example.

Patterns of vertical communication often vary significantly between parent companies and their foreign subsidiaries and can create problems. Consider the case of a Swedish multinational company that establishes a U.S. subsidiary and wants to identify patterns of vertical communication in U.S. corporate culture to avoid conflict and misunderstandings. The Swedes need only consult with selected North Americans who work in U.S. subsidiaries to learn the following:

U.S. Company

- Who sends information: Employees in the corporate hierarchy.
- What information: Information related to role in corporate hierarchy.
- Up to whom: Individual to whom employee reports in hierarchy.
- How often: As deemed appropriate by superior.
- In what way: Written communication preferred: face-to-face and telephone interaction possible.
- With what effect: Variable, depending on reaction of superior.

In contrast, the Swedish parent company would most likely answer the preceding vertical communication questions differently, with the following patterns emerging:

Swedish Company

- Who sends information: Employees in the corporate hierarchy.
- What information: Information related to employee's role in the hierarch or tangential to corporate role.
- Up to whom: Anyone in corporate hierarchy who can assist in problem solving: not limited to direct report.

- How often: As often as the employee pleases.
- In what way: Face-to-face interaction preferred; written communication and telephone less desirable.
- With what effect: Assistance.

The difference in vertical patterns between Swedish and American companies can cause confusion and misunderstanding if they are not identified early in the parent/subsidiary relationship. For example, Swedes transferred to the United States, who are unaware of American communication patterns, might "end run" a superior without realizing that a communication pattern has been violated. Similarly, the Swedish penchant for face-to-face transaction for transmitting upward communication may not work in U.S. companies that revere written memoranda, particularly when sending messages upward.

There are many company benefits using SPA. Notably, patterns can be isolated that can lead to misunderstanding and conflict. Seminars then can be developed for employees at headquarters and foreign subsidiaries that provide concrete recommendations for communicating messages either within the subsidiary or between the subsidiary and headquarters. What should result is an enlightened employee work force which is sensitive to the pattern of effective corporate communication in headquarters/subsidiary transactions. This should ease problems of employee transfers and expedite information flow within subsidiaries and to the parent company.

IMPLEMENTATION

The operational questions of SPA focus on four communication areas: vertical communication, lateral communication, decision-making, and power structure. The extra-organizational questions assess two communication areas: sending information to an organization and receiving information from an organization. Questions are as follows:

Operational Communication Patterns (Communication Within a Company)

I. Vertical Communication
   A. Who sends what information up to whom, how often, in what way, and with what effect?
   B. Who sends what information down to whom, how often, in what way, and with what effect?
   C. Who receives what information, from whom, how often, in what way, and with what effect?

II. Lateral Communication
   A. Who sends what information to whom, how often, in what way, and with what effect?
   B. Who receives what information from whom, how often, in what way, and with what effect?

III. Decision-making
   A. How are decisions made?
      1. Top down
      2. Consensus
      3. Bottom up
      4. Mixed system
   B. Who/What makes the final decision on each level/department?
   C. Influencing decisions.
      1. Who are information gatekeepers?
      2. What are the networking rules (i.e., contacts, friendships, rewards)?

IV. Power Structure
   A. Type of power structure
      1. Top down
      2. Bottom up
      3. Consensus
      4. Mixed
   B. Who/What is the power source in departments/levels?
   C. What are the patterns for deferring to power in each department/level?
   D. What is the power style of a leader: dictatorial/democratic/laissez-faire?
   E. What are the characteristics of the power source (i.e., age/gender/national culture)?

Extra-Organizational Communication: (Communication Between Headquarters and Foreign Subsidiary)

I. Sending Information to an Organization
   A. Who sends what information, to whom, how often, in what way, and with what effect?
   B. Response time expectation.
   C. Perceived credibility of message receiver.

II. Receiving information from an organization.
   A. Who receives what information, from whom, how often, in what way, with what effect?
   B. Response time expectations.
   C. Perceived credibility of message sender.

EVALUATION

To evaluate SPA, it is necessary to: 1) isolate patterns of operational and extra-organizational communication between foreign subsidiaries and headquarters; 2) instruct the corporate personnel in different patterns of operational and extra-organizational communication; and 3) test personnel's understanding of operational and extra-organizational communication patterns. Personnel can be tested on their ability to apply SPA and their awareness of operational and extra-organizational communication patterns. Favorable employee assessments should result in fewer communication problems between headquarters and foreign subsidiaries.

APPLICATIONS TO SMALL BUSINESS

Small businesses increasing their international trade are also subject to communication problems with foreign distributors, agents, joint ventures and solely-owned subsidiaries. These communication problems wreak havoc on morale and profits in much the same way as they do for larger corporations. As a result, small businesses need to utilize SPA, since it can help these companies transact business internationally.

SPA can be used for isolating and identifying communication problems a small business is having with an agent, distributor, joint venture, or subsidiary. Communication protocols and practices of agents and distributors can be readily identified through SPA; operational and extra-organizational communication patterns can be isolated in joint ventures and subsidiaries. Since international joint ventures are particularly attractive for small businesses, it is important that they understand who they are doing business with—the foreign partner's communication patterns and business patterns.

CONCLUSION

Headquarters and subsidiaries have always had their share of communication problems; these issues increase in number and complexity with international subsidiaries. The primary reason for these communication problems is the lack of understanding of operational and extra-organizational communication in the parent company and the subsidiary. Systematic Pattern Analysis is a method for determining how and where communication patterns differ in headquarters and foreign subsidiaries.

SPA is essentially composed of a series of questions for isolating patterns of operational and extra-organizational communication. By using SPA, parent companies can reconcile and prevent communication problems with foreign subsidiaries. SPA is a necessary ingredient for corporate success overseas.

REFERENCES/SOURCES

Adler, Nancy. "Cross-Cultural Management: Issues to be Faced." *International Studies of Management and Organization* 13 (1983): 7-45. An examination of cross-cultural management issues.

Amano, Mary. "Organizational Changes of a Japanese Firm in America." *California Management Review* 2 (1979): 51-59. A look at management issues in a Japanese corporation in the U.S.

Hofstede, Geeat. "The Cultural Relativity of Organizational Practices and Theories," *Journal of International Business Studies* 14 (1983): 75-89. Discusses factors in organizations that make them products of their own national culture.

Ruben, Brent. "Human Communication and Cross-Cultural Effectiveness." *International and Intercultural Communication Annual* 4 (1977): 98-105. An examination of cross-cultural factors that affect global communication.

Shuter, Robert. "When the Manager is a Stranger in a Familiar Land." *Wall Street Journal* (November 24, 1985): 55. A discussion of organizational issues facing foreign corporations operating in the U.S.

———. "The International Marketplace." In Gudykunt and Asante, eds. *Handbook of Intercultural Communication.* Beverly Hills, CA: Sage Publications, 1989: 77-93. A detailed examination of global communication issues.

Dr. D. Robert Shuter
Center for Intercultural Communication
Marquette University

Dr. Robert Shuter is director of the Center for Intercultural Communication at Marquette University and chairperson of the Department of Communication and Rhetorical Studies. He is the author of three books and over sixty articles which have appeared in the *Wall Street Journal, New York Times, International Management,* and other leading journals. He is an international consultant who has worked extensively with European and U.S. corporations, and is the president of Interaction, an international management consulting firm. He has appeared on "Wall Street Week With Louis Rukeyser," "Financial News Network," and other national television programs.

Alternative Approaches to Dispute Resolution In International Business

OVERVIEW

The complex and dynamic arena of international business calls for well-trained and informed professionals who can comprehend the causes and escalation of conflict and can offer strategies and skills for its successful management and resolution. Increased commercial interdependencies and conflicts have created significant interest in and need for alternative approaches to dispute settlement. As a result, Alternative Dispute Resolution (ADR) which includes mediation, arbitration, and facilitated interactive problem solving have become utilized by executives in the practice of negotiation. Since the costs of commercial disputes can run into millions of dollars, pounds, etc., business executives are beginning to participate in cheaper and fairer solutions to commercial domestic and international business disputes. Sometimes referred to as a quiet legal revolution, ADR produces great long term consequences for international business relationships.

EXAMPLES

Recent interest in ADR has been spurred by frequent encounters with the exceedingly slow and expensive litigation process which ultimately produces a loser for every winner. Companies are currently contracting the services of several private mediation and arbitration firms to assist in conflict resolution which is less procedurally complex than litigation. ADR professionals assist corporate managers to determine the appropriate problem solving, arbitration, mediation, and/or litigation alternatives in order to determine the best course of action in a given dispute situation. Corporate executives have claimed that the ADR mechanisms (as opposed to strict adversarial legal processes) resolve and manage not only pending, but also mitigate future conflicts resulting in more just and enduring results concerning disputes.

Industry and commerce have been slow to embrace the concept of ADR. There is still considerable inexperience with ADR processes and the traditional adversarial mindset and culture of litigation continues to be a barrier. However, many companies today actively embrace and promote ADR. Some corporate clients of ADR firms include Ford (Europe), British Telecom, Black and Decker, RTZ, Midland Bank, BOC Group, Prudential, British Telecom, ICI, Trafalgar House Construction, John Mowlem Construction, Grand Metropolitan, and several leading law firm and accountancy firms. The Center for Dispute Resolution (CEDR) is a British nonprofit organization backed by industry and professional advisors dedicated to reaching better commercial solutions through ADR mechanisms. Recruits have increased significantly since 1990 and there are currently more than 250 members who participate in and promote ADR services. CEDR has several established links with a growing number of UK and international ADR organizations.

In the first two years of CEDR, 230 cases were referred to CEDR and more than £30 million in potential legal costs were saved and substantially more if management time was included in the calculations. However, although the Confederation of British Industry (CBI) supports CEDR efforts and considerable ADR success in dispute settlement has been recorded, there continues to be a lack of awareness and skepticism about what ADR has to offer. In the U.S., the success and exposure of ADR has been enhanced by the resolution of several business disputes involving well-known companies. For example, the four year IBM/Fujitsu computer software copyright dispute, Borden's $200 million trust action against Texaco, and American Can's $41 million action for breach of contract against Wisconsin Electrical Power are among mediation successes.

Many corporations are becoming clients of private U.S. based Judicial Arbitration and Mediation Services, Inc. (JAMS), Endispute, Judicate, Inc., and U.S. Arbitration and Mediation, Inc. Increasingly, major U.S. corporations are announcing that they will submit a major area of domestic and international litigation to some form of mediation or arbitration instead of using legal litigation. Many U.S. companies include Pacific Gas and Electric Company, State Farm Insurance, Cigna Corporation, Reebok International, Ltd., and NationsBank.

One ADR example in the UK involved an automotive equipment manufacturer and distributor who agreed with an American inventor to manufacture and market in the UK a sterilizer which was invented and patented for the dental industry. The UK company required several changes and contacted a London product design consultant to make the appropriate design changes. Since the design changes took a lot longer and cost more than anticipated, the automotive equipment company believed it had lost its market share and the inventor terminated his agreement with the UK company. The UK company then sued the design consultant for negligence and breach of contract and lost profits. The traditional method of negotiation and litigation preparation did not lead to a settlement regarding the determination of liability and damages. Before the trial was to commence, the parties agreed to make an attempt to settle the dispute by mediation. Mediators were nominated and the mediation which involved a series of private and open caucuses between the mediators and the respective sides took one day. It was reported that both sides were satisfied and pleased to avoid continued costly litigation and trial. The costs of trial and potential unsatisfactory results were saved.

BENEFITS

Some of the ADR benefits include bottom line corporate savings in legal bills, executive time, and improved relationships among disputants. As long as the dispute continues in the litigation process, more billable hours are generated for law firms and agencies who benefit from the continued dispute. However, the attention in litigation is not on resolving the dispute, but often on delaying action and legalistic efforts which can obscure the "truth" and prevents parties from disclosing the most vulnerable aspects of the conflict. Through assisted mediation, the vulnerable aspects are almost always the place in which resolution is found. ADR professionals provide effective coordination and inquiry in conversation which becomes essential in the resolution process. Even if mediation fails, the cost is a day's work and litigation can be ultimately pursued.

IMPLEMENTATION

As the need for facilitation, mediation, and/or arbitration services arises in the international commercial context, ADR professionals can assess and design the appropriate dispute resolution techniques which can achieve more cost-effective and satisfying results than traditional administrative procedures or litigation. The following steps are suggested for the company who considers the use of ADR services in such a dispute.

Prior to employing an ADR firm, contact the various institutes and centers which serve as clearing houses of ADR services. Investigate published ADR studies which indicate the success rate and client lists of those who have participated in dispute resolution processes. In addition, research what potential and actual financial savings have been reported by clients who have contracted ADR services as opposed to the potential litigation costs.

Corporate managers can also investigate and project the time savings that may be attributable to mediated grievance procedures and consider the potential participant satisfaction as a result of an ADR procedure. Investigate whether the participants are willing and capable of addressing and resolving both the "official" grievances and the underlying causes of the grievance, and whether the participants want to take the responsibility to "own" the outcomes (facilitated by the mediator) which will be created by the disputants. Investigate the willingness of the disputants to pursue a more informal conflict resolution procedure wherein the parties will discuss grievances with a problem-solving perspective and be receptive to mediation that will encourage a range of compromise and outcomes.

Once commitment has been made by the disputants to hire an ADR firm, it is critical to research the mediator concerning training, research, and networks. Also acquire information about the specific role mediators or arbitrators from the dispute resolution firms adopt in the process. For example, will the ADR professionals inform the parties at the outset of the contractual strengths and weaknesses of each of the parties' grievance positions and will the mediator or arbitrator, either officially or in private, provide an outcome prediction. Also, will the mediator and/or arbitrator act as referee, guide, or facilitator.

During the ADR process, remember that ADR grievance approaches have compiled an impressive, though limited, track record and that the communication-facilitation, formulation, and substantive compliance process can be demanding, but rewarding.

EVALUATION

Evaluating the process and results of ADR techniques can be derived from various levels. In general, evaluation will include attention to:

- the activities and contributions of the ADR professionals

- the impact of the mediation, facilitation, or arbitration on the nature of the parties' perceptions and their future interaction

- what kind of change can be described by the participants or by an independent observer.

Evaluation is critically linked with the original goals which must be stated at the outset of the mediation or arbitration by the participants. The subjective criteria (which usually cannot be empirically determined) concerning the satisfaction of the parties will range from ineffective, unfair to effective, or fair concerning both the process and the outcome. The measurement and precise meaning of satisfaction is based on perceptions of entitlement and distribution of resources. Most often, however, a mediated outcome is deemed fair when the parties' expectations are met or when the allocation of scarce resources is consistent with the principles of equality, equity, or need determined by the disputants at the outset and throughout the mediation.

Another subjective criterion for assessing mediation outcomes is efficiency. Therefore, the timeliness, minimization of costs, and outcomes which maximize the benefits of each party requires an initial assessment at the outset of the mediation by each of the disputants. Criteria regarding effectiveness refer to the implementation and permanence of a settlement, whether the participants consider the outcome as stable and realistic, and if the agreement offers opportunities to avoid similar disputes in the future.

Objective criteria rely on indicators which may be assessed empirically by an observer or any of the mediation participants. Objective criteria concerning observed success or failure involve notions of change and judgments about the extent of altered behavior observed upon termination of the mediation. If parties continue to interact in the same conflictual manner after the agreement is reached, the process has failed. If parties embrace a formal outcome that settles many of the issues in the dispute and do produce more productive interactions, then the mediation has been successful. Questions about evaluation of the outcomes should be discussed by the disputants at the outset of the mediation process. Each mediation should be evaluated in terms of the criteria which are significant to the terms and specifics of each case.

APPLICATIONS TO SMALL BUSINESS

The ADR process is very useful for small and medium sized firms who may not have had significant experience with international suppliers, contractors, and work force. Therefore, the prospects for conflicts to arise, and capability to utilize significant legal and management resources for such conflicts are limited. ADR consultations will assist small business executives in finding the most cost and time-effective solution to the various conflicts which arise, and to provide a quick alternative to litigation. In addition, ADR professionals can assist with the design of self-supporting dispute resolution programs as joint ventures and contracts are negotiated in an attempt to anticipate and implement resolution procedures as conflicts arise.

CONCLUSION

When parties in a commercial conflict want to pursue alternative dispute settlement other than the costly, public and sometimes traumatic legal approach, corporate executives will take advantage of the services offered by the burgeoning industry of private mediation and arbitration. Corporate clients can also expect a barrage of new solicitations from private mediation firms which are competing more intensely than ever to lure companies away from the traditional legal approach to dispute resolution.

REFERENCES/SOURCES

The American Arbitration Association (AAA), 140 West 51st Street, New York, NY 10020-1203 (telephone 212-484-4000) is a national, nonprofit dispute resolution service provider with regional offices in 40 cities of the U.S. AAA is the oldest (founded in 1926) ADR organization and serves as a clearing house for information, publishes newsletters and a journal, and runs conferences.

The Society of Professionals in Dispute Resolution, 1100 Connecticut Avenue, N.W., Suite 700 Washington, DC 20036 (telephone 202-833-2188) is an international association of dispute resolvers from various backgrounds and sponsors an annual conference, publishes newsletters, and has several local and regional chapters.

Endispute, Inc., 1201 Connecticut Avenue, NW, Suite 501, Washington DC 20036 (telephone 202-265-9572)

Center for Dispute Resolution (CEDR) London, England (telephone 011-44-71-430-1852)

Bercovitch, J. "Problems and Approaches in the study of Bargaining and Negotiation." *Political Science* 36 (1984): 125-144.

Burton, John. *Conflict: Practices in Management and Resolution.* New York: St. Martin's Press, 1987.

Carnevale, Peter J. "The Usefulness of Mediation Theory." *Negotiation Journal* (October 1992): 387-391.

Friedman, Raymond A. "From Theory to Practice: Critical Choices for Mutual Gains Training." *Negotiation Journal* (April 1992): 91-98.

Goldberg, S. B., F. E. A. Sander, and N. H. Rogers. *Dispute Resolution: Negotiation, Mediation, and Other Processes* 2nd ed. Boston: Little, Brown, 1992.

Goodpaster, Gary. "Lawsuits as Negotiations." *Negotiation Journal* (July 1992): 221-239.

Kennedy, John H. "A Kinder, Cheaper Route to Justice." *Boston Globe* (December 26, 1993).

Kressel, K. and D. Pruitt. *Mediation Research: the Process and Effectiveness of Third-Party Interventions*. San Francisco: Jossey-Bass, (1989).

Pollock, Ellen Joan. "Mediation Firms Alter the Legal Landscape." *Wall Street Journal* (March 22, 1993).

Rice, Robert. "Out-of-court Settlement." *Financial Times* (February 2, 1993).

Rogers, N. and C. McEwen. *Mediation: Law, Policy, Practice*. Rochester, NY: Lawyers Cooperative Publishing Company, 1989.

Shapiro, Debra L., Blair H. Sheppard, and Lisa Cheraskin. "Business on a Handshake." *Negotiation Journal* (October 1992): 365-377.

Slaikeu, Karl A. and Ralph H. Hasson. "Not Necessarily Mediation: The Use of Convening Clauses in Dispute Systems Design." *Negotiation Journal* (October 1992): 331-337.

Karen S. Walch
Assistant Professor
American Graduate School of International Management

12.

International Personnel

An Overview to Selecting Expatriate Managers

OVERVIEW

The selection and development of expatriate managers and staff is critical to the long run success of a business operation outside of the parent country. While this is equally true for domestic operations, the unfamiliar environment, culture, and language of a different country add to the vital importance of these personnel decisions.

Several surveys have shown that a higher proportion of expatriate managers from Europe and Japan are successful than are managers from the United States. Hence multinational corporations (MNCs) need to give special attention to the selection and preparation of U.S. managers for assignments abroad.

Technical or job competence is necessary, but not sufficient. Certain personal qualities, plus family support for the move abroad, are also necessary. Based on past experience and available research, the following guidelines on qualifications for successful adjustment and performance abroad are highly recommended:

- Interpersonal skills, empathy, and openness are needed in order to relate effectively with people in the host country.

- Interest in other cultures, and a willingness to learn the language, are essential to facilitate communication and personal adjustment.

- Intensive training in cross-cultural relations will help prepare the expatriate for work and living in an unfamiliar culture. This orientation instruction could be combined with intensive language training.

In order to evaluate these personal characteristics, as well as relevant educational programs, decision makers should examine past experience and behavior. For example, has the individual shown some interest in other cultures? What do people who work with the candidate think of his or her interpersonal skills?

EXAMPLES

A Mexican plant of General Motors provides a good example of a careful selection process of expatriate managers where attention to language skills is stressed. Initially, the plant manager personally interviews final candidates at the candidates' present work locations. The final candidate is invited to visit the subsidiary plant location with his or her spouse for several days, where the living and working situation is covered as forthrightly as possible. The individual accepting the position is sent for two weeks of intensive Spanish instruction just prior to his or her arrival, and receives further intensive instruction after several months on the job. At the plant, Spanish classes are held several times a week, either in a group or individually. The spouse is given the opportunity to attend the same intensive instruction.

A new expatriate plant manager altered the plant's management policy. After the new manager's arrival, all the management meetings in this plant were converted from English to Spanish (over a five-month period). During the first month of the transition, Spanish was required one day per week; the second month, it was required two days; the third month, three days, etc. This method allowed for a gradual transition that was effective.

The plant's comptroller, a career international manager, described the goal regarding languages: all managers, whether American or Mexican, should become bilingual. The Mexican managers must be able to communicate effectively with other units of the company.

In public international organizations, such as the United Nations, some language study each day is part of the job. It is common for Europeans working abroad to consider language study an integral part of life: when they have mastered one language, they often start another.

Many studies of U.S. MNCs indicate that the lack of personal relation abilities to deal effectively with other people, both inside and outside the company, is a principal cause of job failure. However, the personal relation skills criterion is often not emphasized in the selection decision.

Summarizing a review of available studies involving a large number of MNCs, Simcha Ronen (1986) concludes that interpersonal-relational skills, adaptability and family support, as well as technical ability, appear to be the most critical variables to be considered in developing an effective selection and education/development strategy for international assignments.

The experience of expatriate managers in a "maquiladora" or in-bond plant on the Mexican border clearly demonstrates that those who create trust and mutual respect with their subordinates are most effective. Their results contrast sharply with those managers who have a superior attitude and whose style is manipulative. Communication of attitudes and sincerity between people working together occurs in many ways in addition to the spoken word.

BENEFITS

As in any position, the closer the candidate's personal and professional qualifications match the requirements for successful job performance, the greater likelihood the individual selected will turn out to be successful in a specific assignment. To the extent that a candidate has a genuine interest in learning about another culture (including learning the language), the probability of satisfactory adjustment to the new situation is increased.

There is a striking difference in the relationship between local nationals and expatriates who can communicate in their language as compared with those who cannot. The former make friends in the local community, as well as having better rapport with employees at all levels. The latter not only tend to limit their association to their compatriots, but they remain totally dependent on the subset of local personnel who are bilingual.

The benefits to expatriates who do not have to depend on bilingual local nationals are significant. For example, local personnel promoted because they are bilingual may not be the best qualified people available. This limitation is especially important at the higher managerial levels. Obviously, the potential pool of available host country candidates is greatly increased when the added restriction of being bilingual is not required.

Expatriate managers who take a genuine interest in the development of their staffs and who inspire trust are respected and emulated as leaders.

In addition to personal characteristics, adequate preparation through cross-cultural orientation training should be stressed. Orientation programs that are longer than two or three days are preferable for they facilitate the manager's transition as well as his subsequent job performance.

IMPLEMENTATION

The emotional maturity of a candidate is closely related to the criteria recommended above. While this basic characteristic is difficult to measure, one important clue is the presence or absence of a sense of humor. As President Dwight D. Eisenhower said after many years of overseas assignments, "I take my job seriously, but I try not to take myself seriously."

Providing for reentry into the domestic operation is necessary to attract good candidates. A balance has to be struck with the number of years in an overseas assignment. The longer the time overseas, the greater the contribution the individual can make. On the other hand, more uneasiness is created about losing touch with career opportunities at home.

Before taking the assignment, clear instructions are necessary to insure attainment of specific objectives. Requiring adequate language skills for communication should be one objective. Training and developing a counterpart to fill a position within a specified number of years is another. Unambiguous instructions will help to keep the priorities straight in the press of daily activities and problems.

Evaluation of candidates is usually done with available records and through interviews. Current and former supervisors should be consulted because they know the individual well. Interviews in general have a poor track record for predictive validity unless they are carefully planned. A growing number of companies are using an interview technique called "adaptability screening."

After a final candidate is selected, preparation consists of two phases: pre-departure education and post-arrival development. Before taking up the new assignment, cross-cultural orientation is needed by both the candidate and spouse.

Cross-cultural training should be as extensive as possible. Many U.S. managers working in other countries tend to believe they are superior to their foreign counterparts; this can have a negative impact on interpersonal relations. This common attitude is partly due to lack of understanding and appreciation of the host culture. Work abroad should be viewed as a two-way exchange where technical knowledge is traded for learning how to adapt and manage effectively in an unfamiliar environment.

Language may be the most important thing an MNC can provide to the expatriate and spouse to ensure a successful assignment. Initial language instruction is most effective if it is intensive—four to six hours per day—and taught to individuals or couples by tutors. The use of language tapes are also very helpful for learning to speak by self-study. Language instruction in the host country is facilitated by living in the new environment.

EVALUATION

The purpose of evaluating the effectiveness of selection and development strategies is to improve upon them. Systematic follow-up with, and feedback from, each expatriate manager and his colleagues will permit specific diagnosis of the strong and weak points of each individual's adjustment and overall performance. As experience accumulates, the areas needing more attention in future selection and training decisions can be highlighted. Adjustments in the selection criteria and in the type and length of preparation programs can be made accordingly. Further follow-up will serve to validate the effectiveness of these steps. The cycle is continuous as long as expatriate managers are needed.

In the evaluation process for expatriate managers, the views of local staff should not be overlooked. This latter source of information has the added value of bringing to light ways in which expatriates can manage more effectively in that culture.

Evaluations of several companies indicate that the staffing practices of U.S. MNCs are generally unsystematic and unsophisticated. Further, repatriation has not received the attention it merits.

APPLICATIONS TO SMALL BUSINESS

These guidelines apply equally to small and large businesses. Because of the smaller number of expatriates involved, the decisions regarding selection and development become even more critical for small businesses.

If only one or two managers are needed to work in another country, it would be advisable to find candidates who need less personal development. Someone who has already had work experience abroad, and/or who knows the language, will greatly reduce the training time and effort that would otherwise be needed. The sharing of experiences among several small businesses will serve to provide further guidance and a basis for improving the initial strategy as experience accumulates.

CONCLUSION

Managing human resource functions is perhaps the most serious operational challenge for MNCs, according to a U.S. Presidential Commission. Use of the above guidelines will serve to improve success in the selection and development of effective expatriate managers. This, in turn, will strengthen the organization and reduce the high costs, both human and financial, of expatriates whose job performance is less than optimal. Because the responsibility for effective use of all available resources rests on management's shoulders, the quality of the management team is fundamental to overall success.

Although past surveys have indicated that expatriate managers are often chosen primarily on the basis of their technical competence, equally important are personal characteristics, family support, and adequate preparation for the assignment.

The lack of language skills and cross-cultural understanding has handicapped U.S. business in competition with other industrialized countries, but these shortcomings can be overcome by appropriate management development, and by greater emphasis on international business.

REFERENCES/SOURCES

Brislin, Richard W., Kenneth Cushner, Craig Cherrie, and Mahealani Yong. *Intercultural Interactions: A Practical Guide.* Beverly Hills, CA: Sage

Publications, 1986. Provides a helpful aid to anyone who is interested in training those who are preparing for cross-cultural experience. Emphasizes the "critical incident" technique with 100 incidents.

"Gauging a Family's Suitability for a Stint Overseas." *Business Week* (April 16, 1979): 127-130. Describes an interview assessment technique called "adaptability screening."

Hall, Edward J. *The Silent Language*. Garden City, NY: Anchor Press/Doubleday, 1973. *Beyond Culture*. Garden City, NY: Anchor Press/Doubleday, 1976. These books deal in turn with nonverbal communication in other cultures, and an understanding of the influence of culture on behavior.

Hofstede, Geert. "Motivation, Leadership, and Organization: Do American Theories Apply Abroad?" *Organization Dynamics* 9 (1983): 42-63. Presents the practical results of a major international research study, which show the need for sensitivity to cultural differences.

Howard, C. G. "The Expatriate Manager and the Role of the MNC." *Personnel Journal* (October 1980): 840-844. Contains suggested elements needed for any repatriation program.

Johnson, M. B., and G. L. Carter, Jr. "Training Needs of Americans Working Abroad." *Social Change* (1972). Indicates the relative importance of training needs as perceived by both American expatriates and host country nationals in Asia.

Kealey, D., and B. D. Ruben. "Cross-Cultural Personnel Selection Criteria, Issues, and Methods." In D. Landis, and R.W. Brislin, eds. *Handbook of Intercultural Training*: *Issues in Theory and Design.* Vol. 1. Elsmford, NY:

Pergamon, 1983:155-175. Summarizes studies of factors influencing overseas effectiveness.

Noer, D. M. *Multinational People Management: A Guide for Organizations and Employees.* Washington, DC: Bureau of National Affairs, 1975. Includes information on interviewing international candidates, and preparing for later reentry.

Presidential Commission of Foreign Language and International Studies. *Strength Through Wisdom: A Critique of U.S. Capability.* Washington, DC: U.S. Government Printing Office, 1979. Presents the results and recommendations of a blue ribbon commission's assessment of educational capabilities and commitment.

Robinson, Richard D. *Internationalization of Business: An Introduction.* Chicago: Dryden Press, 1984. Presents a comprehensive treatment on the internationalization of business as well as attention to staffing.

Ronen, Simcha. *Comparative and Multinational Management.* New York: John Wiley and Sons, 1986. Presents a review of relevant research studies and surveys of MNC experience to date.

Rubin, B. D., L. R. Askling, and D. J. Kealey. "Cross-Cultural Effectiveness: An Overview." In D. S. Hoopes, ed. *International Communication: State of the Art Overview.* Pittsburgh: Society of Intercultural Education, Training and Research, 1977. Presents results of an empirical study on the effectiveness of North Americans overseas.

Samovar, L. A., R. E. Porter, and N. C. Jain. *Understanding Intercultural Communication.* Belmont, CA: Wadsworth, 1981. Explains why the ability to apply domestic management skills is severely restricted by not understanding the culture and by certain personal attitudes.

Tung, Rosalie L. *Key to Japan's Economic Strength: Human Power.* Lexington, MA: Lexington Books, D. C. Heath, 1984. Provides a comprehensive description and analysis of the human resource management practices in Japanese MNCs.

———. "Expatriate Assignments: Enhancing Success and Minimizing Failure." *Academy of Management Executive* (May 1987): 117-127. Compares the overseas assignment practices of U.S. firms with those of European and Japanese MNCs, and suggests steps to enhance expatriate success rates.

———. *The New Expatriates: Managing Human Resources Abroad.* Cambridge, MA: Ballinger, 1988. Presents the most comprehensive and authoritative book published to date based on research comparing experience with expatriate managers in the U.S., Europe, and Japan.

Zeira, Y. "Ethnocentrism in Host Country Organizations," *Business Horizons* 22(5) (1979): 66-75. Stresses selection criteria for prospective senior international managers.

James E. Boyce
School of Business and Engineering Administration
Michigan Technological University

Systems for Selecting International Personnel

OVERVIEW

An increasing number of American managers find themselves working in foreign countries as their companies expand into new markets. As the demand for overseas personnel increases, so does the need to screen and select new candidates.

Selection criteria used to hire a manager for an overseas position needs to be greater than for a manager for a domestic position. An expatriate manager must adjust to a variety of factors including: differing job responsibilities even when the same job title is used; language and cultural barriers that make training local personnel difficult; family matters, such as spouse employment and family readjustment; simple routine activities which may become frustrating in the new culture; and the lack of traditional support systems such as religious institutions and social clubs.

The importance of careful selection is brought into focus when the results of incorrect choices are seen. Reviewing the placement decisions of American multinational companies, Edwin Henry found that companies reported 30% of their decisions to be mistakes, primarily because of the employee's failure to adjust to the new culture. Lee and Larwood studied the acculturation process of expatriate managers in multinational corporations and found that upon entering a new culture, the expatriate manager tends to adopt a role he or she *expects* to be appropriate, so as to minimize potential conflict with local personnel. Henry suggests that a manager might avoid some of the conflict due to "misbehaving" in a new culture by engaging in anticipatory socialization, "wearing the other culture's shoes," and by learning more about the new culture. Selecting the right person for an overseas assignment requires discovering who can adjust.

EXAMPLES

Several interesting examples of selection systems are used by various organizations. A classic example is the extensive system used by the Peace Corps. The Peace Corps has a relatively low attrition rate of 12%, and of these, only three to 4% are attributable to selection errors. According to Edwin Henry's study, the Peace Corps receives an average of 5,000 applications a month. The initial screening is based on four kinds of information: a rather extensive and elaborate application form; a placement test to assess general intelligence, language aptitude, and a language achievement test; college or high school transcripts which are typically used for placement rather than screening; and references from up to fifteen separate sources. Although the general tendency for referees is to provide positive views of a candidate, Henry reports that for Peace Corps volunteer positions, they will often provide ample and candid comments. Based on these four sources, screeners assess a candidate using the following questions: is the applicant medically sound?; does the applicant have a skill that is needed overseas, or a background that indicates he may be able to develop such a skill within a three-month training period? (This question is designed to match the candidate with the job required by a foreign government such as a botanist, small businessman, medical worker, etc.); is the applicant personally suitable? This last question focuses on the flexibility, maturity, and emotional stability of the candidate.

Based on the four-element selection, the Peace Corps staff determines an appropriate candidate and his or her preferences for volunteer work. At the same time, requirements transmitted from foreign governments are classified and positions for candidates are established. At this point, candidates are asked if they wish to pursue a particular position and are invited to begin training. This comprehensive method has a high rate of success in placing Peace Corps volunteers.

Another example described by Richard Hays suggests focusing on a potential candidate from three different angles including: *environment*—factors associated with the specific national environment to which an expatriate may be assigned; *task*—factors associated with the specific job to be performed; and *individual*—factors associated with the personality and situation of the person being considered for the assignment. In other words, candidates are selected on the basis of all of these dimensions rather than solely on job competence. Interestingly, Hays also distinguishes among types of positions the expatriate might hold and suggests that the selection procedure might need to be further adjusted according to position. For instance, a position with an operational element, requiring performance in a pre-existing structure, does not need an applicant with strong interpersonal skills. A structure reproducer, an individual who builds a structure in the foreign locale similar to the domestic structure, does need interpersonal skills. Thus, the selection system should focus on the cultural environment, job elements, and individual talents.

Cecil Howard examined the selection system of a variety of U.S. companies. He suggested that selection should be based on qualifications according to *position* (Can candidate X do the job?), *management* (Is candidate X a good overall manager?), *personal* (Will candidate X be a good representative of the U.S.?), and *environment* (Will candidate X be able to adjust to the new culture without becoming completely immersed in it?). As with the system described by Hays, the selection system examines a candidate's qualifications according to the foreign locale, candidate abilities, and proven expertise. It does not place as much emphasis on non-work characteristics as does the Peace Corps model.

BENEFITS

The primary benefit of accurate cross-cultural selection is the reduction of managers who perform poorly after arriving in a new culture. One reason for the failure of a manager overseas is culture shock, which reduces the manager's capacity to perform effectively in a new work setting. A manager who experiences a large amount of culture shock will often become overly critical of others, rationalize his mistakes, and isolate himself. Eventually, a manager suffering from severe culture shock will become withdrawn and alienated from the new culture.

A sensitive manager can thus strengthen the relations between the home and foreign offices. So a selection process that fosters a more global, or cosmopolitan, perspective in a manager will benefit the home office. A manager who is knowledgeable about other cultures and ways of life is better able to understand the differences among heterogeneous employees. And, of course, managers who know a foreign language can often leave nations with the impression that they possess a special interest in the country.

A good selection system also reduces costs of operation by avoiding improper choices for work assignments. Heenan and Perlmutter report that in some companies as much as 75% of the communications between the home office and an overseas employee concerns non-business issues such as buying furniture, personal finances, and schools. This type of inefficiency is greatly reduced by the implementation of a good selection system.

A good selection system also identifies employees with growth potential. Overseas work can be used as a way of cultivating and broadening a manager who may be viewed as a "rising star." Promising employees of the Bechtel Corp. are routinely sent overseas to season them for subsequent domestic promotions.

IMPLEMENTATION

The methodology for implementing a selection system requires developing a valid and fair system. Validity refers to the evaluation of the candidate on selection criteria related to subsequent job performance. As an example, universities and colleges use a student's high school grades and SAT scores to predict college success. The extent to which these predictors relate to a student's grades in college indicates the validity of the predictors. On the other hand, fairness refers to the relative proportion of candidates selected from various subgroups (e.g., ethnic, gender, religious) in a given culture. A test can be valid but still unfair since fairness refers to *how* the system is used.

Given that a company wishes its selection system to be fair and valid, the first step is to perform a job analysis of overseas positions. Such an analysis should focus on *job-related factors*, breaking the job into component elements and requisite skills, and *cultural factors*, examining factors such as perceived power distance across hierarchical levels as they relate to job performance. The second step is to determine whether a national is qualified for the position. If a local employee can fill the position, then the search should be discontinued.

A company should validate its selections system by applying the criteria to current employees, then compare their known success record to the success that the election system projects. A prospective candidate should be evaluated using criteria which have been shown to be fair and valid. To establish this, use the proposed selection system on a group of personnel, at least 30 employees, and determine the job performance of these individuals after several months. Scores on the selected criteria are then statistically related (correlated) with the job performance indicating the validity, called *criterion-referenced validity*, of the selection system. The usefulness of the new selection system is judged according to how strongly the validity compares with the former system.

Although it should be emphasized that the following criteria do not necessarily constitute a legally valid system, here are some of the selection criteria a company might use: *position*—can the candidate handle the responsibilities and duties of the job?; *management*—is the candidate an effective motivator and communicator?; *personal*—is the candidate medically sound and is his or her family cooperative and supportive of the move?; and, *environment*—is the candidate flexible and willing to face radically different ways of doing things? Screening factors are often employed by companies such as the manager's independence, sincerity, technical knowledge, attitude, spouse's opinion, desire to go abroad, ability to be trained, adaptability, history and literature, prior overseas experience, and youthfulness. Again, these factors should be used as guidelines rather than an intact system.

EVALUATION

A company needs the means to determine whether its selection system has been effective. Although a specific evaluation procedure depends on the particular program being evaluated, there are several useful methods: administering pre/post evaluation tests to determine the impact of selection; using a control group to contrast the impact of the selection system; and, using objective measures of the employee's effectiveness during and after selection.

An important concern in evaluating a selection system is the way employee performance is assessed. How is success overseas measured? Employee performance can be measured by job performance, interpersonal relations, cultural adjustment, or some combination of the three factors. Before evaluating a selection system, the company must decide what constitutes an effective employee. It is also important to examine short versus long-term effects of the selection system. If an employee performs effectively in the short-term, this does not guarantee the excellent performance will continue. Likewise, short-term performance failures may indicate slow adjustment, rather than a lack of ability.

In evaluating a selection system it is important to distinguish between the impact of selection versus training. Very few companies separate selection and training programs when evaluating success. Unfortunately, this means that an accurate evaluation of the selection system cannot be made without accounting for the impact of the training program. For instance, if a manager who was selected and trained is evaluated as a poor performer, it is not clear whether the selection system or the training program is at fault. Ideally, a company having an intact training program should establish the validity of a selection program by examining how well the new system predicts good and poor performers in contrast to the existing system.

APPLICATIONS TO SMALL BUSINESS

The relevance of a cultural selection program for the small business can be viewed from two perspectives. First, a small company must be extremely careful about not offending foreign nationals because the locale may constitute an important part of the company's sales or operations. The economic importance of a large company to a community may cause nationals to tolerate many errors. A small company, however, cannot afford to offend a foreign host. In addition, the large company can create a self-contained society in the foreign locale whereas a small business cannot afford this convenience, so adjustment to the new culture is crucial. Another benefit of an effective selection program to a small business is that it can be implemented on a small scale. It should be noted, however, that if the selection is only for a few employees, a small business might save money by hiring out the services of a specialized consulting firm to select the overseas candidates.

CONCLUSION

Intercultural selection of managers for cross-cultural and overseas settings will enhance a company's capacity to deal *intra-culturally*. Poor or inappropriate intercultural appointments are detrimental to the relations between the home office and the foreign office. The introduction of a well-designed and carefully executed selection program can reduce the level of culture shock an individual experiences and, thereby, increase his or her performance in the foreign culture.

REFERENCES/SOURCES

Goldstein, I. L. and M. Sorcher. *Changing Supervisory Behavior*. New York: Pergamon, 1974. A general overview of various forms and theory behind training the adult learning.

Harris, P. R. and R. T. Moran. *Managing Cultural Differences*. Houston: Gulf Publishing, 1986. An excellent overview of cross-cultural issues relevant to the global manager. It contains numerous specific examples useful to a personnel officer.

Hays, R. D. "Expatriate Selection: Insuring Success and Avoiding Failure." *Journal of International Business Studies*, 5 (1974): 25-37. A presentation of various factors which are reported by companies concerning why their employees either succeed or fail overseas.

Henry, E. R. "What Business Can Learn from Peace Corps Selection and Training." *Personnel*, July-August 1965: 17-25. A discussion of the general importance and significance of a training program to companies.

Hofstede, G. *Culture's Consequences*. Beverly Hills: Sage, 1984. A global examination of the work values shared by over 40 countries including a listing of a survey used to determine these values.

Howard, C. G. "Model for the Design of a Selection Program for Multinational Executives." *Public Personnel Management*, March-April 1974: 138-145. A proposed selection system for work assignments including specific criteria categories and sources of information concerning the categories.

Ivancevich, J. M. "Selection of American Managers for Overseas Assignments." *Personnel Journal*, March 1969: 189-200. A critical discussion of the criteria on which candidates are judged for overseas work.

Lee, Y. and L. Larwood. "The Socialization of Expatriate Managers in Multinational Firms." *Academy of Management Journal*, 26(1983): 657-665. A critical discussion of the impact of socialization and role models on the behavior of a manager going overseas.

Muniz, P. and R. Chasnoff. "The Cultural Awareness Hierarchy: A Model for Promoting Understanding." *Training and Development Journal*, October 1983: 24-27. The presentation of a general framework with which to understand the role of training within the context of self versus other understanding.

Tung, R. L. "Selection and Training of Personnel for Overseas Assignments." *Columbia Journal of World Business*, Spring 1981: 68-78. A review of the general forms of cultural training available as well as a model to be used in selecting individuals for overseas work.

Willis, H. L. "Selection for Employment in Developing Countries." *Personnel Administrator*, July 1984: 53-58. A discussion of general issues facing the personnel administrator in developing a selection system.

Dr. P. Christopher Earley
Department of Strategic Management
and Organization
University of Minnesota

C. Carstens Smith
Department of English
University of Arizona

Dr. P. Christopher Earley received his Ph.D. in Industrial/Organizational Psychology from the University of Illinois. He is currently Associate Professor of Management at the University of Minnesota, and he serves on the editorial boards of several journals. His research areas include work motivation, job feedback, and intercultural perspectives in organizational behavior.

C. Carstens Smith holds a master's degree in English as a Second Language from the University of Arizona.

Selecting Foreign Assignees

OVERVIEW

The idea of living and working in a foreign country can be very appealing while sitting in one's home country. The lure of travel, greater responsibility, and increased salaries (due to tax assistance and standard of living premiums) encourages people to consider foreign assignments during their career without a complete understanding of the implications. Naturally, their performance, once in the foreign assignment, is very important to the sponsoring company; a substantial financial investment is made when an employee is sent on a foreign assignment. Consequently, the company should first be extremely selective when a foreign post must be staffed by a home country employee, and second, determine who in the organization (if anyone) best fits the requirements of the job in that particular country.

EXAMPLES

As World War II ended, many countries graciously accepted foreign executives into their countries to manage multinational corporations' (MNC) operations. But as the 1950s progressed, leaders became concerned about foreigners conducting business in their local economies. They felt they might be losing control of their economies, and therefore accepted fewer foreign executives. In the early 1980s, the rapid growth of MNCs and international joint ventures produced a demand for executives with international experience and a willingness to serve outside their home country. Education and development of other-country nationals has lessened the demand for U. S. executives to go abroad but U. S. MNCs still value a manager's international experience. In addition, countries have become creative at encouraging MNCs to enter their local economies, and recognize the necessity of foreign executives assigned to the local office of an MNC, at least in the formative stage of operations. With the 21st century looming ahead, it becomes all-important for MNCs to think and act in a global manner. Their ability to respond to changing markets, both worldwide and regionally, will be essential to continued growth and profitability. Consequently, the MNCs' reliance on good international managers, in both home and host countries, will be a key to their success.

BENEFITS

The reasons for sending an employee on an extended foreign assignment (two or more years), could include the following: a) to establish a new office in a foreign country; b) to find a qualified successor to head operations in a subsidiary while training the foreign nationals; c) as a career development tool grooming an employee for future advancement or; d) for professional knowledge not available locally. Each of these motivations present issues that must be addressed: appropriate skills, selection criteria, training requirements and career planning.

Why is it so important to select the correct individual for a foreign assignment? A study of Swedish expatriates indicated the preliminary costs of selection and relocation exceeded $50,000 per executive. Additionally, 25% returned home before their assignments were complete. The most common reason stated for premature re-entry was "difficulty in adjusting." These figures highlight only some costs; not cited is the potential damage to the subsidiary's business as a result of a manager's inappropriate behavior or lack of cultural understanding. Finally, a foreign assignee (FA) who returns may be viewed by peers as having "failed" or the FA may be disgruntled with the lack of support received from the company. He may then pursue other business opportunities as a result of this perceived lack of support. This would pose a further loss to the company.

Let us now turn to the elements which can influence success, both for the company and for the employee: selection criteria, training requirements and career planning (repatriation).

IMPLEMENTATION

Selection Criteria

In an effort to screen potential candidates, MNC leaders can ask a few questions to determine whether candidates are adaptable to new situations and could potentially adjust to a new culture. The questions are as follows:

1. How easily and quickly has the employee adapted to changes in the domestic workplace?

2. How well does the employee cope with unexpected stress?

3. How tolerant is the employee toward opinions, attitudes and behaviors that differ from his/her own?

4. How well does the employee relate to a variety of audiences?

5. Does the employee genuinely like people of all types, shapes, sizes and colors?

In utilizing these questions as a guide, corporate leaders may eliminate candidates who would be ineffective in a foreign environment. By focusing on a smaller number of candidates, they can pay greater attention to selecting the best individual for a job, and then ensure maximum support and training to achieve success. Success in domestic assignments should not automatically qualify one for foreign assignment.

Recognizing cultural differences is only the first step. Before candidates are evaluated, interviews should identify the management style most likely to be successful, along with the technical expertise required to complete the job. Only after these two elements are clearly stated, should the company begin a detailed evaluation of candidates. As interviewers establish the requirements, they will reduce the opportunity for failure resulting from unclear objectives. Success or failure should be determined at the selection phase. The next step in candidate evaluation is to determine who, if anyone, possesses the desired traits.

Desired Traits

First, the FA's technical expertise must be sufficient to assure success, regardless of his ability to adapt to the culture. The FA must also possess the ability to train and supervise resident nationals, because training a successor may be the primary objective of the job. Organizational skills are also important because it is likely the FA will have to select nationals for supervisory roles; English fluency does not qualify a foreign national as a leader. The FA must have interpersonal skills to adapt to the new environment and culture. A willingness to understand the people and culture will lead to adaptation and rapid acceptance by local people. Finally, the FA must be able to call upon a wealth of knowledge from previous experiences to solve problems, as support staff typically is not present.

The employee's past record will highlight these abilities, but further information should be gathered through discussions with past supervisors and extensive personal interviews with the candidate. Although current foreign language proficiency is not a high priority selection criteria, the candidate must demonstrate some language capability. Other factors which will assist in determining a candidate's qualification are the FA's knowledge of the business environment in the host country, and previous success in a foreign assignment.

Finally, standardized testing will provide a method of screening candidates willing to take a foreign assignment, but whose personalities may not lead to cultural adaptation. In this case, it may not be in the company's or employee's best interest to take the assignment. Not all companies use tests when selecting FAs, but when used, the tests themselves should be evaluated regularly to measure their effectiveness.

Although it is the FA who will be conducting business in the foreign location, equally important to success (both the individual's and the company's) is family cohesiveness and the spouse and family's ability to adapt to new environments. While the FA benefits from his company's identity and the importance of his work in the new environment, the family members must independently establish their own identities in the new culture. This is more difficult for the family than for the FA because they must confront the language barrier and cultural differences without the support of established networks of colleagues and friends. One of the most common reasons for early repatriation is the family's difficulty in adapting. For this reason, families should be screened in interviews, and where possible, evaluations of the strength of family relationships should be conducted. Such evaluations are imperative since many FAs experience divorce or separation either during the assignment or shortly after their return, often as a result of the stress experienced while living in a foreign country. Family's views on living in foreign countries, their personal goals, and their ability to adjust are key elements to determining success of the foreign assignment.

Training

In a study by Baker and Ivancevich, a majority of the firms represented by overseas managers reported their companies did not administer pre-departure training programs. Extensive discussion by the respondents indicates that a lack of knowledge of a country and its people can lead to culture shock upon arrival. This inhibits the FA's effectiveness, and can lengthen the time it takes for an individual to become effective in a new position.

There are many elements appropriate to easing the transition from home country to the country of the foreign assignment. Specifically, overseas managers believed that environmental differences between the two countries, the people and their customs, and the national attitude towards foreigners and foreign-owned business should be highlighted. An added benefit would be some command of the foreign language; one cannot supervise and delegate if the employees have difficulty understanding because of language problems.

Companies can hire a myriad of foreign culture consultants, as well as language schools such as Berlitz, to train FAs and their families. One recent development is the integration of these two services (language and culture instruction) by institutions such as Dartmouth and Middlebury College. They each offer a 10-15 day session that presents language basics and cultural norms and mores in order to minimize embarrassing actions in the new country. A similar approach is a cultural immersion camp where business practices, etiquette, culture and language are all integrated for the FA, and sometimes the family as well.

Royal Dutch Shell employs 5,000 expatriates in 100 countries. Employees going on assignment to foreign countries undergo a one-week residential training course that highlights special business mores that the executives will experience. In addition, foreign country experts at the home office prepare briefing packets for new assignees.

One pitfall appears to be that even though families are viewed as keys to successful foreign assignments, very few programs integrate families into pre-departure training. The trend is improving, but perhaps not rapidly enough. If the family has some limited knowledge, it can better fit into the culture, and become more readily accepted by the local people. By demonstrating that they are making an effort to know the language, the people and their culture, all members of the family will be more approachable than if they take a distant stance toward the culture.

Repatriation

Many companies view the task of assigning an employee to a foreign post as complete once the employee has been selected and trained, failing to understand the importance of giving the FA career goals and paths. This is one of the most anxiety-producing aspects of foreign assignments. Even if comprehensive career discussions have taken place, the FA needs to know what is in store for him once he completes his overseas assignment.

Just as the assignee may experience some culture shock in entering the new country, he may also experience culture shock upon return to the home country. In addition, if inflation has exceeded average rates, he could have financial difficulties. Housing which was affordable before expatriation could be well out of reach upon repatriation. Finally, while out of the home country, the FA's peers may have received significant promotions, and the FA may perceive he was overlooked.

These issues can be addressed through the financial package that is offered when the assignment is first considered. Specifically, the company can manage the FA's property while he is away, or offer low-interest mortgage loans upon his return. Although the financial package may not cover all expected events and future costs, the employee will feel more secure knowing that he still has a home. To combat culture shock, MNCs should allow a period of reacclimation for family re-orientation and professional adjustment upon return to the home country.

Considering the anxiety produced by unknown career plans, extensive discussions should take place between the company (FA's career manager) and the FA at all phases of the assignment: pre-expatriation, during expatriation, and before repatriation. Although management is not likely to promise a specific position, open communication regarding corporate and individual expectations should be aired. In this respect, both parties will have a clear understanding; the employee is not surprised by management expectations of his next job, and management can state its position before the assignee accepts the foreign assignment.

Many companies are tempted to send mediocre employees on foreign assignments. This is a disservice to the individual, the company and its shareholders, and only the best employees should be sent on foreign assignments. One effect of sending top executives abroad is that home country managers will wait for the FA's return and compete for their services. Finally, management should provide a permanent position upon return, rather than placing the returning employee in a temporary position until a job becomes available.

It is important to remember that employees are valuable assets, and that much money has been spent to train and educate them in the company business practices. An even greater investment is made if they are sent on a foreign assignment, so managers should take great care to ensure that FAs are trained before departure, carefully attended to during expatriation, and experience a smooth repatriation.

RELATED ISSUES

Surprisingly, most of the literature on the subject references the FA as a male. The few articles that do discuss the opportunities and difficulties women might face in specific regions focus attention on the special issues they face in accepting foreign assignments. Dual-career couples will place further stress on international assignment selection since two career paths must be managed.

Alcohol and substance abuse are key concerns for companies sending employees abroad. A foreigner is already under some scrutiny; if he abuses substances in the host country, the perception may be even worse than in the home country. The stress caused by a new culture might cause individuals to succumb to alcohol or drugs to alleviate their anxiety. Managers should incorporate an understanding of the implications of these actions and their consequences into the information used in the decision process.

Equally important are financial considerations for the employee and family. The employee and family should have a complete understanding of foreign assignment premiums to adjust for standard of living differences, and interest rate and home purchase assistance packages available upon his return. Consideration of salary payments and tax obligations in both home and host country currency may protect the family's financial position against currency changes. Some companies may offer fixed conversion rates to accommodate currency exchanges to prevent penalizing the FA financially for accepting the assignment. All financial aspects of the foreign assignment should be thoroughly evaluated during consideration of the assignment.

These issues must be considered as future research is conducted on foreign assignments and candidate selection. Further adjustments are likely to be necessary to accommodate the trends of increasing numbers of dual-career couples and women in management.

EVALUATION

In order for MNCs to experience continued growth and respond to changing markets, good international managers must be able to empathize with various cultures, and understand differences between markets. One method is to staff the corporate headquarters with foreigners from various parts of the world who have experience running the company's subsidiary operations. A second approach is to groom a number of home country nationals through international assignments so they may also understand the various influences of culture and behavior on world markets and business decisions. Naturally, an optimum approach would be to have a mixture of foreigners and home country nationals. In both cases, careful selection of managers is required.

The first step in selecting an employee for a foreign assignment should begin well before a position is available. Each functional head throughout the corporation (worldwide) should submit to a central personnel manager a list of high potential candidates (HPCs), identifying the ultimate position each individual could achieve. Independent of this group, the company should structure (or contract with a consultant) a series of classes to educate employees about various cultures around the world, including places where operations currently do not exist.

Once this program is established, the HPCs should then enroll in a class periodically, to give them a flavor for the various cultures which compose the world market. In addition, this will provide some eye-opening experiences for the HPCs and perhaps pique interest in a particular country or region.

The response and participation of the HPCs during these sessions should be noted, in case they are considered for an international assignment at some later point in their career. This work will ease selection when a foreign post must be staffed. Employees would already be somewhat sensitized to the differences that exist between cultures, and may even assist in defining whether interest in a post exists. (Unrelated to foreign assignments, home-country managers who deal with foreigner operations should participate as well in order to increase their cultural sensitivity.)

Once a foreign post becomes available, managers should determine the technical expertise required and the most effective management style for that culture. These two elements will provide the first selection criteria to match against the pool of HPCs. The questions cited earlier to test for adaptability and adjustment should also be used as a secondary screen. Managers should then evaluate the candidates through the use of standardized tests, interviews, success in cultural courses, and discussions with previous supervisors on the following areas: cultural empathy, adaptability, maturity, education, adaptability of family, and language ability. These qualities, when evaluated in the context of the country with the available post, will provide a guide for selection of the candidate with the best mix for the situation.

Once a selection is made, the employee should be given the opportunity to decline the post without fear that his future career advancement will be jeopardized by the decision. This is crucial as it will act as another balance to ensure the company is receiving the candidate best qualified and willing to take the foreign assignment.

During the consideration phase, managers should discuss specific assignment duration and potential job opportunities and position levels upon return. Dual-career couples will have a particular dilemma determining what efforts they should request of the company for the individual whose career is interrupted. The company should entertain reasonable requests as families may not tolerate major sacrifices, especially if one party is willing to take the assignment and the other has conditional requirements. A happy, cohesive family is key to success. After the employee accepts the post, final pre-departure training should begin, in language and cultural immersion.

Dependent upon personal choice, the company should conduct a series of classes for the employee and family for the purpose of cultural education, language development, business and social etiquette and practices of the local culture. This can be done with company experts (including recent expatriates from that region, in concert with language tutors), or through the use of outside consultants. Each HPC should be able to select the process he desires. After this series of events, the employee and family will be adequately prepared for duty.

During the course of the assignment, the MNC should be given regular trips back to the home country for the employee and family to maintain personal and business relationships, and to allow for continued career discussions with the employee's career manager. This communication will reinforce discussions conducted prior to the employee's departure, and should reduce some of the FA's career-related anxiety.

Before the period of assignment is complete, home managers should begin work to find the appropriate job in anticipation of the FA's return. In beginning the search prior to assignment completion, a replacement can be found for the FA if necessary, and a permanent position begun immediately upon return to the home country. This position should be consistent to that discussed prior to expatriation, depending on performance while on assignment.

APPLICATIONS TO SMALL BUSINESS

Small businesses must be concerned about the staffing of their foreign locations, especially as they initially expand into foreign markets. Staffing with the most qualified executives increases the likelihood of the small business' penetration into the foreign market. If an organization does not employ individuals who are capable of handling new situations in foreign cultures, it may never become apparent that their product offerings are accepted in the newly expanded markets. Therefore, it is perhaps even more critical for small businesses wishing to expand, to employ individuals whose skills provide the greatest likelihood of success. The organization may not receive another opportunity in that market if the initial efforts fail, not to mention the cost associated with the failed venture.

CONCLUSION

These steps, if used as a guide, should achieve an above average rate of success when sending employees on foreign assignments. An FA can become a valuable asset in the management of foreign operations of the MNC.

MNCs must conduct further research to integrate the implications of dual-career families, financial implications, and appropriate cultural instruction and indoctrination. If one begins with an honest, sensitive, adaptive, intelligent individual, the foreign assignment will be a joy to the FA for the work and personal experience, and to the company for the rewards it will ultimately yield.

REFERENCES/SOURCES

Adler, N. J. "Pacific Basin Managers: A Gaijin, Not a Woman." *Human Resource Management* 26,2 (Summer 1987): 169-191. A study of two expatriate women managers in Asia is used to evaluate whether women can be successful in these roles.

Baker, J. C. and J. M. Ivancevich. "The Assignment of American Executives Abroad: Systematic, Haphazard or Chaotic?" *California Management Review* 13, 3 (Spring 1971): 39-44. A study of selected firms' approaches to foreign assignee selection to determine appropriate corrective action in present selection practices.

Harvey, M. C. "The Other Side of Foreign Assignments: Dealing with the Repatriation Dilemma." In *The Multinational Enterprise in Transition*. Phillip D. Grub, *et al.*, eds. Princeton, NJ: Darwin Press, 1986, 226-242. Repatriation is often forgotten as an important component of foreign assignments. Harvey highlights some problems and steps to make repatriation a successful experience for the assignee.

Hubbard, G. "How to Combat Culture Shock." *Management Today* (September 1986): 62-65. Knowing what to expect when entering a foreign culture and how to respond to make the transition easier.

Kepler, J. Z. *Americans Abroad: A Handbook for Living and Working Overseas.* New York: Praeger, 1983. Assists in identifying skills and attributes of the "ideal" expatriate businessman.

Kruse, T. "How Do You Ensure Success of Managers Going Abroad?" *Training and Development Journal* (December 1985): 22-24. Suggestions for successful staffing of overseas plants and offices, preparing assignees and families for cultural differences and providing the maximum potential for success.

Machan, D. "Ici on Parle: Bottom-line Responsibility." *Forbes* (February 8, 1986): 138-140. Knowing a foreign language should improve performance while on foreign assignment, but may not help one get the assignment.

Oddon, G. and M. Mendenhall. "Seven Questions to Ask Before Sending an Employee Overseas." *Training and Development Journal* (May 1986): 24. Key questions which act as a barometer of success when evaluating foreign assignee candidates.

Teague, Burton W. "Selecting and Orienting Staff for Service Overseas: A Research Report From the Conference Board's Division of Management Research." New York: Conference Board, 1976. A review of actions and concerns associated with selecting and orienting staff for service in foreign countries.

Torbiorn, I. *Living Abroad.* Chichester, NY: John Wiley and Sons, 1982. Implications of the experience of living abroad as a foreign assignee and the anxiety the assignee is likely to experience.

Zeira, Y. and M. Banai. "Selecting Managers for Foreign Assignments." *Management Decision* 25,4 (1987): 38-40. A review of selection procedures and criteria for expatriates which takes more account of the opinions and needs of the host country.

Michael Troppe

Preparing Managers for Intercultural Assignments

OVERVIEW

The importance of training in preparing an individual for an intercultural work assignment has become increasingly apparent in multinational corporations. In general, intercultural training may be defined as any procedure intended to increase an individual's ability to cope and work in a foreign environment.

The need for companies to prepare operatives to work in a different culture is illustrated in a study conducted by E. R. Henry (1965). After reviewing placement decisions of American multinational companies, Henry found that companies reported 30% of their placement decisions to be mistakes, primarily due to the failure of the employee to adjust properly to the new culture. Lee and Larwood (1983) looked at the process of acculturation occurring for expatriate managers in multinational corporations. They found that, upon entering the new culture, the expatriate manager tends to adopt a role he or she expects to be appropriate to minimize potential conflict with local personnel. They suggested that a manager might avoid some of the conflict due to "misbehaving" in a new culture by engaging in anticipatory socialization, by wearing the other culture's shoes, or by learning more about the new culture.

An interesting story reported by Baker further illustrates a pitfall of a manager not receiving adequate training prior to travelling overseas. He reports the story of an American manager who attended a party while working in a Mid-East country. During the party, the manager inquired as to the health of a native colleague's family. Within the context of the particular culture, such an inquiry is only permitted among individuals who know one another quite well. As a result of the cultural faux pas, the manager alienated his colleague and damaged existing work relations. Although most locals will overlook this type of incident, the subtlety of interpersonal exchange shapes the impression a visitor makes on his hosts.

Ironically, many companies consider a "training program" to consist of a handout detailing the population, economy, and political system of a country even though this is clearly inadequate preparation for overseas work. At the other extreme, cross-cultural training has often come to denote a series of expensive training interventions, which can only be conducted by organizational consultants. Between the poles are different training methods that may be conducted by company personnel with minimal cost.

EXAMPLES

Prior to presenting several specific examples of cross-cultural training programs, it is important to discuss how cultural training differs from traditional university education. Traditional university education has the following goals: *communication*—to master written, and to a lesser degree, verbal communication at an abstract and general level; *decision making*—to develop critical judgment and to test assertions and assumptions using hard facts; *ideals*—to value the great principles and ideals of western society, such as social justice, progress, and scientific truth; and, *problem solving*—to search for truth and knowledge and to discover the true, correct answer. On the other hand, cultural training views these goals somewhat differently: *communication*—to understand and communicate directly and through non-verbal means, including gestures and facial expressions so as to listen to the concerns, values, and motives of others; *decision making*—to develop conclusions and take actions on inadequate, unreliable, and conflicting information as well as to trust feelings, impressions, and beliefs in addition to "facts"; *commitment*—to become involved in relationships and inspire confidence in others; *ideals*—to value the causes and objectives of others from a radically different social environment; *problem solving*—to problem solve as a social process designed to develop a decision needed to achieve a common goal.

From this comparison of a traditional university model to a cross-cultural model of training, it is apparent that they differ in several important ways. First, a cultural approach emphasizes the general relativity of "truth." One person's fact is another person's fiction. For instance, in South Korea a contract is assumed to be valid only so long as the situation in which the contract was developed remains stable. If a company has contracted for computer memory chips at $3.00 each and a shortage arises, then the Korean manager may feel free to raise the price even if a written contract exists. To the Korean manager a contract is not the binding reality that the American manager perceives. Thus, a good cultural training program should emphasize relative similarities and key differences between societies rather than absolutes.

There are numerous examples of training programs used by organizations. ARAMCO, a Saudi-Arabian corporation, uses an extensive orientation program for an employee and his or her family in preparing for work overseas. The ARAMCO orientation program consists of two parts: practical information, such as local transportation, shopping, day-to-day finances; and, a comparison of the Saudi people, their beliefs and customs, with the American culture. In their book, *Managing Cultural Differences,* Philip Harris and Robert Moran discuss the Canadian International Development Agency's (CIDA) predeparture program for their overseas volunteers. CIDA's training aims to impart several objectives, including: communicating respect, being non-judgmental, personalizing knowledge and perceptions, displaying empathy, practicing role flexibility, and tolerating ambiguity.

Another interesting example of training is illustrated by the InterFuture Scholars Program, an educational program sponsoring American undergraduates who conduct independent research in overseas settings. This program incorporates experiential learning with specific technical skills. Prior to travelling overseas, an InterFuture Scholar participates in three five-day preparatory conferences during which he or she refines a specific research proposal to be conducted in the U.S., a European nation and a developing nation (e.g., Kenya, Surinam, Nepal). In addition, the InterFuture Scholar undergoes a series of area studies and exercises to prepare for living three months in each locale (with little formal supervision). The scholar is also expected to participate in several repatriation activities upon returning to the U.S. designed to help re-entry into the home culture. Ironically, few training programs place much emphasis on the repatriation of the overseas employee.

BENEFITS

The key benefit of a cross-cultural training program focuses on the negative emotional state called "culture shock." Culture shock generally is thought to reduce an individual's ability to function in a new cultural setting as the result of a perceived difference between how events *actually* proceed and how they are *expected* to proceed. If, for instance, an American visits a developing country and expects to use the local library's photocopier, there is likely to be some shock concerning the availability of high technology machinery. The accumulative effect of such discordant events is a stress state that results in culture shock.

The primary benefit of cross-cultural training is the reduction of the culture shock. A manager who experiences a large amount of culture shock will often become overly critical of others, rationalize his or her mistakes, and isolate him or herself from others. Eventually, the manager suffering from severe culture shock will become withdrawn and alienated from the new culture. A specific example of the impact of culture shock on an individual is relayed by Chris

Lee, who describes his experience in attending a presentation by Dudley Woodberry for a Detroit-based consulting firm. Woodberry opened his workshop in Urdu, a Pakistani and Indian language, which led the audience to experience feelings of frustration, defensiveness, and apprehension.

Another benefit of cross-cultural training is the foreign office's belief that the home office cares about them, as well as giving them special training for advancement in the company. Cultural training should foster a more global cosmopolitan perspective in the trainee, which will benefit the home office. A manager who is knowledgeable about other cultures and ways of life is better able to understand the differences among heterogeneous employees from the same culture.

One final benefit of training relates to the cost if an employee *is not* properly trained. Some consultants report that in companies not using cultural training as much as 75% of the communications between the home office and the overseas employee concerns non-business issues such as buying furniture and tending to personal finances. This type of inefficiency is greatly reduced by the implementation of a cultural training program.

IMPLEMENTATION

The implementation of a cross-cultural training program consists of six major steps. First, a company must carefully research the target locale; culturally-defined factors affecting interpersonal relations, local needs and national politics. In addition, many different facets of the culture must be explored and researched. Second, intercultural organization development should be applied to establish policies and procedures to be used in the local setting. Third, an employee chosen for an overseas assignment should undergo an initial orientation concerning the new work setting. If appropriate, an employee's family should participate in a briefing concerning the country, job and living conditions. Fourth, predeparture training should be conducted with the employee, involving the family. This training should consist of specific exercises to enhance the employee's interpersonal skills. Fifth, an in-country follow-up should be conducted after the employee has been overseas for a short period. The follow-up should include further training and counseling, if needed, as well as opportunities to experience the new culture in an informal setting, e.g., social events. Finally, the training program should provide some form of repatriation phase for the returning manager. This portion of the program should facilitate the employee's re-entry into the home office structure and home culture. Furthermore, the program should provide repatriation counseling for the employee and his or her family.

The training methods used during the pre-departure phase are numerous. In her extensive research into expatriate personnel, Rosalie Tung established an interesting grouping of preparation methods, based on a continuum of methods ranging from low to high rigor, defined as the amount of emotional involvement or activity the trainee experiences during the training. At the lowest level of rigor is the area studies program, consisting of a factual presentation to the trainee of the country's environment, geography, history and politics. This approach assumes that knowledge of another group promotes empathy. Area studies, however, are not particularly useful for trainees who have extensive contact with the local personnel. A second form of training is referred to as a culture assimilator consisting of 75 to 100 programmed episodes describing specific intercultural encounters. The episodes have been judged by experts to be critical to successful functioning in the local culture. The third form of training focuses on language skills. Although a trainee may learn a great deal about a new culture through its language, this is a long and laborious approach to intercultural training. Fourth, a training program can use sensitivity training which focuses on helping the trainee better understand him or herself so that unfamiliar modes of behavior will be both obvious and less threatening.

Finally, field exercises can be used to confront a trainee with the experience of entering a new culture. One example of a field exercise is the placement of a trainee in an ethnic community for several hours with the purpose of learning something about the local community. Through the experience of being immersed in a completely new community the trainee receives a "mini-cultural experience."

Several additional methods are described by Harris and Moran in their book, *Managing Cultural Differences*. For instance, a role-playing exercise using an American and a non-American contrast the expectations of each culture. Another method is self-confrontation, which consists of self-observation on videotape of an encounter with a foreigner. Finally, there are a series of intercultural sensitivity simulations, or games, which can be used to expose a trainee to the experience of entering a new culture. One example of an intercultural game is *BaFa BaFa*, developed by Dr. Garry Shirts, in which participants play members of either a trading culture or a friendly, patriarchal culture. The game's title is derived from the trading culture's language used for trading. During the course of the game, representatives are sent from one culture to the other in an attempt to discover how the other culture operates.

EVALUATION

It is important that a company establish a means to determine whether its training program has been effective. Although a program to evaluate training effectiveness will depend on the specific job assignment, several useful methods include: pre/post evaluation instruments; use of a control group who did no training; objective measures of trainee performance during and after training using sources; and peer and supervisory ratings after overseas placement.

An example of how to evaluate a cultural training program is illustrated by a study conducted by this author of a program used by a west coast electronics firm to prepare employees for work in Seoul, South Korea. The training consisted of: a control group contrasted with three training groups; a paper-and-pencil approach focusing on critical incidents, field experiences and role-playing; and a combination of these two methods. The trainees underwent a five-day training program approximately one month prior to going overseas. The evaluation consisted of a self-report of their reactions to the training after program completion along with a follow-up assessment of the trainees' performances (self and supervisor-rated) after having worked overseas for three months. In addition to performance measures, the trainee's level of culture shock he experienced and his cosmopolitan perspective were assessed. This study illustrates the use of a control group, self-rated measures, and supervisor-rated measures collected at different points in time.

APPLICATIONS TO SMALL BUSINESS

The relevance of a cultural training program for the small business can be viewed from two perspectives. First, a small company must be extremely careful about not offending foreign nationals because the locale may constitute an important part of the company's sales or operations. The clout of a large and powerful company can justify the forgiveness of many sins; a small company, however, cannot afford to offend a foreign host. In addition, the large company can act as a self-contained society in the foreign locale, whereas a small business is not afforded this convenience. Another benefit of a training program to a small business is that it can be implemented on a small scale. It should be noted, however, that if the training is only for new employees, a small business might save money by hiring a specialized consulting firm to conduct the training.

REFERENCES/SOURCES

Baker, J. C. "Foreign Language and Predeparture Training in U.S. Multinational Firms." *Personnel Administrator* (July 1984): 68-72. A general discussion of some intercultural training techniques.

Earley, P. C. "Intercultural Training for Managers: A Comparison of Documentary and Interpersonal Methods." *Academy of Management Journal* 73 (1987). An example of the methodology useful in evaluating a training program.

Goldstein, I. L. and M. Sorcher. *Changing Supervisory Behavior.* New York: Pergamon, 1974. A general overview of various forms and theory behind training the adult learning.

Harris, P. R. and R. T. Moran. *Managing Cultural Differences*, 2d ed. Houston: TX: Gulf Publishing Co., 1987. An excellent overview of cross-cultural issues relevant to the global manager. It contains numerous specific examples useful to a personnel officer.

Henry, E. R. "What Business Can Learn from Peace Corps Selection and Training." *Personnel* (July-August 1965): 17-25. A discussion of the general importance and significance of a training program to companies.

Hofstede, G. *Culture's Consequences.* Beverly Hills: Sage Publishing, 1984. A global examination of the work values shared by over 40 countries including a listing of a survey used to determine these values.

Kolb, D. and R. Fry. "Toward an Applied Theory of Experiential Learning." In *Theories of Group Processes*, ed. by C. L. Cooper. New York: John

Wiley, 1975. A discussion of the various forms of interpersonal training available, their impact on an individual, and the philosophy of experiential learning.

Lee, C. "Cross-Cultural Training: Don't Leave Home Without It." *Training* (July 1983): 20-25. General discussion of some benefits of cultural training and some programs available.

Lee, Y. and L. Larwood. "The Socialization of Expatriate Managers in Multinational Firms." *Academy of Management Journal* 26 (1983): 657-665. A critical discussion of the impact of socialization and role models on the behavior of a manager going overseas.

Tung, R. L. "Selection and Training of Personnel for Overseas Assignments." *Columbia Journal of World Business* (Spring 1981): 68-78. A review of the general forms of cultural training available as well as a model to be used in selecting individuals for overseas work.

Dr. P. Christopher Earley
Department of Strategic Management
and Organization
University of Minnesota

Dr. Christopher Earley received his Ph.D. in Industrial/Organizational Psychology from the University of Illinois. He is currently Associate Professor of Management at the University of Minnesota and serves on the editorial boards of several journals. His research areas include work motivation, job feedback, and intercultural perspectives in organizational behavior.

Compensation in International Settings

OVERVIEW

An integral part of many companies growth is overseas expansion of manufacturing or marketing services. Although much attention has been focused on the development of an overseas market for domestically produced goods, organizations have begun to realize the importance of emphasizing personnel policies and practices. This is especially evident if one considers the issue of compensation for foreign personnel. Compensation refers to the various forms of pay and benefits provided to an employee. Compensation also includes non-monetary rewards, such as verbal rewards and work status, used by managers to reward day-to-day activities. Compensation can be viewed from two perspectives: compensation of foreign personnel; and compensation of home personnel who work overseas. Typically, methods of compensating home personnel working overseas are straightforward. Compensating foreign personnel (foreign nationals) working for a company in their native country is more complicated.

An article by Steven Kerr of the University of Southern California entitled, "The Folly of Rewarding A While Hoping for B" is a splendid illustration of the dilemma of cross-cultural compensation. The focus of Kerr's article is that a manager often will make the mistake of rewarding an employee's work performance using the rewards the manager values. Unfortunately, the key to appropriate and successful compensation is to provide rewards valued by the *recipient* rather than the *provider*. Managers often view particular rewards as important to employees even though they may not be rewarding to the employees. Thus, it is apparent that a very important aspect of effective compensation is to determine what is rewarding to an employee from a particular culture.

A second important aspect of compensation concerns its impact on the community in which a company operates. For instance, a company might enter a new market and pay exorbitant salaries for personnel, draining local talent from the area. If this occurs in a developing country, where U.S. operations are moving, the drain can be seriously detrimental to local companies. Obviously, a multinational corporation must concern itself with the image that might develop if it consistently lures away local talent. Thus, an equity issue arises within the local community.

EXAMPLES

An understanding of values and culture is necessary to interpret why certain forms of compensation are favored over others. A thorough analysis of the fundamental values of various cultures was developed by Geert Hofstede in his study of over forty countries.

Hofstede (1984) proposed that cultures differ along four fundamental dimensions: power distance, individualism, uncertainty avoidance, and masculinity/femininity. *Power distance* refers to the extent to which a superior and his subordinate influence each other's behavior. *Individualism* refers to how an individual views himself relative to the collectivity to which he belongs. An individual who is a member of a highly collectivistic society is emotionally dependent on his or her collectivity. *Uncertainty avoidance* refers to the extent to which individuals in a society can tolerate ambiguity. Finally, *masculinity/femininity* refers to the way individuals approach interactions with one another. "Masculine" cultures tend to be characterized by more competitiveness and aggressiveness than more "feminine" ones.

These four dimensions can be used to characterize a variety of countries. For instance, the United States is a high individualistic and moderate power distance culture. One might argue that an appropriate reward in the U.S. is a prize that is competitively won or lost. In a low individualistic culture like Israel, however, a competitive contest might be viewed as a divisive trick which is to be resisted. The cultural background of the recipients will influence the nature of workplace compensation.

An example of the differential values held by employees concerning rewards is Preiss' survey of American and German engineers. Preiss showed that American engineers were oriented toward their companies, careers, and private lives; German engineers were, however, oriented toward a professional (specialist) career, earnings, cooperation, and security. As examined above, the German engineers' performances for specialist development, security, and anxiety avoidance is consistent with the high uncertainty avoidance observed in Hofstede's survey.

In a study of reward perceptions of American, English, and Ghanaian (West African) workers, this author found several differences among the countries. The study was conducted in three foreign subsidiaries of the same multinational corporation. At the time, the home office believed that all workers placed great importance on social interaction with their supervisors. It was believed that social interaction was valued comparably in all three countries, even though no one had ever bothered to find out whether or not this was true. After implementing an international personnel program to encourage the use of interaction between supervisors and shop floor workers, the company observed mixed results. After observing, interviewing, and surveying shop floor employees, it became evident that the employees in the three countries differed in their attitudes toward interaction with their superiors. English workers resented, rather than revered, general conversation with their superiors and, further, assumed that conversation was simply a device to "spy" on the workers. On the other hand, the Ghanaian workers responded very favorably to this form of intervention; U.S. workers fell somewhere between the two extremes. While the English shop floor workers are part of a class-oriented society that structures the nature of acceptable interactions, the Ghanaians are from a largely tribal society (the Ashanti tribe) that places great value on kinship and social interaction. As a result, the program of social rewards was valuable in Ghana but not in England.

BENEFITS

The first and most obvious purpose of an effective compensation system is to maintain worker motivation. As exemplified in the study discussed above, English workers do not respond well to praise, whereas American and Ghanaians find praise important. In the study, the American manager operating in England should have relied on rewards other than praise to encourage worker motivation in that country. An additional benefit of effective compensation is the assurance of an equitable system both within and across cultures. In terms of individual productivity, an equitable system should ensure that employee compensation is appropriate within a given culture. It also should balance specific cultural norms within a system to ensure fairness across *all* cultures under consideration.

A final benefit of a compensation system is the availability of alternative, non-monetary rewards. An effective compensation system must include rewards other than money; an effective system uses an array of rewards valued by a particular group of people. For instance, a manager working in Israel might choose to capitalize on prevalent collectivistic values by providing group-level recognition for achievement or group-level rewards for individual effort.

IMPLEMENTATION

IMPLEMENTATION

Developing and implementing an effective compensation system involves five basic steps.

1. A manager determines the basic values of the employees involved in the new system. This can be accomplished through a variety of methods including: (1) a *survey of the employees* to assess cultural values and beliefs administered by a trained professional using a standardized measure (such as the one listed in Geert Hofstede's book, *Culture's Consequences*); (2) *ethnography,* an examination and analysis of a culture by a professional; (3) *library research,* including traditional documentary research using resources such as the *Human Relations Areas Files*, which is a collection of descriptions of many cultures; and (4) *interviews* of prior job incumbents to determine their view of a country's culture.

2. Use identified cultural values as the basis for developing a list of rewards. These rewards should be culturally accepted as well as practical for a manager to use. The list should include those rewards that can be used in tandem (e.g., recognition award and verbal praise). Once established, the list is used as the basis for the actual compensation system.

3. Define which jobs are to be compensated. This determination is based on two tools: job analysis and evaluation. These tools are used to decide the appropriate amount of monetary compensation and other forms of reward. For instance, verbal praise might be used for *all* high performing employees whereas a year-end bonus might only apply to a subset of employees. It should also be noted that the job analysis

provides a legally defensible basis for inequitable compensation across cultural settings for the same job. For instance, it is a common practice to provide additional wages for overseas work in a hazardous setting.

4. Determine who provides rewards and in what fashion. In a high power-distance culture such as the Philippines, it is necessary and appropriate for compensation to come from superiors, whereas in a low power-distance country such as Sweden the work group may act as the compensating agent.

5. Address the special case or situation that does not seem to obey the previous scheme. Some forms of compensation, particularly monetary, are strictly regulated by the political powers governing a particular region. Most industrialized nations have some form of minimum wage and benefits package required for all of its citizens. In putting together the final form of a compensation package, the labor laws and prevalent customs of a culture must be incorporated.

EVALUATION

To evaluate the utility of a new compensation plan it is important, first, to assess the current levels of performance and compensation satisfaction in the organization. This base level is used as the standard by which future changes are judged. A manager can determine base levels by reviewing and recording employee performance during a six to twelve month period or by examining archival performance records. Existing levels of satisfaction with pay can also be measured using standardized surveys such as Smith, Kendall, and Hulin's *Job Description Index.*

After determining the levels of performance and compensation satisfaction, the new compensation plan should be implemented using only one group of employees while another group acts as a control or comparison group. In order to avoid resentment among employees in the control group, management must make it clear that should the test prove successful—meaning increased productivity or job satisfaction—the new plan will be extended to everyone. The advantage of creating a comparison group is that if differences in performance occur over the implementation period, then the manager can determine whether these changes were due to the compensation plan or to some other unexpected event. If performance shifts for the comparison group, as well as for those receiving the new compensation plan, then the manager can infer that some unexpected event occurred.

The last phase in evaluating the compensation plan is to observe its impact over a period of six to twelve months, and to compare the actual results with the desired results. It is important for a manager to define the "desired results" prior to beginning the evaluation phase. Further, it is important to consider the impact of external influences, such as governmental regulations and local labor market conditions.

APPLICATION TO SMALL BUSINESS

The advantage of a culturally-adapted compensation scheme to the small business is three-fold. First, this type of scheme is tailored so that small business can capitalize on worker differences, since rewards provided to employees are adapted according to individual and cultural needs. Second, equity across employees can be maintained by a carefully thought out system. The importance of perceived equity, or fairness, of a compensation system cannot be stressed enough since an inequitable system will inevitably lead to pay dissatisfaction and turnover. And third, a well-designed compensation scheme represents a means by which important, key personnel may be induced to stay with the company. A small business can tailor compensation to the high performer so as to retain this employee.

REFERENCES/SOURCES

Baker, J. C. "Foreign Language and Predeparture Training in U.S. Multinational Firms." *Personnel Administrator* (July 1984): 68-72. A general discussion of some intercultural training techniques.

Harris, P. R. and R. T. Moran. *Managing Cultural Differences*. Houston, TX: Gulf Publishing, 1975. An excellent overview of cross-cultural issues relevant to the global manager. It contains numerous specific examples useful to a personnel officer.

Henry, E. R. "What Business Can Learn from Peace Corps Selection and Training." *Personnel* (July-August 1965): 17-25. A discussion of the general importance and significance of a training program to companies.

Hofstede, G. *Culture's Consequences*. Beverly Hills: Sage Publishing, 1984. A global examination of the work values shared by over 40 countries, including a listing of a survey used to determine these values.

Lee, Y. and L. Larwood. "The Socialization of Expatriate Managers in Multinational Firms." *Academy of Management Journal* 26 (1983): 657-665. A critical discussion of the impact of socialization and role models on the behavior of a manager going overseas.

Milkovich, G. T. and J. M. Newman. *Compensation*. Plano, TX: Business Publications, 1987. An excellent introduction to the general area of compensation and how it fits into the organization structure.

Muniz, P. and R. Chasnoff. "The Cultural Awareness Hierarchy: A Model For Promoting Understanding." *Training and Development Journal* (October 1983): 24-27. The presentation of a general framework with which to understand the role of training within the context of self versus other understanding.

Tung, R. L. "Selection and Training of Personnel for Overseas Assignments." *Columbia Journal of World Business* (Spring 1981): 68-78. A review of the general forms of cultural training available as well as a model to be used in selecting individuals for overseas work.

*P. Christopher Earley
Department of Strategic Management
and Organization
University of Minnesota*

Dr. Christopher Earley received his Ph.D. in Industrial/Organizational Psychology from the University of Illinois. He is currently Associate Professor of Management at the University of Minnesota and serves on the editorial boards of several journals. His research areas include work motivation, job feedback, and intercultural perspectives in organizational behavior.

13.

The Impact of Culture on International Operations

Adapting Foreign Operations to Cultural Diversity

OVERVIEW

Cultural diversity is neither a management technique nor a management concept. Cultural diversity can best be described as a phenomenon resulting from the intermingling of individuals from different cultures. Culture is, "whether organizational or national. . . a set of taken-for-granted assumptions, expectations, or rules for being in the world. As paradigm, map, frame of reference, interpretive scheme, or shared understanding, the culture concept emphasizes the shared cognitive approaches to reality that distinguish a given group from others" (Adler and Jelinek 1986). In the business world, cultural diversity is represented in multinational corporations by the expatriate, national and third-country national employee.

EXAMPLES

The recognition of the potential impact of cultural diversity on the business world did not take place until the 1950s. Up until this period, American economists and management theorists pointed to the success of U.S. business as legitimizing the development of a universal management theory (Jamieson 1982-83). Sociocultural factors were not considered to influence business behavior or management practices.

As Americans became involved in the process of reconstruction after World War II, problems arose because Americans found that their beliefs and assumptions about behavior were not shared in other countries. By the mid-1950s Japan was being scrutinized with interest by her American and European competitors. Japan's success in the international marketplace stimulated interest in studying the influence of cultural factors on economic performance.

By the 1960s American companies were becoming established abroad. The experience of these multinational corporations pointed to the demise of a cultural convergence theory and the development of a cultural divergence theory. Child (1981), Laurent (1983), and Hofstede (1983) conducted research which supported cultural diversity and the associated culturally specific management practices.

Examples of business situations in which cultural diversity may be found include multinational corporations employing expatriates and/or nationals in their subsidiaries in foreign countries, multinational corporations employing nationals in other countries, and multinational corporations employing third country nationals in their international operations. Generally, the multinational corporation employing expatriates, nationals, or third country nationals is described as the "mother-company" with her headquarters located in the "parent-country." The country in which the multinational corporation has operations is defined as the "host-country."

Although companies having subsidiaries or formal representation in other countries are likely to experience cultural diversity, companies in the U.S. may also find themselves dealing with individuals and groups from different cultures. For example, Miles Laboratory, a West Germany owned company, regularly hosts West German scientists and business people from the mother-company, Bayer, as delegate employees to the U.S. subsidiary. Miles also sends U.S. employees to the West Germany location as delegates. Other American owned corporations also sponsor foreign nationals at their U.S. locations, such as Eli Lilly and Cummins Engines.

BENEFITS

Review of a Delphi study conducted by Adler (1983) resulted in the following "major benefits of multiculturalism that organizations could potentially realize in the future as enhanced abilities to: 1) be more creative and innovative, 2) deal more sensitively with foreign customers, 3) attract the best personnel from around the world, 4) assume a more global perspective of opportunities, 5) create a unifying organizational culture based on the best of all members' national cultures, and 6) adapt more effectively to environmental change."

Number five above, the creating of a unifying organizational culture based on the best of all members' national cultures, can be thought of as developing "cultural synergy—the positive interaction between multiple national and ethnic cultures within a single organizational context" (Adler 1980, 1986).

IMPLEMENTATION

Corporations experiencing cultural diversity must make decisions about strategic issues at the organizational, or "macrolevel," and the individual, or "microlevel." Strategic issues to be addressed at the macrolevel include:

1. Making policy decisions about the applicability of the parent company's structures and strategies to various host-country operations.

2. Coordinating management values and ethical standards across cultures.

3. Managing the relationship between multinational corporations and host-country government and political systems.

4. Determining the locus of control between headquarters and foreign subsidiaries.

At the individual level, multinational corporations need to address the following issues:

1. Training of managers to be sensitive to cultural considerations.

2. Locating and selecting professionally and culturally competent job candidates.

3. Developing equitable, worldwide compensation packages and assessment systems.

4. Managing the international transfer of spouse and family as well as of the employee.

5. Creating clear career paths for international managers, including repatriation programs.

EVALUATION

The implementation, or the managing of a culturally diverse population, requires "competent internationalists [who] are able to recognize the contribution made by managers of various nationalities. . .[who] are able to develop solutions to problems face[d] by multinational corporations by using these contributions and cultural diversity as a resource, rather than as a barrier to be overcome" (Moran, 1985).

At the microlevel, a competent internationalist must possess the cognitive, affective, and behavioral skills necessary to deal with cultural diversity. The skills and abilities recognized as most necessary for managing in a multicultural organization include: 1) a strong self-concept and emotional maturity, 2) ability of the spouse to adapt, to be self-motivated, and to learn the local language, 3) awareness of the history, sociocultural patterns, and legal and political systems of the countries in which the organization operates, 4) ability and willingness to relate to people from other cultures, 5) managerial competence and experience, 6) knowledge of the people and power relationships within the organization, 7) ability to view the world from multiple perspectives, and 8) ability to behave differently in different cultural settings.

Multinational corporations must develop strategies and techniques for evaluating the international manager's skills related to cross-cultural experiences. Because of the equalitative nature of several of these skills, such as the ability to view the world from multiple perspectives, evaluation strategies may require the inclusion of qualitative assessment techniques along with the traditional quantitative methods.

Strategic planning at the organizational level must include an evaluation plan for each of the identified strategic issues, such as policy decisions about applicability of parent-company's structures/strategies to the host-country operations. The strategic issues associated with an international organization are complex and require continuous attention and ongoing assessment to ensure success in the global market. Thus, dual-directional communication between headquarters and its foreign subsidiaries is critical to successful strategic planning.

APPLICATIONS TO SMALL BUSINESS

Each of the strategic organizational issues which was defined at the macro- and micro level is an appropriate concern of small businesses currently experiencing, or preparing to experience, situations of cultural diversity. Each issue should be explored and addressed in relation to the specific situation of the small business. The benefits and potential disadvantages of cultural diversity within an organization are as relevant to the small business considering international expansion as they are to the larger, already established multinational corporation.

CONCLUSION

Cultural diversity impacts an organization in the areas of motivation, training, decision-making, leadership, management techniques, group dynamics, policy-making, etc. The phenomenon of cultural diversity results from the intermingling of individuals or groups from different cultural backgrounds. Cultural diversity is based on the theory of cultural divergence rather than convergence. It follows that culturally specific management techniques are recommended over the application of universal management practices.

Although cultural diversity offers opportunities for more creative use of human resources, it is not without its disadvantages. Potential problems of multiculturalism which may affect an organization include: 1) difficulties in coordinating policies and practices across cultures, 2) difficulties in integrating people from different cultures, 3) host-country resentment of multinational organizations, and 4) cultural dominance or ethnocentrism—use of one cultures' perspective in managing the entire organization" (Adler 1983).

As worldwide expansion and competition increase, more and more corporations are finding themselves in the global marketplace. A more global and less ethnocentric vision combined with a recognition of cultural diversity and the ability to deal with the complex international management issues arising from this phenomenon will be critical to the success of these enterprises. A successful multinational organization will be one that adopts strategies to take advantage of the power of cultural diversity and explores the opportunities that cultural differences might provide (Schein, 1986).

REFERENCES/SOURCES

Adler, Nancy. "Cross-Cultural Management: Issues to be Faced." *International Studies of Management and Organizations* 1-2 (1983): 7-45. Presents and analyzes findings of a Delphi study. Discusses multiculturalism, advantages and disadvantages of cultural diversity, and skills/attributes needed by international managers.

Adler, Nancy and Mariann Jelinek. "Is 'Organization Culture' Culture Bound?" *Human Resource Management* (Spring 1986): 73-90. Investigates the organization culture concept and questions its ability to integrate culturally diverse perspectives within its current conceptual framework.

Chakravarthy, Balaji S., and Howard V. Perlmutter. "Strategic Planning for a Global Business." *Columbia Journal of World Business* (Summer 1985): 3-10. Reviews four generic planning systems available to a MNC for meeting the complex strategic planning decisions required by globalization of business. Discusses the context in which each of the systems should be used.

Child, John. "Culture, Contingency and Capitalism in the Cross-National Study of Organizations." In L. L. Cummings and B. M. Shaw, eds. *Research in Organization Behavior,* Vol. 3. Greenwich, CT: JAI Press, 1981. Presents findings resulting from the review of cross-cultural studies which focused on two trends: convergence studies with their emphasis on organizational issues at the macrolevel, and divergence studies with their focus issues at the microlevel.

Hofstede, Geert. "The Cultural Relativity of Organizational Practices and Theories." *Journal of International Business Studies* (Fall 1983): 75-89. Presents the results of a 40-country study of the behavior of employees from different cultures working within a single organization. Supports the divergence theory of cultural diversity.

Jamieson, Ian. "The Concept of Culture and its Relevance for an Analysis of Business Enterprise in Different Societies." *International Studies of Management and Organizations* (Winter, 1982-1983): 71-105. Traces through history the role of culture as a factor influencing management and business theory.

Laurent, Andre. "The Cross-Cultural Puzzle of International Human Resource Management." *Human Resource Management* (January 1986): 91-102. Contributes to the framing of the new domain of international human resource management by investigating the cultural diversity of management conceptions across nations. Suggests critical steps necessary for a truly international conception of HRM.

Maisonrouge, Jacques G. "Education of a Modern International Manager." *Journal of International Business Studies* (Spring/Summer 1983): 141-146. Discusses the traits of international managers which lead to success or failure. Discusses the qualities or skills needed by mangers in today's international business world.

Moran, Robert T. "The Composite of Qualities that Makes for the Best Internationalists." *International Management* (March 1985): 65. Indicates that competent internationalists are those who perceive cultural diversity as a resource rather than a barrier.

Schein, Edgar H. "Epilogue: International Human Resource Management: New Directions, Perpetual Issues, and Missing Themes," *Human Resource Management* (Spring 1986): 169-176. Summary of the concerns and issues discussed during the 1985 Symposium on International Human Resource Management. Discusses the power of cultural diversity in relation to the future success of global organizations.

Triandis, Harry C. "Dimensions of Cultural Variation as Parameters of Organizational Theories." *International Studies of Managment and Organizations* (Winter 1982-83): 139-169. Reviews dimension of cultural differences that have implications for organizational functioning, with emphasis on managerial behaviors.

Zeira, Yoram. "The Role of the Training Director in Multinational Corporations." *Training and Development Journal* (March 1979): 20-25. Describes the unique human problems faced by the training director of an international corporation.

Dr. Sue A. Miller

Ethical Dilemmas in Transacting Business Across Cultures

OVERVIEW

The concept of the "Global Village" is popular and attractive, but deceptive. It encourages international businesspeople to see themselves easily talking with, reasoning with, and entering into satisfactory agreements with people anywhere in the world. However, the Global Village lacks certain essential attributes of the traditional village. Most importantly, no one can assume or insist that other "villagers" accept his values and norms. Basic concepts are defined differently in different cultures and dictate different behaviors. As global business strategies are developed, the transferability of ethics and ways of doing business becomes a continuing conundrum.

Business negotiations between Westerners and representatives of the People's Republic of China illustrate cultural barriers and subsequent dilemmas. When Americans re-entered China in 1972, they were told that the big ethical dilemma, doing-business-with Communists-who-want-to-destroy-us, had been resolved. China's political system was not a threat; the new ideology was pragmatism. Buying, selling, and investing in China could be considered "normal business decisions."

In crushing the pro-democracy movement in June 1989, the government brought the ethical-political issue back to the attention of Western business people. Is it a basic screening question? Should it be? In the last few years, entrepreneurs and managers have spoken freely about making money. Deng

Xioaping himself had been quoted: "To be rich is glorious."

The action of the Peoples Liberation Army at Tiananmen Square made many Americans uncertain about their commercial commitments and ambitions in China. Some advocate pull-out. Some condemn the government. Some compare involvement in China with involvement in South Africa in terms of human rights violations. Others say reality demands they stay. Roger Sullivan, President of the US-China Business Council has observed, "Companies are loathe to abandon the joint ventures that are already in effect. They spent a lot to get them in place. . .So companies will try to keep them alive."

For those who opt to stay or the few who choose to pursue new ventures, much of the "informed advice" on Sino-American commercial negotiations has assumed that if only Westerners understood the Chinese negotiation model, they could "play the game." However, recent research strongly suggests that Westerners cannot play the Chinese negotiation game without encountering ethical dilemmas. Open-ended interviews with Chinese officials, Chinese and American managers in joint ventures, and American businessmen in the process of negotiating commercial agreements with the Peoples Republic of China strongly suggest there are key words that create many ethical dilemmas. These words include progress, friendship, truth, compromise, agreement, and fairness. Chinese and American negotiators agree that these ideas are "good"; however, the negotiators find that serious problems arise when the operational meanings of the terms become clear. What is "proper behavior"? What is "good behavior"? Differences in understanding frequently lead to anger, frustration, and feelings of betrayal.

EXAMPLES

Some old China hands have said that the basic Chinese model of negotiation is quite similar to a basic American model (Pye, 1982; Solomon, 1985).

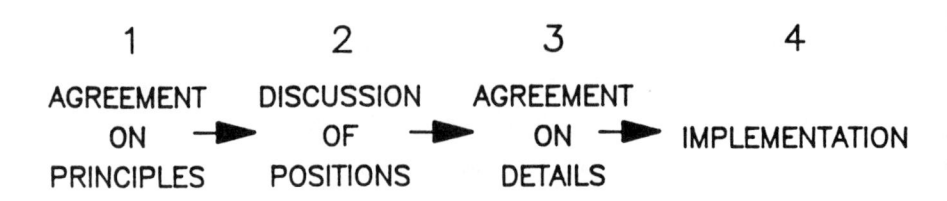

```
    1              2              3              4
AGREEMENT    DISCUSSION     AGREEMENT
    ON    ⟶      OF     ⟶      ON     ⟶   IMPLEMENTATION
PRINCIPLES    POSITIONS      DETAILS
```

Figure 1

Stages in the Linear Model of Negotiating

Thus Western negotiators have prepared themselves to proceed step by step: First, they lay the groundwork and present a general statement of their principles and objectives. Second, they get down to details. Third, they formalize the agreement; and finally they implement the agreement.

There are two critical problems with this model. First, it assumes the Western value of progress — movement in a single direction. To go backward is bad. Second, at each step there are key words that are not easily translated from one culture to the other.

To Westerners, "good progress" is rapid progress. The American businessman wants to move from Principles to Details to Contract to Implementation. However, when he comes to China, he finds himself in "endless receptions" and "endless meetings." He finds "valuable business time" is being taken by trips to the Great Wall and the Ming Tombs. And he suspects the Chinese are avoiding the business problems.

The model of linear progress in the Western negotiator's mind is part of his frustration. In real negotiations, movement is uneven and not always in the same direction. He thinks he's settled details and about to finalize an agreement when Principles come up again. The Western businessman needs a model that is descriptive rather than normative. This more accurate and more useful model is one that is "encompassing" rather than linear.

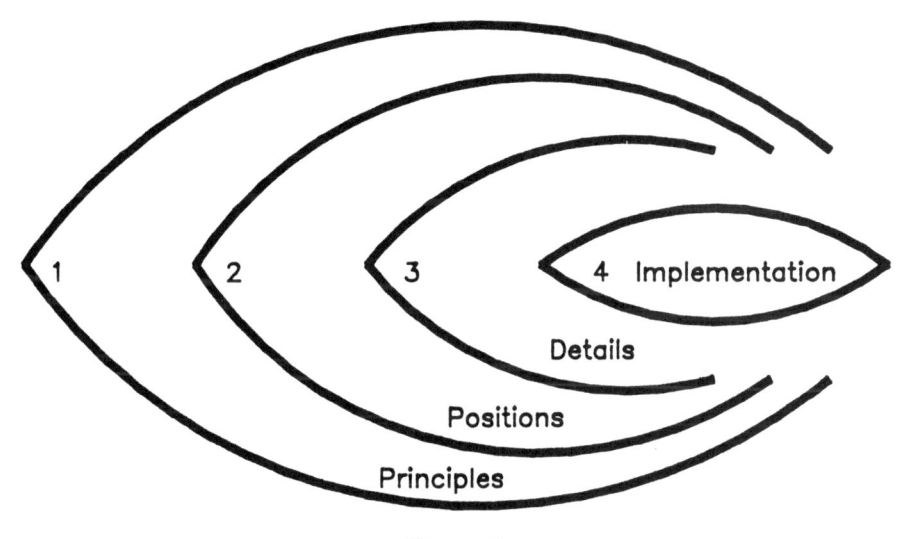

Figure 2
Stages in the Encompassing Model of Negotiation

In the encompassing model, the stages are still present, but it is obvious that they do not simply occur one after another. The most important stage, Defining Principles, envelopes all other stages. Progress comes from agreeing on basic terms. What is it about Defining Principles that makes it so important? The key word is "friendship" and it does not translate across the cultures.

IMPLEMENTATION

In their statements of principles, the Chinese stress friendship, helping, national development, growth, and the enhancement of the life of the Chinese people. Western guests tend to follow the lead of their hosts, repeat the principles, and thereby, appear to adopt the stated principles. They view the principles as equivalent to the "mission statements" of corporations—wonderful words that have little impact on day-to-day operations. They do not expect these good intentions to have significance for decisions such as plant location, employment policies, or sourcing.

The opening phase of negotiations not only establishes friendship as a principle, but also initiates a friendship relationship. To the Chinese, the word means a continuing relationship in which favors are exchanged. The exchanges are evidence of reliability, and provide a procedure for developing trust.

In traditional Chinese perspective, friends want to meet the needs of friends. Friendship means accepting their rules of the game, deferring to their priorities, accepting their definitions of need, and understanding any lapses in their performance of their part of the agreement.

Misunderstandings about the nature of friendship are critical to conflicts that have emerged. Western negotiators go through rituals designed to assert friendship (toasts, hosting and being hosted, exchange of gifts), but they are not prepared to take on the obligations of Chinese friendship. Even in the new anti-corruption atmosphere, some favors are to be extended. In particular, friends will not cause friends to lose face. This has operational impact on such issues as qualifications of employees (managerial and worker). A friend should not ask too many questions about the availability of the engineers, technicians, or financial specialists that are supposed to be available. A friend will not refuse to provide the latest technology just because he doesn't believe they need and/or can maintain it.

The key words in Stage II are honesty and compromise. Negotiators focus on facts and figures, give and take. But what if there are no real facts and figures? And what if "giving in" is losing face? The Chinese "know" that a friend will not cause a friend to lose face. What are the ethical dilemmas? The Westerner is being asked to overlook missing data—data that apply to his need for profit. The Westerner is being asked to do all the giving—and overlook his need for profit.

The key word in Stage III is agreement. To the Westerner, to agree is to settle principles and details and have a working document. To the Westerner, to agree is to have a contract, to have mutual commitment to what has been decided. To the Chinese, it is more complex. First, the infrastructure of contract law does not exist. And continually, there is friendship. A friend would not enforce some abstract principle on a friend who finds it impossible to perform as promised. Explanations should be accepted. For example, recent changes in policy may make it "necessary" for China not to implement some agreements. The Westerner should understand—after all he agreed to be a friend and he said he would support the development of the Chinese nation and the growth of the Chinese people.

The key word in Stage IV is fairness. As Westerners go to start up trade or establish the joint venture, they find themselves saying. "The Chinese are not fair." The Chinese deny this. They believe it is fair to ask you to hire and train more workers and to fulfill the traditional Chinese obligations to workers—food, housing, day care, education, clothing. It is fair to ask you to change the site to one more "needy."

Another critical misunderstanding at Stage IV may center on the definition of the goal. Western negotiation literature identifies two fundamental models of negotiation. The competitive model sees one's gains coming at the expense of the other. Both sides of the negotiation view their goals as mutually exclusive. This is a zero-sum, I-win-you-lose model. There is a limited amount of goods or services available and the winner will get his share at the expense of the loser.

A key element of the win-lose model is determining the other side's resistance point, the point beyond which that side won't go in negotiating the deal. The resistance point is based on a calculus of the utility one expects from the outcomes less the costs. Negotiation is a process of attempting to alter the other's resistance point by influencing his perception of utilities and costs.

EVALUATION

A big factor in any win-lose negotiation is information. Both sides need information about their own as well as the other's utilities, costs, and resistance point. Both sides seek to gain more information about their adversary and also attempt to hide or obscure their own resistance points. When Westerners look at Chinese negotiating behavior they see classic zero-sum tactics and impression management. The Chinese are thought to hoard information. They do much more listening than talking (Lubman, 1983). They are so unclear about their goals that they will literally change the topic of the negotiation in midcourse. They further screen their goals by obscuring the positions/relevance of the members of their negotiating team. They appear unwilling to reciprocate concessions. They draw attention to competitive offers and use dilatory tactics to reduce their adversary's resistance.

A second model of negotiations is integrative bargaining or joint problem solving. To achieve integrative bargaining, it is necessary to believe that joint effort will achieve a better solution for each side. Integrative bargaining is often called win-win because both sides get something they want from the agreement.

The Chinese have a cultural tendency to see interests as mutual, to insist both sides have a stake in a larger outcome. However, the Chinese perspective of mutual interests leads them to want to involve Westerners in the achievement of what Westerners often view as strictly Chinese outcomes.

The Chinese come into negotiations with a long-term perspective, expecting long-term involvement of the Western corporation. The negotiated settlement is only the beginning of negotiations to achieve the final goal. Negotiations under these circumstances tend to be rambling and diffuse. Westerners cannot play this game. They come to China to achieve specific and highly segmented goals. China is not the puzzle, but only one piece of a puzzle. The expectation of negotiators is that they can find the one piece they need and move on. Thus, they want to identify specific commitments and they expect adherence to these commitments. Similarly, they expect to adhere to their own commitments, but they seek no further involvement. To the Chinese, limited commitment is a violation of the principle of friendship and unethical conduct.

CONCLUSION

To enter commercial negotiations with the People's Republic of China today, Western representatives must first decide to cross a political-ethical barrier. They must decide that the benefits of low-cost labor, market potential, and/or "maintaining a presence" are more important than incidents of June 1989. Once this decision has been made, other ethical issues may also effect the progress of deal-making. Western efforts to accommodate the Chinese negotiation model can lead to significant ethical dilemmas and unsatisfactory business results. The lack of shared assumptions and meanings can turn Western efforts at accommodation into something bordering fraud in spite of (and maybe even because of) the best intentions.

REFERENCES/SOURCES

Banthin, J. and L. Stelzer. "Business Negotiations with the Chinese: Working Toward a Strategic Model." Paper presented to the annual meeting of the Academy of Management (New Orleans, August 1987). An introduction to and elaboration of the encompassing model of negotiation.

Fenwick, A. "Equity Joint Ventures in the People's Republic of China: An Assessment of the First Five Years." *The Business Lawyer* 40 (1985): 839-878. Emphasizes the evolving nature of joint venture law.

Fisher, R., and W. Ury. *Getting to Yes*. Boston: Houghton Mifflin, 1985. A classic discussion of bargaining strategies.

Grow, R. F. " Japanese and American Firms in China: Lessons of a New Market." *The Columbia Journal of World Business* 21 (1): 49-56, 1986. Focuses on the Chinese response to Western marketing efforts.

Hendryx, S. R. "The China Trade: Making the Deal Work." *Harvard Business Review* (July-August): 75-84, 1986. An optimistic view of the difficulties of doing business with the Chinese.

Ikle, F. C. *How Nations Negotiate*. New York: Harper and Row, 1964. Strategies and practices of international negotiations. Ranges from geo-politics to interpersonal relations.

Lewicki, R. J. and J. A. Litterer. *Negotiation*. Homewood, IL: Richard D. Irwin, Inc, 1985. An academic examination of bargaining and negotiation.

Lubman, S. B. " Negotiations in China." In *Communicating With China.* ed. R. Kapp, Chicago: Intercultural Press, 1983: 59-70. The insights of a lawyer with practical experiences negotiating with the Chinese.

———. *Chinese Commercial Negotiating Style*. Cambridge MA: Oelgeschlager, Gunn & Hain Publishers, 1982. A study of Chinese negotiating behavior that emphasizes psychological and cultural factors.

Solomon, R. *Chinese Political Negotiating Behavior*. Washington, DC: The Rand Corporation, 1985. A model of Sino-American negotiating based on observation of the U.S. opening to China during the Nixon presidency.

Weiss S. and W. Stripp. *Negotiating With Foreign Businesspersons: An Introduction for Americans With Propositions on Six Cultures*. New York: New York University, 1984. Faculty of Business Administration, Working Paper

Series. Empirically based descriptions of "dimensions" of international negotiating behavior.

Dr. Joanna M. Banthin
New Jersey Institute of Technology

Dr. Leigh Stelzer
Seton Hall University

Dr. Joanna Banthin is an Associate Professor of Management in the School of Industrial Management at the New Jersey Institute of Technology. Her major teaching and research fields are international business, technology transfer, and business-government relations. Her current research is on U.S.-Chinese trade. Dr. Banthin has been in China as a teacher, researcher, and consultant. She has lectured at the University for International Business and Economics and maintains a research relationship with Beijing Polytechnic University. She earned her Ph.D. at the University of Michigan; she has also done graduate work in international economics and international finance at the Fletcher School of Law and Diplomacy and the Massachusetts Institute of Technology.

Dr. Leigh Stelzer's primary research field is Sino-American commercial relationships. He has published articles in a number of journals and presented papers at the Academy of Management, International Academy of Management and Marketing, and other national and regional meetings. Dr. Stelzer has been in the Peoples Republic of China and Hong Kong as a teacher, researcher, consultant, and member of a State of New Jersey trade Delegation. In 1986 and 1988, Dr. Stelzer taught at one of China's premier business schools, The University for International Business and Economics, in Beijing. Dr. Stelzer has published extensively in the field of public policy and business-government relations.

Profiling Your Negotiating Counterpart

OVERVIEW

Most people who travel overseas for their organizations participate, on a regular basis, in cross-cultural negotiations of one form or another. In fact, research indicates that today more than 50% of the international manager's time is spent negotiating.

Negotiation is a process in which two or more entities come together to discuss common and conflicting interests in order to reach an agreement of mutual benefit. In international business negotiations, cultural dimensions have an impact on every aspect of this process. Therefore, in preparing for and analyzing an international negotiation, it is essential to review these dimensions in order to better understand one's counterpart, his strategy and values.

Negotiators from different countries are neither unreasonably complex nor completely similar to businesspeople in one's own country. Those from other countries have a different past and a different present in terms of political system, education, business strategies, negotiating protocol and customs, as well as values and approaches to business relationships. These differences, however, have a profound effect on the negotiating process.

A successful international negotiation is a "win-win situation" in which both parties gain. Many factors effect its outcome, such as how consistent one's actions are with one's counter part's values, the approach used, the negotiators' attitudes, and the negotiating methods employed. International negotiation comprises all of these factors.

EXAMPLES

International negotiations occur when individuals from different cultures try to reach agreements on issues of mutual interest. A U.S. businessperson purchasing pipe from Japan is involved in international business negotiations. Consultants working with the United Nations to develop training materials for use in Pakistan are involved in negotiations. Government officials in Canada determining French/English legislation are involved in international negotiations.

Preparation for successful international negotiation requires a careful assessment of one's foreign counterpart. For example, do Japanese negotiate with the same strategies and approaches as Americans do? Mostly, they do not. Are Chinese, French or German negotiators selected by their organizations to participate in negotiations for the same reasons as Americas are? In part, yes.

Cultural dimensions set the tone for international negotiation. The French seem to consider negotiation as a grand debate; at the conclusion, well-reasoned solutions are found. Brazilians expect socializing before getting down to business and prefer behind-the-scenes bargaining. Russians tend to base their arguments on ideals and see little benefit in developing relationships.

BENEFITS

In a special briefing on the "Challenge of a Changing World Economy: What Will It Mean for Multinational Companies?" the Center for International Business in Dallas stated:

In only 30 years U.S. economic performance at home and abroad has gone from a rating of A+ to C-. . .simultaneously the global economy has become more integrated and interdependent. . .we are forced to deal with problems that truly can only be measured in global terms.

American negotiators who wish to improve U.S. performance must adequately prepare for business transactions overseas. They must become more skillful in the international marketplace by learning to be more effective negotiators. Through better U.S. negotiation, one could expect the following results:

1. The U.S. percentages of world gross national product should increase as fast as those of the 50 largest foreign companies.

2. The overall competitive position of U.S. firms in international markets should improve.

3. One should see an increased demand for U.S. exports.

Understanding the American negotiating styles and strategies, along with those of potential counterparts is a first step toward improving U.S. performance.

A 1986 questionnaire sent to a number of large corporations asked what kinds of programs, seminars, and consultations they would support. An overwhelming number of respondents reported a need for improved negotiating skills. Furthermore, 74% said they would support a negotiating training program designed for dealing with foreign governments and businesses. There are a number of international consulting organizations that offer excellent negotiating training programs.

IMPLEMENTATION

Successful international negotiation should begin with a careful assessment of one's foreign counterpart and a thorough assessment of oneself.

For American negotiators preparing to participate in international business negotiations, a first step is to become aware of the characteristics that they bring to the negotiating table. This combination of characteristics has been described as the "American John Wayne" style of negotiating. Some of these American negotiating traits are:

1. I can go it alone. Many U.S. negotiators seem to believe they can handle any negotiating situation by themselves, and they are outnumbered in most negotiating situations.

2. Just call me John. Americans value informality and equality in human relations. They try to make people feel comfortable by playing down status distinctions.

3. Pardon my French. Americans aren't very talented at speaking foreign languages.

4. Check with the home office. American negotiators get upset when halfway through a negotiation the other side says, "I'll have to check with the home office." The implication is that the decision makers are not present.

5. Get to the point. Americans don't like to beat around the bush and want to get to the heart of the matter quickly.

6. Lay your cards on the table. Americans expect honest information at the bargaining table.

7. Don't just sit there, speak up. Americans don't deal well with silence during negotiations.

8. Don't take no for an answer. Persistence is highly valued by Americans and is part of the deeply ingrained competitive spirit that manifests itself in every aspect of American life.

9. One thing at time. Americans usually attack a complex negotiation task sequentially; that is, they separate the issues and settle them one at a time.

10. A deal is a deal. When Americans make an agreement and give their word, they expect to honor the agreement no matter what the circumstances.

But what do these American negotiators find across the table? Most often different characteristics. The following list offers important variables to consider in international negotiations.

1. The negotiating process. In the U.S., negotiation is seen as a competitive process of offers and counter-offers. In some cultures, negotiation is more a wide-ranging discussion and agreement takes place rather subtly.

2. Negotiator selection. U.S. negotiators are chosen principally for their technical expertise and their negotiating experience. In other parts of the world, selection is based not only on the negotiator's experience, but also on status and personal qualities.

3. Significance of issues. In international negotiation, typically there are substantive issues such as price and delivery schedule to be discussed. But relationship issues, such as compatibility of styles as well as procedural issues must also be considered. Some cultures emphasize

relationships first, whereas Americans tend to want to "get down to business."

4. Role of protocol. The extent to which rules concerning dress, titles and other formalities are adhered to varies from culture to culture. Generally, American negotiators are considered informal by their counterparts, whereas many foreign negotiators consider protocol extremely important.

5. High or low context communication. Every culture uses words to communicate. However, low context cultures such as Americans value frankness and interpret communication on its face value. Other cultures value ambiguity, and meaning is found not only in words, but in reading between the lines.

6. Methods of persuasion. Negotiators attempt to influence each other to accept certain viewpoints. But the way one supports an argument will vary across cultures. U.S. negotiators tend to rely on facts and are often surprised to find that their foreign counterparts rely on ideology, dogma, tradition, or emotion.

7. Role of the individual. Individualism and grand performance are valued by Americans, French, and Swedes. It is not so prized by Asians in general or by Chinese and Japanese in particular. In these cultures, the group is paramount.

8. Establishing trust. Business relationships thrive on trust. But trust is established in different ways. Americans tend to assume an environment of trust until the other party's behavior gives them reason not to. Negotiators from other cultures believe that trust is earned, or that trust is established by building personal relationships.

9. Risk-taking. All negotiators are risk-takers, because there are always unknowns and changes. However, one's propensity to take risks is also determined, in part, by culture. Americans tend to take risks in negotiations more readily than their foreign counterparts.

10. Use of time. For Americans, time is to be saved, spent, used and valued as money. Others see time as a rather plentiful commodity, and believe that detailed plans cannot affect the course of inevitable events.

11. Decision making system. Americans tend to make decisions quickly and they are made at high levels in an organization. The Japanese ringi system is slow and involves all those concerned with the issue. In France, decision making is highly centralized and in any organization, decisions are made only by those who have clear authority and power.

12. Forms of agreement. Americans like written, legally binding contracts which don't change except by mutual agreement. In contrast, some foreign negotiators prefer liberal contracts which provide general guidelines for determining future details. Others simply place their trust in verbal agreements.

CONCLUSION

The foreword of the 1984 report entitled "What We Don't Know Can Hurt Us," prepared by the American Council on Education by C. Peter McGrath, states:

> We Americans no longer have the luxury of time and distance to justify our lack of concerted attention to the serious and dangerous lag—a

shortfall in our international competence.

With the global interdependent economy, it has become imperative to understand our world trade partners. The question that arises now is what can be done to give negotiators a more thorough knowledge of foreign counterparts. First, we must recognize that the U.S. negotiators' lack of knowledge means a loss of business. A remedy is to provide negotiators with effective programs involving briefings and cross-cultural communication. Through proper training, U.S. negotiators can master the necessary intercultural skills to effectively manage international business relations.

John F. Kennedy said, "Let us not be blind to our differences—but let us also direct attention to our common interests." Skillful international negotiators work toward mutual benefits, recognizing and managing effectively cultural differences.

REFERENCES/SOURCES

Casse, Pierre. *Training for the Cross-Cultural Mind.* 2d ed. Washington, DC: Society for Intercultural Education, Training and Research, 1981. Presents ideas and exercises to use in cross-cultural training programs.

Cohen, Herb. *You Can Negotiate Anything.* Secaucus, NJ: Lyle Stuart, 1980. A popular, easy book to read with many examples and illustrations.

Fisher, Glen. *International Negotiations: A Cross-Cultural Perspective.* Chicago: Intercultural Press, 1980. An excellent overview of some of the cross-cultural factors involved in international business negotiations.

Fisher, Roger and William Ury. *Getting to Yes.* Boston: Houghton Mifflin, and New York: Penguin, 1981. Discusses a strategy for developing win-win business negotiations.

Graham, John L. and Roy A. Herberger. "Negotiators Abroad—Don't Shoot from the Hip." *Harvard Business Review* (July/August 1983): 160-168. Very informative for Americans to read and reflect on the points presented in this short paper.

Harris, Philip R. and Robert T. Moran. *Managing Cultural Differences*. 2d ed. Houston, TX: Gulf, 1987. A classic text widely used in business schools and by human resource managers.

Moran, Robert T. *Getting Your Yen's Worth: How to Negotiate with Japan, Inc.* Houston, TX: Gulf, 1985. A practical guide for negotiating with Japanese businessmen.

Pye, Lucian. *Chinese Commercial Negotiating Style*. Cambridge, MA: Oelgeschlager, Gunn & Hain, 1982. A practical guide for persons negotiating with Japanese businessmen.

Weiss, Stephen E. and William Stripp. "Negotiating With Foreign Businesspersons: An Introduction for Americans With Propositions On Six Cultures." New York University, Graduate School of Business Administration, December 31, 1984.

Films

Doing Business in Japan: Negotiating a Contract. Vision Associates, 665 5th Avenue, New York, NY 10022 (212-935-1830). Illustrates the issues of international negotiations through the inability of American and Japanese negotiating teams to comprehend and deal with cultural differences. The film also examines other subtle issues involved in negotiating.

The Going International Film Series, by Lewis Griggs and Lennie Copeland, 411 15th Avenue, San Francisco, CA 94118 (415-668-4200). Offers six presentations that present a variety of international negotiating situations and demonstrates how a negotiating team's inability to understand and manage cultural differences can result in failure.

Dr. Robert T. Moran
American Graduate School
of International Management

Dr. Robert T. Moran is an Organizational Management Consultant in cross-cultural training, organizational development, and international resource management. He is Director of the Program in Cross-Cultural Communication, and Professor of International Studies at the American School of International Management. As an international consultant, he has designed and conducted seminars for Aramco, Arthur Andersen & Co., AT&T, General Motors, Honeywell, Intel, Miles, Exxon, Volvo Truck Corporation, and Singapore Airlines, among many others.

Cultural Keys to Successful Negotiating

OVERVIEW

With more companies "going international" to enhance their profitability and expand their market base, negotiating the sales contract, purchase agreement, or joint venture is a key element in determining the success of the operation. All too often, business executives fail to take the steps necessary to ensure success. Thus, the negotiation process ends in failure, or an agreement is reached without one or both parties understanding fully the reasons why. By sound planning in advance, ensuring that all documents are translated correctly, and a clear understanding of the environment in which the company will be dealing, what might have been a failure will turn to a successful long-term agreement for the benefit of both parties concerned.

EXAMPLES

While there are many reasons for failure in the negotiation process, the three most common errors occur in terms of culture, language, and environment. While all three play a very important role in the success of business ventures beyond national boundaries, all too often business executives take them for granted by saying that "business is business throughout the world." Perhaps some illustrations can best explain the significance of these three elements.

A major U.S. manufacturer began negotiations in 1984 with a Japanese company to sell its industrial products. While this was not the first occasion for the firm to do business in Japan, it was the first major opportunity to sell more than a $100 million dollars worth of its products. Furthermore, it was the first time that this major American firm had dealt with their Japanese counterpart, one of the top ten corporations in Japan. Negotiations proceeded for over two years resulting in many trips by the American executives to Japan with each trip adding to their frustration because negotiations seemed to be getting nowhere. They understood that the Japanese wanted their product, which was top ranked in the world market, pricing seemed to be satisfactory and the American firm could deliver on time. Why, the corporate staff wondered, could that contract not be signed? The Japanese said they needed more time to think it over.

The problem was rooted in cultural differences. The American team had been composed of some engineers with product expertise, the director of international marketing, the local sales representative and a staff of attorneys to see that the contract conformed with U.S. and Japanese law. The American team was accustomed to quick decisions and "doing business the American way." In short, they failed to recognize that one of the keys to success in doing business in Japan is doing things the Japanese way.

When the U.S. company was about to give up, after spending over a $1 million dollars in developing plans, travel and expenses, and executive time, they turned to an outside consultant. Getting things "on track" was a very simple procedure as soon as top management could be convinced of the necessity of taking a different approach.

First, the team composition was changed. The new team consisted of the Chief Executive Officer and Chairman of the Corporation, one senior engineer, the Director of International Sales and Marketing, and one attorney. In addition, the Americans retained their own qualified interpreter who understood Japanese custom, Japanese business, and the engineering technology. Secondly, instead of going to Japan for just a few days, it was predetermined that they were willing to spend at least two weeks, if necessary, in order to insure success of the negotiations process. Reaching this agreement was not easy because the American CEO stated that he could not be gone for that long; however, given the size of the potential order and the firm's substantial investment, there was little choice. Third, they decided that they would do business "Japanese style" to the best of their abilities.

Since this was the first meeting of the American and Japanese CEOs, a very formal exchange took place at the headquarters of the Japanese corporation. After introductions were made and business cards exchanged, the two senior executives exchanged pleasantries for about fifteen minutes over a cup of tea and began to become acquainted. At the conclusion of their brief meeting, the Japanese host invited the American team to have dinner at a Japanese restaurant that evening. During the course of the dinner, no business was discussed as the Chief Executive Officers and other corporate officials got to know one another better.

The American team's CEO responded by inviting the Japanese delegation to dinner the following evening and stated that his team would like to have the opportunity to see some of the sights of the Tokyo area, indicating their interest in learning more about Japan. When they met for dinner the following evening, after their tour, the American CEO commented on his impressions of Tokyo and some of the historic sights that he had seen.

This approach impressed the Japanese team and the following day discussions were begun on the sales contract, which had been stagnating for two years. The negotiation process continued for two days, followed by a weekend when the Japanese hosts invited the American team to visit the ancient city of Kyoto and to golf. On Monday the negotiation process resumed, and business discussions were preceded by an informal discussion of the sights that had been seen in Kyoto. Everything proceeded smoothly and the following day the contract was signed. The Japanese team then hosted a dinner party to celebrate their new working relationship. Toasts were made to further business in the future.

The moral of the story is simply that culture plays a large role in the negotiation process. Nothing in the contract was changed from what had been originally proposed; however, there was a meeting of the minds, a mutual respect developed between the two Chief Executive Officers, and a personal relationship evolved in addition to the business relationship.

Language also impedes successful negotiations. An American company wished to enter into a management contract with an Eastern European firm for the production of parts that would be assembled into a product being produced both in Europe and the United States. The reason for selecting the Eastern European firm was that costs of production were much less, and by buying parts in that country, it would open the opportunity for the U.S. firm to sell some of its other products there. The Eastern European firm lacked foreign exchange, and by selling to the American firm they would be able to use the foreign exchange earned to buy the needed equipment.

Everything seemed to move smoothly and the contract was signed. However, since the American company did not have its own interpreter, the negotiators relied upon the one provided by the Eastern European company. Problems arose as plans for production began to progress. The Eastern European firm had interpreted "appropriate technology," which the American company agreed to provide, to include sending their engineers and production personnel to the United States for training. Furthermore, they also interpreted the term to include all future technology that might be applied to the product. The end result was that the American firm, if it wished to continue the contract, would be responsible for travel, training and all expenses of those being trained, as well as providing future technologies at no cost.

Language problems are particularly troublesome in China. Often negotiations end in failure because U.S. executives have not translated their brochures, specifications, and other data into Chinese in advance of their trip. Secondly, all too often they fail to obtain a qualified interpreter who understands business terminology and will act as their representative. Rather, they depend upon the interpreters provided by the Chinese company, or they hire a local interpreter on their own. While these individuals may speak English well, they may be unfamiliar with business and business terminology. As a result, misunderstandings occur and the negotiation process fails.

The third factor is that of the environment in which the business arrangement is to take place. In China—an extreme example—immense bureaucracy and many layers of administration retard the progress of negotiations. Not only does the local company concerned have to approve, but it may have to get local authority as well. After this is gained, it may be referred to a ministry in Beijing. All of this, of course, takes time, patience, and an understanding of how business is done in China. Furthermore, the Chinese have not yet become acclimated to do business "western style" where decisions are made expeditiously.

Another problem which also occurs in China is that the company will not have the foreign exchange allocation to make the purchase. Again, foreign firms often follow-up on inquiries that are received when, in fact, the Chinese are just looking for information and possible sources from which to acquire goods should they acquire an exchange allocation. Again, time and money are wasted; appropriate inquiries in advance could have put some reality into the high expectations for quick and easy sales that cannot materialize.

BENEFITS

The benefits that result from having knowledge of the culture, language requirements, and environment are significant. First, companies should do their homework on the economic, social, political, technological, and business environment of the country with which they wish to do business. Even if there is political and economic instability, it does not mean that business cannot be conducted. On the contrary, if what you are trying to sell or undertake is of importance to the country, the prospects for your company can be excellent.

The same is true concerning the cultural environment. Whether in Latin America, the Middle East or Asia, most individuals are very proud of their country and their culture. Not only do you need to know how business is conducted, but you need social graces, keeping in mind that you are the foreigner and being a good guest is indeed important. With this knowledge and approach, your chances of success will be improved considerably.

IMPLEMENTATION

The following steps are suggested for the company wishing to negotiate a business deal in a foreign country for the first time. Not only are these steps good business procedures, they are also good common sense. They can be divided into actions to take before, during, and after the negotiations process.

Prior to beginning negotiations, the company should obtain a good understanding of the firm with which they wish to do business, including the scope of its operations, the backgrounds of key personnel, and the business environment within that country. This can be done by contacting other firms that have had successful experience in that country, the Department of Commerce Desk Officer, and a specialist who is familiar with the culture and environment. In preparing for negotiations, particularly in a developing country, the firm should be prepared to negotiate a part of the deal in other products as well as more cash. A third important factor is to obtain the services of a qualified interpreter in the event that no one in the company has language fluency. Finally, the negotiating team should be selected carefully, keeping in mind how the other side will view the team's makeup. Both the level and function of each team member should be carefully considered.

During the negotiation process, cultural etiquette must be observed. While your host knows that you are a foreigner, and will overlook some blunders, major blunders must be averted. After all, being a good guest is an important factor in the success of the negotiation process. The team leader (usually the CEO if a small firm) needs to assure that the appropriate procedures are followed as the negotiation process continues.

As follow-up after the contract is signed, you should maintain contact with the original negotiators. The informal process includes sending the appropriate greeting cards for various occasions. While Americans exchange holiday greetings at the end of the year, much of Asia celebrate the Chinese New Year. While few firms would make the blunder of sending a Hanukkah card to a Moslem executive, many Christians will send a Christmas card when it just is not appropriate. However, sending a Chinese a New Year greeting card or a "Year-End" card to a Japanese is appreciated.

EVALUATION

At each step of the negotiation process, management should evaluate what they have done, how it applies, and where there is need for additional work. Priorities must always be kept in mind, while realizing that the timetable for the negotiation process may need to be extended as circumstances dictate. Each situation is unique, and the procedures that apply in one country do not necessarily transfer to another, just as there may be differences between one company and another within the same country. Consequently, a continual evaluation before, during and after the negotiation process is essential to positive business relationships.

APPLICATIONS TO SMALL BUSINESS

The procedures outlined for successful negotiations are extremely significant to the small business enterprise. Many small and medium-sized firms have not optimized their potential for dealing in the international business arena. Often it is because they lack the contacts or the personnel able to develop the contacts for them. On the other hand, there are many opportunities internationally that can be even more profitable than business at home. However, most small firms have limited budgets and cannot afford to make big mistakes. Consequently, if the firm does not have international expertise, retaining a good consultant to assist in the negotiation process can be a very worthwhile investment.

CONCLUSION

Planning for the negotiation process is the most crucial step that management can take in ensuring the successful end result when negotiating cross culturally. While it cannot guarantee success in all cases, it certainly can minimize the prospects for failure. Again, understanding the culture, the language, and the business environment is essential.

REFERENCES/SOURCES

A major reference for negotiations is the International Negotiation Institute, Inc., located at 301 North Harrison Street, Building B, Suite 347, Princeton, New Jersey 08540. Telephone (609) 921-1658. Resources available from the International Negotiation Institute include the following services and products:

- Training programs in negotiations
- Developing and implementing the personal computer based Negotiation Experience Information Bank
- Assistance in preparing for negotiations

- Multi-media products including audiotapes, videotapes, and printed material on various aspects of the negotiation process.

Alder, N. J. et al. "Business Negotiations in Canada, Mexico and the U.S." *Journal of Business Research* 15 (October 1989): 411-29.

Fisher, Glen. *International Negotiations: A Cross-Cultural Perspective.* Chicago: International Press, 1980.

Graham, John L. and Roy A. Herberger. "Negotiators Abroad—Don't Shoot from the Hip." *Harvard Business Review* 14 (July/August 1983): 47-61.

———. *Smart Bargaining: Doing Business With the Japanese.* Cambridge, MA: Ballinger Publishing Company, 1984.

McCall, J. B. "Negotiating a Foot into the Chinese Door." *Management Decisions* 21, 2 (1983): 3-13.

McCreary, Don R. *Japanese-U.S. Business Negotiations: A Cross-Cultural Study.* New York: Praeger, 1986.

Mendosa, E. "Conduct When Negotiating Overseas." *Business Credit* 90 (June 1988): 26.

Moran, Robert T. *Getting Your Yen's Worth: How To Negotiate With Japan, Inc.* Houston: Gulf, 1985.

Pye, Lucian. *Chinese Commercial Negotiating Style.* Cambridge, MA: Oelgeschlager, Gunn and Hain, 1983.

Ware, James P. *Bargaining Strategies: Collaborative Versus Competitive Approaches.* Boston, MA: President and Fellows of Harvard College. Distributed by HBS Case Services, Harvard Business School, 1980.

Yao, E. L. "Venturing Through China's Open Door." *Business Marketing* 73 (February 1988): 63-64.

Zimmerman, Mark. *How To Do Business With The Japanese.* New York: Random House, 1984.

Dr. Phillip D. Grub
Business Consultant and Professor Emeritus
The George Washington University

Dr. Phillip Grub is a consultant on Asian business, particularly Vietnam, China, Indonesia and South Korea. He holds the rank of Professor Emeritus from the School of Business and Public Management and the George Washington University, and was also the holder of the Aryamehr Chair in multinational management. He has worked in Asia since 1955 when he was a journalist in Japan. Throughout his career in academe he has authored or co-authored 16 books, over 300 articles, and numerous case studies, monographs, and working papers. His articles have appeared in a variety of publications including *The Wall Street Journal, The Wall Street Journal Weekly, The International Economy Magazine, Business Horizons* and numerous other U. S. publications, as well as in publications in Europe, Asia and South America.

Cultural Differences on Sexual Harassment in the Workplace

OVERVIEW

As local, national, and international companies around the world expand markets or globalize their operations, the personnel issues related to gender relations will have an ever greater impact on market success, productivity, morale and profit. The financial and relational toll taken by complaints of sexual harassment is a very real concern for foreign or domestic businesses operating in the USA, and is an increasing concern globally. Sexual harassment in the workplace has become one of the major personnel issues of the 1990s with financial, personnel, and opportunity costs that can be staggering.

By 1993, 90% of the Fortune 500 companies had reported complaints of sexual harassment by employees. The costs of dealing with such complaints are estimated at $6.7 million to the average large company. Some estimates put future cost to USA businesses at $200 million dollars per year over the next five years.

The costs in human terms are substantial. Employee morale, as well as job effectiveness, is reduced. Mental anguish, depression, and stress-related problems cause staff turnover, absenteeism, and low levels of productivity. The working environment is eroded as relationships between male and female coworkers are diminished by the loss of trust and respect.

Globalizing companies seeking to generate business abroad have real costs and opportunity costs resulting from ruined client relations, broken negotiations, lost sales, etc. because of the reaction of foreigners to what they perceive as sexual harassment in the host culture. The ensuing anger, distrust, frustration and harmful sexist stereotypes lessen global market opportunities.

The issue of sexual harassment in the workplace is not peculiar to the U.S., but is of international concern. Recently, the Commission on the European Community created a Recommendation which was sent to participating governments. The Recommendation addressed gender related workplace issues, including sexual harassment, calling it an "invisible" violation of worker's rights which occurs far more extensively than generally recognized due to underreporting and fear of career damage. The Recommendation's goal was to facilitate the process for defining sexual harassment and for creating corporate and private sector laws that allow for remedy by harassment victims and hold individuals and corporations responsible and liable.

In most Asian countries, sexual harassment is not considered a major workplace issue by policy makers, but women's groups are working to enhance social awareness and change social and business behavior. In countries such as Taiwan, groups are working to pass discrimination laws. In others, such as Japan, labor standard laws and equal employment opportunity laws exist and recently have been used to contest incidences of discrimination. For example, in 1992, a female employee of a small publishing company was the first person to win a sexual harassment case in Japan.

In the U.S., Scandinavia and some European countries, policies on sexual harassment relate to both women and men. However, in most countries the issue is concerned, almost exclusively, with the treatment of women; therefore definitions and policy reflect this cultural fact. In discussing this topic, it is important to note that individuals in a given culture will often act outside the cultural norms, therefore one must be careful about turning cultural generalities into stereotypes.

Cultural Differences on Sexual Harassment in the Workplace

What is sexual harassment?

Until 1976, a label for the concept of sexual harassment did not exist, but the reality of sexual harassment did. Without a means to identify the experience, women were unable to articulate the ordeal encountered by many in the workplace. With the legal substantiation of the concept, groups, particularly in the U.S., were able to capture public opinion and reshape public policy toward defining harassment as socially and legally unacceptable. In the past two decades, sexual harassment has been identified as a growing social and legal concern for women and men in almost all societies around the globe.

Sexual harassment is defined, to a large degree, by the social and cultural mores of individual societies and nations. Common to all cultural definitions of sexual harassment is the perception of the abuse of power by one in authority. Power can be derived from superior position, physical strength, or aggressiveness in asserting of personality. However, cultural definitions often vary as to what constitutes an abuse of power, particularly when definitions include more than misuse of superior position.

In the United States, work related sexual harassment is generally defined as verbal or physical conduct of a sexual nature that relates to: a condition for being offered or keeping employment, being rewarded or punished in employment decisions, and interfering with work performance or creating a hostile working environment. Most harassment complaints are a result of gender related verbal misconduct that is emotionally threatening or sexually humiliating, creating a hostile environment. In clarifying the physical and verbal conduct that determines a "hostile environment," the U.S. Supreme Court, in *Harris v. Forklift Systems Inc.*, cited frequency of the conduct; its severity; if it is physically threatening or humiliating; and if it unreasonably interferes with work performance as legally accountable. Significantly, verbal behaviors, as well as physical acts, that are perceived by the recipient as physically or emotionally harmful, and affecting job performance, are illegal and subject to due process.

In Europe, Community regulatory and legal commissions, and not individual countries, are pushing the impetus for change in this area. In the 1992 Report on discrimination and sexual harassment, the EC developed a related code of practice. Defining it broadly, sexual harassment involves unwanted direct physical, verbal or nonverbal conduct, as well as conduct that ridicules or intimidates employees on the basis of their gender. *This definition moves well beyond the traditional European perspective in which sexual harassment is understood as pressure upon employees to provide sexual favors in return for job benefits.* In addition, the European Court has ruled that EC directives regarding discrimination and sexual harassment are binding on member nations, regardless of their internal rulings. In spite of this, there is wide disparity in treatment of women in the workplace among member nations.

In most Asian countries, with some exceptions, women are more recent entrants into the business community. Therefore, traditional, and strongly held cultural views on the subservient role and place of women in society still dominate business expectations and are only recently being challenged. The concept of sexual harassment has been viewed in terms of inappropriate forced physical conduct. Women's groups are working to create an expanded understanding of the nature of sexual harassment and substantiate its cultural existence, develop social policy that condemns it, and create legal definitions, as well as legal restrictions, on its practice.

Why is sexual harassment perceived as a social "problem" in some cultures and not others?

Comments and behaviors considered to be sexually abusive in one culture may not be considered so in another. A culture's perceptions of what constitutes harassment have little to do with economic development and should not be judged as such. They are derived from the past and current cultural realities of each society. It is important that one suspend judgment of gender relations, roles and related behaviors until one understands the social influences affecting the behavior. What is considered to be harassment may be a compliment in a given culture. What one "feels" in an encounter may not be what was "meant."

Understanding the nature of sexual harassment goes beyond a set of legal or social definitions because it is a behavioral response to the dimensions of such cultural values as power, equality/hierarchy, dependence, individuality/collectiveness, fairness, gender roles, and the importance of interactional/relational context. Therefore, understanding different cultural perceptions means also appreciating the application of such values. One can look to Hofstede's work on dimensions of national culture and Hall's model of culture contexts to give valuable insights into why different views exist on what constitutes harassment across cultures.

Three basic differences can be identified among cultures as to what comprises sexual harassment in the workplace:

1. Whether harassment is limited to physical conduct.
2. What constitutes verbal harassment.
3. Whether one can freely seek redress within some form of due process.

The first two differences exist on a continuum from flirtation to abuse.

Most cultures agree that threat of physical force for sexual favors is aberrant behavior. However, in certain cultures the power inherent in one's business or social position entitles one to privileges of physical contact that more equalitarian cultures might not accept as appropriate.

An insight into why verbal harassment is such a significant issue in the U.S. is given through application of Hall's concept of high and low context cultures. As a low context culture, words carry a great deal of power and are of primary importance in an interaction. Americans look to words for validation of ideas, actions and even the self. As independent, equal individuals, relationships with others are created through words and subsequent actions. Words give meaning and reality when spoken. Therefore, the power of the misuse of words must be protected against. On the other hand, in high context cultures, which are more hierarchical and socially interdependent, who one is, and what one does, carries more significance in an interaction than the meaning of the words spoken. Though words are important, the greater part of the weight in an interaction is carried in what exists in the interaction's context, i.e. who is talking, how they are expressing themselves, the relationship to the hearer, etc. Self-validation and validation by others is more from one's social position.

EXAMPLES

Asia

Asian cultures view sexual harassment in terms of physical abuse of power. Traditionally, males have held the superior position in the culture and carried the authority and power in the workplace. Power has its responsibilities, but also its privileges, depending on the social position of the female employee. Persistence in physical and verbal attention is commonly experienced by female workers. Sexual harassment in the workplace is rarely made public because public accusations would bring shame on the women's family. Women are still often seen as provoking the attention they receive, rather than the victims. The most common response to persistent unwanted attention is to quit the job. In countries such as Thailand and the Philippines, women involved in family business are given the same professional treatment as males.

Foreign women are usually treated with the respect due their position in the home company. However, respectful treatment of women and their ability to make a deal may not be the same thing, especially for foreign businessmen who do not have international experience. Gender may not be a disadvantage in international companies that are accustomed to dealing with women.

Europe

European countries are not uniform in their perceptions of what comprises sexual harassment. In France, Italy and Spain there is no differentiation between a business woman and woman as sensual human being. In other words, women can expect to receive compliments and be recognized for their sexual differences. In Italy and Spain, there is a high tolerance for flirtation and social banter in the workplace. Many consider flirtation to be a game in which, if nothing is ventured, nothing is gained. These comments and behaviors are not considered inappropriate, in fact a women might be insulted if it does not occur to an appropriate degree. This is why an American woman working in France can complain of harassment, while her French female coworker would respond that there is no sexual harassment in France. However, physical contact or impolite verbal or nonverbal sexual comments would be considered sexual harassment. Harassment was made illegal in France in 1992.

In Germany, laws protect against harassment, but definitions of it are still largely unformed. In business, the glass ceiling exists, as well as discrepancies in pay and opportunity. Few women are in upper management, but remain in support roles. The traditional expectations about women and the home are strong. However, foreign women working in Germany can expect similar treatment as their male counterparts, based on position and expertise, and their appropriate behavior.

Scandinavians have a strong equalitarian cultural tradition. Definitions for harassment are similar to the U.S. and such actions are illegal and socially inappropriate. In business, behavioral expectations are similar for men and women.

English culture is male dominated and, depending on the industry, so is the business culture. Women are rare in upper management and usually serve in support positions. However, harassment laws do exist and harassment of a sexual nature is considered bad taste. Mild forms of harassment such as subtle remarks and discussion of non-professional topics may occur, but English men would not consider this as harassment. Professional behavior by both genders is expected and respected.

Latin America

Latin America cultures are male dominated and hierarchical. Women are viewed, not as subservient, but as special and needing protection. Thus, there is a high degree of respect afforded women, especially those of higher social standing. Like the Latin countries of Europe, the business woman is not seen as distinct from her sexuality and is afforded the appropriate displays of respect and compliments expected in the culture. In the workplace, sexual harassment occurs with women in subordinate positions, but there are effective and appropriate means for women to protect themselves and discourage such attention. There are few laws regarding sexual harassment, as its definitions are just now being created within Latin American countries. It should be noted that Latin America is not uniform in its views on sexual harassment. Countries such as Chile have growing numbers of women in business, and have adopted legal and social sanctions against any form of sexual harassment. Foreign business women can expect the attention and compliments of a sexual nature, but this is not inconsistent being treated as a professional. However, reacting negatively, or responding too positively to such attentions will harm one's credibility.

United States

Men from Latin countries in Europe and the Americas often complain that they are afraid to compliment a women in the U.S. because of a concern for accusations of sexual harassment. They are exaggerating the risk, but the comment points up some important issues about perceptions of sexual harassment that vary across cultures.

In the U.S., equality of treatment is a key concept. If one is to get ahead on individual merit, then fairness in action and opportunity are essential. Language and behaviors that are traditionally identified with indicating or reenforcing the subordination of women, and thus undermining of equality and independence, are inappropriate. If used with frequency, they are considered to be sexual harassment. Social pleasantries do not constitute harassment, unless they are actively discouraged, suggestive, or sexually demeaning.

The independence of American women and men is also indicated by the fact that unwanted touching can be viewed as harassing. In most cultures, touching is either an act of intimacy or demonstration of superior position. The former is inappropriate in the workplace, and the latter is appropriate only if men and women are touched similarly, such as a superior touching the back of a subordinate to usher her out of the elevator.

BENEFITS

When a company utilizes the knowledge that cultural differences exist in acceptable or unacceptable gender oriented behavior, management can be more effective 1) in preparing company representatives traveling abroad to appropriately perceive and productively handle situations that arise, thereby reducing possible risks in developing foreign relations, and 2) in anticipating and minimizing personnel issues related to sexual harassment in the multicultural workplace.

As companies seek international markets, encounters are increasing between men and women from unfamiliar cultural environments. It is becoming crucial that each representative be intellectually informed and behaviorly prepared for the unexpected. The rules for mixed gender interactions, or what is considered the "game" for some cultures, are different between cultures. Representatives need not be intimidated or insulted by customary social behaviors. If understanding and acceptance of differences in mores and expectations for behavior are learned and applied, meaningful business relations can develop. Learning tolerance can lead to the formation of strategic responses to "compliments" or culturally appropriate flirtation. One who applies this knowledge can avoid creating problems where none exist or solving gender related problems that may arise.

The employees in a multicultural workforce are diverse in their beliefs about what is appropriate behavior for men and women working together. In fact, men from particular cultures may not appreciate working with women as peers, nor working as subordinates to women supervisors. This resentment will manifest itself in conduct that may be acceptable in the culture of origin, but not in the global workplace. The intent of behaviors, as well as "complimentary" comments and acts, should be considered within the context of their cultural source and handled in an appropriate and culturally aware manner. Identifying, through cultural awareness, where problems may occur among employees, and understanding the deeper cultural sources of such behavior will assist management in developing a set of corporate steps for avoiding potential problems and may permit management to solve more effectively those problems that do arise in the workplace. This in turn will minimize morale problems, emotional stress, cultural misunderstanding, and develop a more synergistic workplace.

IMPLEMENTATION

Simple awareness of cultural differences in the perception of sexual harassment by management is not enough. First, developing a clear policy for local employees and management on sexual harassment in the organization is a legal necessity. Cascade the policy via discussion groups down through the whole organization. The policy should spell out what the corporate culture considers to be inappropriate behaviors and the repercussion for breaching the policy. Building on this, champion cultural awareness and diversity training for all employees, especially management, and include gender related issues. This will generate appreciation for similarities, as well as differences, that will pay long term dividends. This will break down cultural barriers, promote acceptance, build trust and energize cooperation.

Too often women and men are sent abroad for business without a realistic expectation of the attitudes and behaviors they will encounter, nor a means to effectively respond in the new cultural environment. Missed opportunities is often the result. Opportunities can be maximized through culture specific training. Training should focus on the cultural mores influencing gender relations and the verbal and physical behaviors that are appropriate for business and social settings. It is important to develop the skills to recognize what is acceptable or unacceptable behavior in a given setting and to respond with a suitable repertoire of behaviors. Often, businesswomen who understand cultural differences have an advantage in business dealings. If one knows how to "work" the cultural expectations for behavior in the country, one has credibility as the company's rep and social advantages as a female. The rules for gender relations can be taken advantage of and turned to the woman's gain if there is tolerance, specific cultural knowledge and the behavioral skill sets.

EVALUATION

The success of organizational policy and training in sexual harassment related to culture and other diversity issues will be apparent in the improved morale among men and women in the workplace and improved effectiveness in the global marketplace. In the multicultural workplace, the efficacy of the company's efforts to develop an awareness of sexual harassment policies will be partially dependant on its ability to engender an acceptance of cultural differences and similarities. Increase in team productivity due to synergistic cooperation and a decrease in harassment related complaints will be ways to measure the success of efforts in this area. Success in international interactions will be evident in two ways. One is an increased morale and satisfaction in staff given overseas assignments because of enhanced relational effectiveness and an ability to correctly judge the gender related behaviors of their international counterparts. The second is the increase in contacts, commitments and other positive results from representatives effective in international business encounters.

APPLICATIONS TO SMALL BUSINESS

Small businesses entering the global marketplace need to take particular note of the cultural differences they encounter. Having fewer financial and personnel resources limits choices for who can be sent abroad and also may limit access to the international connections needed. Therefore, the most must be made of each opportunity abroad, or foreign contact at home. Awareness and training are essential to avoid the pitfalls of projecting one's own gender related expectations for behavior on others. In addition, the majority of small business owners met abroad will tend to be interacting based on their own cultural assumptions about behavior. The ability to be prepared to adapt behavior and accept another's culturally appropriate actions, will allow the small business person to compete more effectively in the international arena.

CONCLUSION

How cultures tend to view sexual harassment will be an important issue in the 1990s. Not only will it affect the effectiveness and productivity of the multicultural workplace, it will influence how men and women perceive one another in international encounters. Ignoring the cultural differences in gender relations will only enhance the potential for social and relational problems within the multicultural organization. In international travel, expecting stereotyped behavior and reacting to it from one's own perspective may be personally rewarding, but it will do little to enhance global business opportunities. It is an international reality that different cultures expect different behaviors from men and women in business and social settings. It is also an international business reality that travelers must adapt to most successfully compete. In the future, as transactions of international business culture continue to homogenize the world of business interactions, the need to understand differences in perceptions of sexual harassment may diminish . . . but not in the near future.

REFERENCES/SOURCES

Bustelo, Carlota. "The International Sickness of Sexual Harassment." *World Press Review* 39: 24-25.

CEC. *The Dignity of Women at Work.* Luxembourg: Office for Official Publications for the European Community, 1988.

CEC. *Protecting the Dignity of Men and Women at Work: Code of Practice on Measures to Combat Sexual Harassment.* Luxembourg: Office for Official Publications for the European Community, V/937/92-EN, 1992.

Fisher, Anne B. "Sexual Harassment: What to Do." *Fortune* (August 23, 1993): 84-86.

Gordon, Gloria. "A Worldwide Look at Sexual Harassment." *Communication World* (December 1991): 15-21.

Hall, Edward T. *The Hidden Dimension.* Garden City, NY: Anchor Press/ Doubleday, 1986.

Harris, Philip and Robert T. Moran. 3d ed. *Managing Cultural Differences*, Houston,TX: Gulf Publishing, 1990.

Hofstede, Geert. *Culture's Consequences: International Differences in Work Related Values*, Beverly Hills, CA: Sage Publications, 1980.

Hofstede, Geert. *Culture and Organizations, Software of the Mind.* London: McGraw-Hill, 1991.

Husbands, Robert. "Sexual Harassment in Employment: An International Perspective." *International Labor Review* (November-December, 1992): 535-560.

MacKinnon, Carole. *Sexual Harassment of Working Women: A Case of Sex Discrimination.* New Haven, CT: Yale University Press, 1979.

Paludi, Michele, A. and Richard B. Barickman. *Academic and Workplace*

Harassment, A Resource Manual. New York: State University of New York Press, 1991.

"Sexual Harassment Is Easier to Deplore than to Define." *International Management* (March, 1992): 9-10.

Dr. David O. Braaten
The American Graduate School
of International Management

Dr. David O. Braaten is an associate professor at The American Graduate School of International Management, where he specializes in cross-cultural communication. Previously, he was on the faculty of the International Business Education and Research M.B.A. program in the Graduate School of Business at the University of Southern California. Dr. Braaten has consulted with managers and executives from international companies on the cross-cultural perspectives for a global marketplace. He has worked in Mexico and lectured in Taipei, Taiwan. His Ph.D. in communication arts is from the University of Southern California. He is on the Editorial Advisory Board of the *International Directory of Intercultural Resources.*

14.

Evolving Issues in Global Business Operations

Developing a Global Perspective

OVERVIEW

In recent decades, the United States has been conceding its economic leadership to the Japanese in one industry after another—first it was automobiles, then electronics, then banks. In 1986 the per capita income in Japan exceeded that of the U.S. for the first time. In short, it would not be too much of an exaggeration to say that the situation in the U.S. has reached crisis proportions. "International competitiveness" has became the buzz word in Washington. Although Japanese industry suffered setbacks in the 1990s, and has been widely pressured to revise its trade restrictions, the decline in exports has resulted from economic conditions rather than internal failures of Japanese management. The issues of trade and protectionism were widely debated in the U.S. with respect to the North American Free Trade Agreement and the U.S. ratification of GATT. Ross Perot made NAFTA a focus of his 1992 presidential campaign, while the newly elected Republican majority split over GATT.

EXAMPLES

Protectionism has been prescribed by many as a panacea to help the U.S. regain its international competitiveness. In reality, however, protectionism alone does not work unless the industry granted temporary protection takes full advantage of the opportunity to restructure its existing deficiencies and shortcomings. The case of Harley-Davidson has been widely publicized as an example of how protectionism can help U.S. industry to regain its international competitiveness. However, Harley-Davidson could not have achieved its remarkable turnaround in sales and profits if it had simply luxuriated behind the walls of protectionism. The company took some drastic measures, such as decreasing plant employment by 25%.

Other analysts suggest that the solution to international competitiveness may lie in the formation of global alliances. The proponents of this approach argue that an undue emphasis is placed on our foreign competitors and not enough attention to the formulation of domestic strategies to cope with the challenges of the international arena. Consequently, the efforts and energy of U.S. corporations may be directed at the wrong target, namely, foreign competitors. An alternative strategy is for U.S. companies to collaborate with foreign competitors; some of the most successful multinationals have opted for this approach—IBM, Boeing, General Motors, Nippon Telegraph and Telephone (Japan), and Philips (Netherlands). These companies, which were once strongly opposed to cooperative ventures, either domestic or international, have revitalized their markets through collaborative agreements.

Still others argue that the United States has not lost its competitiveness. For example, Kenichi Ohmae, a leading expert on U.S.-Japanese relations, has even gone so far as to characterize Japan as being uncompetitive vis-a-vis the United States. He based his argument on product presence as a yardstick for global competitiveness. Product presence is defined as the total goods exported by a country combined with goods produced locally by subsidiaries of companies from the same country. In 1984, for example, during the height of Japanese "dominance of U.S. markets," U.S. product pressure in Japan totaled $69.5 billion ($25.6 billion in exports plus $43.9 billion of made-in-Japan American goods), compared to $69.6 billion in Japanese product pressure in the U.S. ($56.8 billion in exports and $12.8 billion in made-in-the-U.S. Japanese products).

The key to regaining or maintaining U.S. international competitiveness is to develop a global orientation. Without a global perspective, there is no way that American managers can take full advantage of the emerging phenomenon of global economic alliances, nor can they continue to manufacture products and render services that are marketable in other countries.

A global orientation entails the ability to think internationally. A major reason for the successful inroads made by select countries in Europe and Japan in the international marketplace in recent decades stems from their ability to think globally. Asian and European companies, for example, moved quickly into Vietnam as soon as it became politically stable, while the U.S. continued its wartime boycott until 1994, and restrained U.S. companies from developing the vast natural and human resources available in Vietnam.

In a way, the Europeans and Japanese companies had to develop an international orientation because of the smaller size of their domestic markets. In the case of Japan, the country is entirely devoid of natural resources and depends on trade to survive. The large land mass of the United States and the abundance of natural resources have lulled many Americans into complacency and self-satisfaction. U.S. companies are perhaps the only ones in the world that have been afforded the luxury of being ethnocentric in their orientation, but that security is rapidly changing.

IMPLEMENTATION

There are six important requisites to the development of an international orientation.

1. *Shed ethnocentric tendencies.* The first step is for American managers to stop viewing business through their own tinted lenses, but rather through the eyes of nationals of others countries. In the ABC documentary, "The Secret Negotiations: Release of American Hostages from Iran," Pierre

Salinger made the poignant observation that the long drawn-out negotiations between the U.S. and Iran could have been attributed in part to the fact that American negotiators approached the crisis with a Western mind set. We thought that government officials were the people to deal with. But in Iran, it is the religious leaders who are the political power.

Similarly, in the economic arena there are innumerable instances where American companies cannot effectively market to another country —where they cannot accomplish their corporate goals simply because of their inability to understand the other country's systems that dictate what is permissible and what motivates the people. A study of how Japanese multinationals try to get inside the cultural fabric of a foreign country provides an example of how dedicated the Japanese are to obtaining a global perspective. A junior executive from one of the largest general trading companies was sent to Spain for one year to learn how to play the Spanish guitar. During that year he was exempted from all administrative and production-related activities. That might seem a bit excessive to Americans, but not to the Japanese company. "A person can only be a good producer by being first and foremost a good consumer. Only when a person understands the innuendos and subtleties of a country and its accompanying culture can he develop products that will be suited to the needs of that country."

2. *Be adventuresome.* In Tung's study (1988) of the expatriation policies of eleven Australian multinationals, several executives attributed the greater ease with which many Australians adjusted to living and working overseas to the "Paul Hogan" mentality. In the Australian hit movie, *Crocodile Dundee,* the hero (played by Hogan) typified the Australian spirit and mentality—adventurous, friendly, and adaptable. The adventuresome spirit was also cited by many European executives as pivotal

to success abroad. Americans tend to feel less secure abroad than their counterparts, and do not venture into remote areas to seek business opportunities, as do the British and French.

3. *Review your limitations.* It is futile and counterproductive for Americans to blame others for their economic woes. A *Time* magazine survey (1985) found that 53% of those polled believed that Japan was being used as a scapegoat for U.S. economic problems. Instead of finger pointing, Americans should engage in soul searching to discover the underlying sources or causes of their country's economic woes. It is only through an accurate assessment of the situation, namely the strengths and weaknesses of one's country and company, that correct strategies can be formulated to meet the challenges of the global arena.

4. *Plan for change.* In the past, many U.S. companies have insisted on 100% equity ownership abroad. Two major developments have rendered this policy inoperative in a growing number of instances. The first is the increasing demand by host governments for some form of equity participation in ventures that utilize their resources. The second stems from the narrowing technological gap between the U.S. and other industrialized countries. To achieve synergies in the areas of research and development for the purpose of financing overseas operations, U.S. companies increasingly may have to enter into collaborative agreements with entities from other advanced nations. The burgeoning incidence of joint ventures, co-production, co-marketing, R&D partnerships, and territory sharing between and among economic entities from several nations are an indication of this development. The joint space research venture between the U.S. and Russia embodies the new spirit of international cooperation. In light of a rapidly changing global environment, U.S. companies have to become more responsive in adapting to

new methods of competition.

5. *Understand other socio-cultural, political, and economic systems.* Americans have had a love-hate relationship toward industrial policy or targeting. On the one hand, the U.S. tends to accuse the Japanese of unfair trade practices stemming from their country's policy of industrial targeting. On the other hand, industrial targeting has been proposed as a key to America's revitalization efforts. In order to determine whether industrial targeting is appropriate for this country, one has to understand the circumstances under which it was formulated in the Japanese context. There are substantial differences between the U.S. and Japan in their socio-cultural, political, and economic systems.

The successful implementation of an industrial policy in Japan requires close collaboration among government, business, and labor. Robert Ballon, a noted Japanologist, observes: "Japanese social dynamics operate on the basis of interdependence. Whereas Western interaction tends to be based on the logic $1 + 1 = 2$, in Japan the formula would be $1 \times 1 = 1$. Thus, in Japan, the reality of government and business is not that of two entities to be somehow added up but rather the reality of one coin with two faces. In other words, two distinct but interdependent institutions, namely the government and business, form one reality, Japan. In Japan the Western notion of laissez-faire, which supposes a gap between the public and private sectors, has never made sense. Although the private sector is not combined with the public sector, the dividing line between the two is not always that clear. Furthermore, the private sector is explicitly endowed with expectations and responsibilities that are public in nature, as in the case of national emergencies in Western countries."

6. *Respect the laws and customs of the host society.* Expatriates and their

families must become sensitive to the customs of their host country if they are to live and work effectively in it. Many Americans often expect foreigners to adapt to their customs and to speak English. Expatriates must realize that local customs and practices, no matter how primitive or strange they might seem, are within the cultural context of the host country the legitimate way to conduct business.

Many of the techniques used for training expatriates for overseas assignments appear to be appropriate for developing an international orientation among U.S. managers.

1. *Area studies programs.* These include environmental briefing and cultural orientation programs. They are designed to familiarize managers about a particular country's socio-political history, geography, stage of economic development, and cultural institutions. The basic assumption behind this approach is that "knowledge will increase empathy, and empathy will modify behavior in such a way as to improve intercultural relationships" (Campbell, 1969). Although there is some indication that increased knowledge will remove some of the fear and aggression that tends to be aroused by the unknown, the evidence that knowledge will invariably result in increased empathy is sparse and usually not the result of rigorous experimental control.

2. *Sensitivity training.* These programs are designed to develop an attitudinal flexibility within the individual so that one can become aware of, and eventually accept, that "unfamiliar" modes of behavior and value systems can also be valid ways of doing things in a different culture. Although the effectiveness of sensitivity training sessions have been questioned, there is some indication that "sensitivity training may well be a powerful technique in the reduction of ethnic prejudice, particularly

among those who are low in psychological anomy" (Rubin, 1967). The Peace Corps is by far the most ardent advocate of this type of training program.

3. *International assignments.* An expatriate assignment can serve at least two useful purposes. First, it allows the person to observe and gain firsthand knowledge and experience about the political, economic, and socio-cultural differences that may exist between the U.S. and other countries. Consequently, one or two terms of overseas assignments are an expedient means to develop a global orientation among managers.

Second, given the smaller size of the administrative organization abroad, an expatriate generally has to take on wider management responsibilities in the overseas position. An increasing number of multinational corporations are beginning to recognize the value of using overseas assignments as a phase in the overall career development program of those possessing potential for senior management positions.

While career issues, such as possible problems associated with repatriation, may plague the effectiveness of expatriate assignments, an overseas assignment, where appropriately designed and engineered, can facilitate the acquisition of an international orientation and assist managers in formulating strategies appropriate for competing in the economic arena.

CONCLUSION

Since attitudes and values are generally well developed by the time people reach adulthood, the argument is made that in order to prepare the next generation of Americans for the challenge of the global economic arena, such an international orientation must be inculcated from childhood. It is heartening to see that Congress is now supporting competitive trade legislation to encompass internal education business centers, and a number of school systems are developing bi-lingual classrooms. Programs such as these provide steps toward achieving global orientation within the U.S.

REFERENCES/SOURCES

Campbell, R. D. "U.S. Military Training for Cross-Cultural Interaction." Office of Naval Research, June 4, 1969.

Deutsch, S. E. *International Education and Exchange: A Sociological Analysis*. Cleveland, OH: Case Western Reserve University Press, 1970.

Moran, R. T. and P. R. Harris. *Managing Cultural Synergy*. Houston: Gulf Publishing, 1982.

Rubin, I. "The Reduction of Prejudice through Laboratory Training." *Journal of Applied Behavioral Psychology* 3 (1967): 20-50.

Tung, R. L. "Selection and Training for Overseas Assignments." *Columbia Journal of World Business* (Spring 1981): 68-78

———. *Key to Japan's Economic Strength: Human Power*. Lexington, MA: D. C. Heath/Lexington Books, 1984.

———. *Strategic Management in the United States and Japan: A Comparative Analysis*. Cambridge, MA: Ballinger, 1987.

———. The New Expatriates. Managing Human Resources Abroad. Cambridge, MA: Ballinger, 1988.

———. "Career Issues in International Assignments." *Academy of Management Executive* 2,3 (1988): 169-179.

Dr. Rosalie L. Tung
Director, International Business Center
University of Wisconsin-Milwaukee

Dr. Rosalie L. Tung was born in Shanghai and educated in England at York University (B.A.) and in Canada at the University of British Columbia (M.B.A., Ph.D.). Immigrating to the U.S. in 1975, she has held faculty positions at the University of Oregon (1977-1980), U.C.L.A. (1981), Wharton School of Finance (1982-1986), and Harvard University. She has published numerous books, including *Key to Japan's Economic Strength: Human Power*, and *The New Expatriates: Managing Human Resources Abroad*, and numerous journal articles. She has served as Treasurer of the Academy of International Business and as a member of the Board of Governors of Governors of the Academy of Management. She is listed in *Who's Who of American Women*, *Who's Who in the East*, and *Who's Who in the World*.

Strategic Planning for the MNC

OVERVIEW

By general consensus a multinational corporation (MNC) engages in foreign direct investment, meaning that the firm has transferred from its home country certain necessary factors of production, and has retained significant control over their use abroad.

Multinational firm strategy seeks to resolve the conflict of the financial return potential of foreign investment with the inherent risks, advantages, and complexities of operating beyond the more familiar constraints and opportunities of the MNC's country of origin. To reduce the risk or to raise returns, multinational strategy must reflect successful planning and execution of:

- Decision strategies for foreign direct investment
- Opportunity/risk scanning strategy
- Market expansion/channel control strategy
- Organization/operations strategy

Not all firms engaged in international business necessarily engage in foreign direct investment. Depending on the firm's technology position, competitive position, and resources, more appropriate forms of international business involvement might include exporting, contract manufacturing (outsourcing), or joint venture arrangements. Shortages of human and financial resources generally preclude the small business from successful MNC operations.

EXAMPLES

The highly successful Toyota/GM joint venture (UMMI) to manufacture the Chevrolet Nova in Freemont, California was a planned prelude to Toyota's $8 billion manufacturing direct investment in Georgetown, Kentucky which came on line in late 1987. However, the earlier, unsuccessful ventures of Chrysler in Europe and of United Fruit/United Brands in Latin America in the early 1980s show that even industry leaders may fail in foreign direct investment due to faulty strategy. Successful foreign direct investment usually means designing specific strategies to cope with dominant competitors. For example, ITT used foreign direct investment and a market expansion strategy to acquire certain undercapitalized and inefficient state-owned telephone companies, achieving rapid international market growth through foreign direct investment while AT&T was preoccupied at home by Justice Department monopoly concerns. Similarly, using an international environmental scanning strategy, Bethlehem Steel invested in pre-extraction facilities overseas after finding prime raw materials sources in the U.S. locked up by such major competitors as U.S. Steel.

Effective organization/operations strategies by multinationals are exemplified by DHL Worldwide Courier Express. DHL used excess baggage capacity on international flights of foreign airlines for it package/mail delivery services to overseas sorting and distribution centers, avoiding costly investment in company/owned fleets, such as those operated by competitors UPS and Federal Express.

An example of adroit multinational market expansion/channel control strategy was provided by Colgate-Palmolive, which manufactured and introduced fluoride toothpaste in Europe prior to Procter and Gamble, which had actually innovated the product for the U.S. market. Using a "fast-follower" strategy, Colgate promoted its products in Mexico by commissioning and supporting soap operas, a marketing concept actually pioneered by P&G.

Unfortunately, cases of strategic failure in new product development also abound. The U.S. firm Ampex developed a high quality reel-to-reel video recorder in 1950, twenty-five years prior to Sony's Betamax. CBSA and RCA then improved upon Ampex's expensive studio version by introducing home videotape machines in the 1960s. Next CBS and RCA lost their lead when Sony introduced a consumer-oriented data-based technology in 1975. However, Sony was in turn overtaken by Japan's Victor VHS format. In a great strategic blunder, U.S. technology innovators have allowed VCR technology and profits to pass from the hands of their companies to foreign "fast followers" with demonstrably greater opportunity scanning and strategic planning capability.

BENEFITS

Properly implemented, strategic planning for multinational firms permits focused activity on the fundamental long-term market share, technology, and profitability goals of corporate activity. A major means to this end is strategic planning and coordination of resources among the MNC's subsidiaries. A comprehensive MNC strategy will facilitate improved performance within such arenas of foreign direct investment as opportunity scanning, response in competitor threat, market expansion, product development, manufacturing, and foreign direct investment expansion. Thus, foreign direct investment strategies at the country level can be fully integrated with and supportive of objectives at the corporate level.

IMPLEMENTATION

A. Initiation/Expansion Strategies in Foreign Direct Investment

The decision to initiate foreign direct investment (FDI), or to expand current foreign direct investment to another country, generally serves one or more of the following basic purposes:

- to achieve firm growth
- to exploit process and/or product technologies or other competitive advantages of the firm
- to earn returns on markets and production consistent with the product life cycle theory
- to maximize corporate return on investment consistent with differences in international capital markets

Firms may initiate or expand FDI for any of the above reasons. FDI motivation seldom reflects interest rate differentials in different countries, since such an assumption fails to explain the strong preferences of U.S. MNCs for foreign direct investment as opposed to foreign portfolio investment. To achieve sales growth, the firm may increase FDI instead of portfolio investment, exporting, licensing, or franchising if high transport costs or trade barriers are a factor. The opportunity to obtain manufacturing economies of scale abroad may also make direct investments more attractive than exporting.

The exploitation of proprietary process (manufacturing) and product technologies may explain some multinational investment, particularly where the firm's proprietary knowledge permits operating advantages over local competitors. Nevertheless, the strength of such technological advantages must be sufficient to overcome such potential drawbacks of operating in a foreign market as higher information acquisition costs, exchange rate risks in repatriation of earnings, political risk, and possible diseconomies of scale due to smaller market size.

Product life cycle-based strategy for MNCs focuses on the strategic implications of new product development, which often occurs in highly developed countries. Subsequent to introduction, successful products attract imitative competitors. Increasingly under competitive pressure in its home market from these follower firms, innovators may begin exporting to unexploited markets in new countries, where demand is initially inelastic. However, competing local producers are soon attracted, so that innovators begin cost-oriented production in these same countries to avoid losing markets to local fast-follower producers. Subsequently, the developed-country innovator may shift production to even lower cost sites, often in developing countries, in order to service both domestic and foreign markets.

To evaluate the performance of foreign investments, MNCs often rely on discounted cash flow techniques. Risk evaluation—particularly in the form or risk-adjusted discount rates and risk-adjusted cash flow—may be used where data availability permits. More often, risk is conceptualized and evaluated but not mathematically specified.

B. Opportunity/Risk Scanning Strategy

Structured environmental/scanning processes can by employed to manage foreign country data more effectively. In the typical MNC—the vast majority of which are not name-recognizable corporate leviathans—staff planners and line executives may have persistent world views not necessarily congruent with factual complexities. Moreover, the production/marketing/finance expertise of many MNCs does not adequately serve a firm's needs to gather and assess strategic information. Consequently, MNC management often puts non-urgent informational, social, and political scanning needs on the back burner.

Threat/opportunity scanning is further complicated by MNC management's tendency to reject or ignore non-critical or mildly threatening environmental information. In particular, data regarding social class malaise and political risk is frequently ignored unless it persists or grows more intense—by which time, however, the environmental situation may have deteriorated substantially. At the core of the scanning problem, then, lie the dual issues of inadequate resources allocated to threat/opportunity scanning, and selectivity of managerial perception. The results are that much data is either ignored, subjectively interpreted, or not acted upon.

Therefore, the CEO and his planning staff must ensure that the MNC has committed necessary resources to ongoing, in-depth, broad-based opportunity/threat scanning. This requires personal CEO involvement. It is especially important that opportunity/threat scanning is based on multiple information sources. Scanning areas must include competitor evaluation, new product development, opportunity analysis, materials sourcing review, human resources availability, project strategy formulation, and foreign exchange/interest rate assessment.

C. Market Expansion/Channel Control Strategy

Strategic market planning permits detailed examination of the firm's major alternatives for marketing in terms of:

- identification of potential markets
- determination of priorities for market entry
- determination of rate of market expansion
- allocation of differential marketing resources among different markets

MNC strategic market planning should be premised on three underlying realities:

1. MNC sales growth directly determines accumulated expertise in manufacturing efficiency and cost reduction, or "experience."

2. Market share, including international market shares, determines ability to

lower costs relative to international competitors.

3. The successful MNC follower firm is the firm which captures a dominant share of world demand in a specific niche or segment.

The power of an experience-based strategy is formidable: if a follower MNC firm accumulates experience at 30% per year, it follows that it will double experience in less than three years and will typically lower its costs by 20-30%. On the other hand, for an innovator firm to maintain market dominance it must reinvest in new plant and process technology to maintain a steeper experience curve slope than its fast-follower MNC competitors. Continuous currency devaluation and lower inflation rates help maintain first-mover advantages, but a faster experience accumulation effect is indispensable. Follower firms may be unwittingly aided by innovator firms which, in seeking higher present return on investment (ROI), maintain a price umbrella to achieve higher return on past investment.

Where the same product is marketed worldwide, the benefits of multinational scale economies and experience curve effects are generally understood. Less well understood are strategic limitations upon standardization of product. Interestingly, the 1980s demonstrated trends toward both product standardization and product differentiation. Standardization strategies for MNCs evoke such global product examples as Sony televisions, the Ford Escort, the Toyota Corolla, and the development of globally uniform hand tool lines by both Matika and Black and Decker.

In spite of recent MNC emphasis on global products, the specific needs of consumers in both developed and developing countries must be met. Multinationals choosing to compete in developing country markets may produce uniform or "global" products if demand can be legitimately viewed as homogenous across all markets. However, in many developed countries such factors as climate, product use conditions, income levels, labor costs vis-a-vis capital costs, and custom and tradition all impact on product design.

In other words—despite the scale advantages of an MNC global product standardization strategy—many MNCs adapt product design, promotion, and advertising outcomes to local conditions of purchase and use, thereby decentralizing many product development and product advertising decisions.

D. Organization/Operations Strategies

A key organization issue for the multinational firm is formalization. Formalization reflects subsidiary dependence on procedures policies and directives supplied by headquarters. Data collection, data interpretation, and type and frequency of reports to headquarters are affected by formalization. Formalization may vary between subsidiaries located in developed vs. semi-developed or developing countries. For example, tactical (short-term) decision-making and day-to-day operations management of MNC subsidiaries in developing countries requires considerable flexibility. Such flexibility insures adequate adaptation of sales and marketing, personnel policies and industrial relations, and product design/manufacturing process to the specific opportunities and constraints of the host country, with its characteristic mix of industrialization and infrastructure development.

CONCLUSION

Given needs for both control and flexibility, organizational conflicts are inevitable. Headquarters, with its emphasis on global or broad geographic areas, will frequently conflict with subsidiary's focus on national and regional issues. One approach to resolve such conflicts is to limit headquarters' role in allocating financial resources and dictating strategy development. In the case of an MNC headquarters role limited to resource allocation and outcomes monitoring, the strategic focus is often on:

1. Divesting or reducing corporate exposure to operating subsidiaries with products incompatible with headquarters' perception of the firm's strategic mission.

2. Search and acquisition of new subsidiaries or lines of business compatible with the firm's strategic mission.

3. Monitoring financial and market share performance of existing subsidiary operations.

A second, more centralized approach is to expand the MNC headquarters charter to include resource allocation, new product development, marketing, and production decisions. Such an expanded, more aggressive headquarters role may result in:

- Supranational product design. The "Europeanization" of tastes in Spain as a result of European Community membership has provided market entry conditions for non-Spanish frozen food lines, while making the fabrication of decorative Spanish building tiles a successful venture in the U.S. and Europe for such Spanish MNCs as Porcelina, SA.

- Internationalization of marketing mix elements including product positioning and advertising themes.

- Standardization and centralization of manufacturing, finance, and R&D management at world or regional headquarters.

- Manufacturing operations are rationalized on a global basis to minimize tradeoffs between scale economies and differential production costs for different countries.

To ascertain the effectiveness of these management techniques, useful measures of financial and market success must be developed. Management's perspectives and practices must transcend isolated international trade and investment initiatives, and engage in that coordinated global strategy which defines the multinational firm.

REFERENCES/SOURCES

Hamel, Gary and C. K. Prahalad. "Do You Really Have a Global Strategy?" *Harvard Business Review* 63 (July-August 1985): 139-148. A practical strategic guide to elevated MNC subsidiary performance.

Kelly, M. W. *Foreign Investment Practices of U.S. Multinational Corporations*. Ann Arbor: UMI Research Press, 1981. A valuable empirical study with clearly presented conclusions.

Mascarenhas, Briance. "International Strategies of Non-Dominant Firms." *Journal of International Business Studies* (Spring 1986): 1-86. Superb strategic analysis especially pertinent to the smaller MNC.

Porter, Michael. *Competition in Global Industries*. Cambridge, MA: Ballinger, 1986. A comprehensive yet incisive analysis of MNC product portfolio-based competition, of considerable value to the managerial practioner, consultant, or researcher.

Dr. H. Charles Chase
Professor in International Business
Towson State University

Dr. H. Charles Chase is a management consultant and Professor of International Management and Marketing in a Graduate M.B.A. Program in Madrid, Spain. His areas of special interest include the evolution of the European Economic Community and the application of practices in strategic management to the improvement of corporate performance in Latin America. His Latin American teaching/research/consulting experiences have included Ecuador (1988-1989) and Puerto Rico (1981-1983). Dr. Chase holds the M.B.A. in International Marketing from Columbia University, and the Ph.D. in Management from the Organizational Behavior Group of the Graduate School of Management, Case Western Reserve University. He has published extensively in the areas of international management and international marketing.

International Market Analysis
Through Electronic Databases

OVERVIEW

The potential for electronic information retrieval applications in international business is enormous. However, studies of database use in international operations reveal very little of these applications. Though one may access mainframes, bulletin boards, and extensive database services from personal computers, few of these applications are widely used in international business dealings.

The extent to which *information technology* (IT) can be used in international business deals depends on the interplay of diverse economic, political, technological, and cultural forces. By its nature, IT stretches well beyond the descriptive analysis of databases as electronic tools to the vital questions concerning the correlation between transnational business and national supervision of the emerging *global information age*.

EXAMPLES

Three dynamic forces profoundly stimulated the development of electronic data storage and retrieval. First, the centrality of information technology to the basic operation of expanding business activities fueled the development of a new economic sector devoted to the production and provision of information technologies, software and services. Second, the emergence of newly-independent nations as major players in the international business system and global political sphere presented opportunities, as well as obstacles, to developed market economies. Third, as the postwar economic expansion began to slow at the beginning of the 1970s, information-based businesses assumed more significance as Western Europe and Japan competed with the United States for lucrative international markets.

MNCs which have emerged in the postwar period as the dominant economic institutions of the global business system, have become increasingly dependent on Third World markets as their foreign sales exceed those of the home markets. This global interdependence, however, suggests profound management issues for MNCs. The development of electronic means of information technology, including databases and networking, makes centralized supervision and control of diverse operations feasible, effective, and cost efficient.

BENEFITS

The compilation of statistical data covering business production, governmental regulations, political inclinations, and social trends is essential for evaluating a prospective market. The database is the tool that gives a company control over prospecting information. Furthermore, a database ensures that information always remains accessible to everyone who needs it. Without a database, information is usually isolated within divisions of the company instead of being instantly accessible to everyone. Computerized database systems:

- Improve the company's competitive edge
- Reduce time requirements
- Reduce clerical requirements
- Assure accurate information

- Reduce company's dependence by storing data for future use
- Increase knowledge and awareness
- Improve their statistical base

There is a growing interest within the U.S. business community in exploring new markets, especially the developing economies, and in establishing joint ventures overseas. Databases can be used to evaluate entry options and to analyze the operations of potential partners, which can be employed for tactical or strategic purposes. The corporate intelligence specialist can compile a company profile that includes an analysis of its goals, its research direction, the composition of its board of directors, and the company's position within a market. Furthermore, international databases are designed in a way to permit broad, multi-industry searching, or searches focused on specific industries or regions.

To be successful, however, corporate intelligence specialists must have more than information retrieval skills. They must be business detectives as well, able to recognize inaccurate information or illogical patterns in their data, which is occasionally made available by companies to public databases for the purpose of misleading competitors.

It is also important for decision makers in transnational corporations to know rules and regulations that act as barriers or as incentives to trade. Country-specific databases are, therefore, essential to serve as tracking devices.

IMPLEMENTATION

A comprehensive database that provides analytical background and market assessment studies may be difficult to construct. On a practical level, three issues need to be addressed: availability of data, reliability of the data, and the benefit/cost ratio of database construction. The availability of data can come from many sources, including governmental or public sector agencies, which provide national accounts and balance-of-payments statistics as well as regulations relating to trade and doing business in the country; and private-sector agencies providing information on the firm level.

The government's national accounts are the primary source of data on the composition of the economy and work force by the different sectors. While national accounts data are useful for gaining insight into the relative importance of the different sectors in the economy, data on international transactions are obtained primarily from a country's balance-of-payments accounts. Another source of data on international transactions is based on surveys of foreign direct investment by government agencies or on financial flows monitored by central banks.

SOFTWARE/DATABASES

Until recently the richness of choice among databases has not readily been available on the international level. Although *International Dun's Market Identifiers* has been available through *DIALOG* since early 1983, its coverage is limited to "leading" companies as defined by sales and/or prominence in the international marketplace. For lesser known firms, one has to consult printed materials, if available, or do a search of secondary sources, hoping to cull an annual sales figure or the name of a CEO from newspapers or trade periodicals. These approaches are time-consuming. Neither allows the ready manipulation and comparison of company information.

In the last few years, international business sources have proliferated, including databases of non-U.S. companies. *Kompass* has a unique classification system that is particularly strong on product information.

Predicasts is a database with convenient access to full text from a broad range of specialized business and industry newsletters. *Predicasts'* new *PTS Newsletter Database,* which became available in June 1988 on DIALOG, contains important information about company development; joint ventures and activities; new products and applied technologies; market and industry trends and conditions; government policies, funding, regulation and legislation; and international trade opportunities.

With the development of a full text newsletter database, the analyst can retrieve information from twenty industries and international regional areas, as reported in more than 120 newsletter titles. The scope of PTS Newsletter Database includes advanced materials, biotechnology, computers and electronics, defense and aerospace, energy, environment, financial services, international trade opportunities, and telecommunications.

This database is international in scope, with initial geographic emphasis on important eco-political regions such as Japan and the Middle East, in addition to North America and Europe. It provides coverage of product and technology development and licensing opportunities from Japan, the Soviet Union, Germany and other nations representing a broad range of markets. Similarly, newsletter coverage tracks key events and activities in the Middle East and provides access to information about Mid-East oil and gas resources and related policies, strategic defense issues, the geo-political conditions and their global implications.

The Middle East Abstract And Index is another database that covers material relating to the Arab World/Middle East region. Detailed abstracts are provided for journal articles and doctoral dissertations. Bibliographic citations, and occasionally brief abstracts, are provided for government documents, speeches, news conferences, interviews, and statistical material. Books and book reviews are also cited. This database provides an interdisciplinary index to topics. Countries included are: Bahrain, Egypt, Iran, Iraq, Israel, Jordan, Kuwait, Lebanon, Libya, Oman, Qatar, Saudi Arabia, Syria, Sudan, Turkey, United Arab Emirates, Yemen, Arab Republic, and People's Democratic Republic of Yemen. Material is drawn from approximately 1,500 English-language periodicals.

Mideast File is a database that covers a wide range of information on all aspects of life and work in the Middle East, derived form sources produced both inside and outside the region. Countries include Libya, Egypt, Sudan, Turkey, Syria, Lebanon, Israel, Jordan, Iraq, Iran, Saudi Arabia, Yemen and the Persian Gulf States. This database covers 340 journals, as well as research reports, official gazettes, government publications, manifestos, interviews, television and radio broadcasts, monographs, books, book reviews, conference proceedings, and dissertations. About 65% of the items are from English-language sources and 20% from Arabic sources. The remainder are from sources found in other languages of the Middle East, like Hebrew and Farsi, or from French or German sources.

Chinese Patent Abstracts In English is produced by the Patent Documentation Service Center of the People's Republic of China. The database includes patents published in the PRC since April 1, 1985. This database is the only comprehensive database dealing with patents in China.

Financial Times Company Abstracts contains information on companies from all countries worldwide, engaged in all industries and all service sectors. The information is derived from the London international editions of the *Financial Times* newspaper. This database is not as comprehensive as other databases; it lacks the in-depth analysis. It is mainly a collection of bits and pieces of news from around the world.

Japan Technology contains abstracts from the major Japanese journals and periodicals in technology, applied sciences, engineering, and business management, as well as articles from Japanese authors published in journals outside Japan. Achievement awards, corporate histories, industrial standards, economic reports, and consequential product news are included. Over 80% of the original articles are in Japanese; all abstracts are in English. Approximately 600 periodicals are indexed and abstracted in this database.

Infomat International Business provides multiple-industry concise abstracts of articles on products, markets, companies, and business trends from over 400 business newspapers and journals, translated into English from ten languages.

Principal focus is on European and Third World sources of activities, especially the Middle East and Latin America.

Japan Economic Newswire Plus contains the complete combination of all English-language newswires as reported by Kyodo News Service, Tokyo, Japan. It includes both the Japan Economic Daily (JED) and Kyodo English Language News (KENS) newswires. This database provides coverage of both general and business news from Japan, as well as international news that relates to Japan. Coverage includes the complete text of official statements issued by international groups, such as the International Monetary Fund, GATT, and OECD conferences. This database is compiled utilizing the services of nearly 2,000 correspondents and additional employees stationed throughout Japan and in 43 overseas news bureaus.

CONCLUSION

The United States has come a long way in providing databases for businesses in Canada, and/or the European Community. As a matter of fact, there is considerable overlap among databases covering these regions. But there are still tremendous gaps in covering the Pacific Rim countries and the rest of Asia, Latin America, the Middle East, and industrializing third world countries everywhere.

With respect to the content of the existing international databases, unlike their domestic counterpart, they are selective rather than comprehensive. Their coverage is often inaccurate, inconsistent, and dated. As a consequence, any business that wishes to expand global markets must develop an information system that is able to secure relevant data appropriate to management needs.

Dr. Zeinab A. Karake
Department of Economics and Business
The Catholic University of America

Corporate Philanthropy as Strategy

OVERVIEW

Companies once needed a kind of "outpost" mentality to be successful in business abroad, recalls Lorenzo Necci, chairman of EniChem SpA, one of Italy's biggest chemical producers. By establishing a self-contained foothold, the company virtually shut out local influence, preferring only to tap its own labor supply.

Times have changed. Now the emphasis is on interaction between guest and host at all professional and social levels. According to Necci, "Companies that cling to an independent mentality are in danger of going the way of the dinosaur as we move toward the 21st century." Olivetti Chairman Carlo di Benedetti believes that the traditional "loner" stance of multinationals has already had its day: "We have entered the age of cooperation because only through cooperation can companies find the resources required in the global marketplace."

Corporations in the 1990s that distinguish themselves as enlightened philanthropists will not be waiting for the grant applications to roll in. Perfunctory grants to local colleges and symphonies will no longer do. Rather, the entrepreneurial ingenuity upon which the company was built will be applied to philanthropic endeavor. These companies will arrive on American shores and determine the niches where they can contribute to the community.

Good corporate citizenship is rapidly gaining momentum in international business circles so that many MNCs now expect to actively participate in their host communities. They do so as the ultimate courtesy, but they recognize something more: philanthropy advances longer-term interests of the company itself. The higher the company's profile as a friendly new neighbor, the greater its staying power. Additional dividends include new knowledge and a deeper understanding of the host countries' public opinions, markets, private and government elites.

It is often difficult for the foreign company to see immediate, tangible, bottom-line benefits flowing from "good works." How can one quantify the goodwill of the community, a good reputation, or employee morale? These are long-term results, analyzed only after a sustained program of philanthropic strategy. Such efforts eventually can be measured by improved productivity of the work force, consumer loyalty, and better relations with government officials. Sales can also be affected either directly through such methods as cause-related marketing, which ties sales with corporate charitable contributions, or indirectly, through favorable treatment by authorities.

EXAMPLES

"The whole purpose of our direct giving program is to increase sales through image enhancement," explains Joan Guilkey, contributions manager for Burroughs-Wellcome, one of Britain's largest pharmaceutical manufacturers. "A newcomer to an American community who skillfully selects voluntary organizations in which to participate, and who then actively participates in these groups, can facilitate acceptance in that new setting, while enhancing awareness of its own products or services."

Several American firms are way ahead of their European and Asian counterparts, perhaps because corporate philanthropy in the U.S. has a long and colorful history. For example, Levi Strauss & Co. established one of the most effective and pro-active worldwide programs. It includes such activities as low-cost medical services in Cotia, Brazil; an adoption service in Toronto; a soccer field for economically disadvantaged 8- to 15-year olds in Dundee, Scotland; computer supplies for a hospice in Dublin; school facilities in Manila. The list is long and the track record a model. This manufacturer seeks out sensitive social problems in areas where it has plants, and aggressively applies solutions.

To reach this point, however, cultural perceptions within the foreign company may themselves need modification. Former cabinet member Elliot Richardson, an expert on international trade, notes that Japanese companies traditionally have felt a high responsibility to their workers. This leads to practices that promote low unemployment, and thus, "understandably, they may have less responsibility to the community." Conversely, because U.S. workers can easily be laid off, American companies feel more responsibility to the communities, because if the unemployed and needy are not their old workers, they are someone else's. "Japan is a more homogeneous country, which is a mixed blessing," observes Richardson. "There are fewer problems of seriously economically disadvantaged people, but this means that there are also fewer people who feel a commitment to correcting this through voluntarism."

Yet, as a result of their dynamic rise to the top of the global economic ladder, indications are that the Japanese have become more sensitive to the benefits of local philanthropy. No longer just anonymous trading companies, Japanese companies are the largest employers and taxpayers in some American towns, and thus are expected to act like any other member of the community. Suddenly the Japanese are seeking guidance and making courageous attempts toward "good corporate citizenship." They accept the fact that without local support, their long-term survival in the United States is questionable.

Sadahei Kusumoto, President of Minolta Corp., has declared that in light of this expectation, other Japanese companies must change their thinking: No longer are they just Japanese companies that happen to be doing business abroad; they are true multinational corporations that affect their host communities. The Japanese government is urging companies to do what it takes to be model citizens. Typical instruments of influence garnering in the U.S.—$10 billion of media marketing in 1988 and $45 million for lobbying in 1988—are too strident to accomplish the mission. The slick advertising and all-out campaigns that previously were designed to influence state and federal legislation now tend to be seen as too transparent or heavy handed. These methods are rapidly being replaced by concerted efforts to win local friends. Japanese executives of U.S. subsidiaries point with pride to their leadership of local United Way drives or invitations onto boards of such national institutions as New York's Lincoln Center and Washington's Kennedy Center.

Because of the considerable dangers that can stem from taking action in foreign cultures, projects to promote cross-cultural understanding must be designed with great care. There is the added concern by local groups regarding foreign management of such projects. Too often, the motives of foreigners are misunderstood.

Even when there is nothing inherently wrong with the program itself, foreign funding and management can produce criticism. In July 11, 1988, *Business Week* ran a sensational front page report—"Japan's Influence in America." Claiming that "never before in modern history has a foreign adversary wielded so much influence in a rival's home ground." The series of articles interpreted the wave of Japanese donations in the U.S. as a Trojan horse. In addition, it is not uncommon for grant-making foundations initiated by foreign subsidiaries to be called upon to defend its gifts. Certainly no American foundation would have to answer to: Are you trying to buy our research? Buy our university?

BENEFITS

Whereas American law permits a significant tax deduction for corporate philanthropy, continental tax systems are only now reaching the point of allowing greater encouragement of charitable gifts by either individuals or companies. For example, Japanese tax reform created the likelihood that the government might abolish longstanding disincentives for corporate giving, but in 1989 tight restrictions on tax exemption were loosened. "Now the momentum is in the direction of tax changes that will allow companies to treat overseas philanthropy as a business expense," said Yoshi Nakamura of the Council for Better Investment in the U.S., a program of 245 companies that wish to promote good corporate citizenship.

Despite these differences, some foreign companies in America are making waves. Shell Oil Co. gave away $19 million in 1988; Campeau Corp., $12 million in 1987; and BP America, $10.5 million in 1987. BP America clearly understands the value of corporate citizenship. With 50% of its total world assets located in the United States, British Petroleum understandably sought ways to integrate itself in the American way of life. Their funding operates on two tiers: large grants that support education and urban development emanate from the Corporate Contributions unit; more regional grants are made by individual related businesses. In 1988, the company launched a pioneering Social Investments program that invested over $3.5 million in six projects. Result? Four hundred units of low-to-moderate income housing were built in Cleveland, the company's American headquarters. According to its president, "We wouldn't be doing this but for the social objectives they serve."

The American Honda Foundation was designed as an extension of principles espoused by Mr. Honda during the company's development. When the first prototype motorcycle was completed in 1949, Mr. Honda shouted, "It's a dream!" Officially the motorcycle was named "Dream Type D." Hence the American Honda Foundation literature describes the foundation as "dreamlike," and invites proposals for projects that are innovative, creative or visionary. Contrary to typical Japanese reverence for the wisdom of advanced age, Mr. Honda encouraged a youthful approach to work. In his retirement statement, he said, "I attribute the company's success to the fact that the firm possesses dreams and youthfulness." Funding patterns follow these general themes. For example, the Kindereconomy project was taken to U.S. grammar schools with American Honda Foundation support. The program was designed to teach (and study) entrepeneurial skills to children, especially among lower income groups. Small societies were set up, in which the children were the shopkeepers and service providers. Social organization was left entirely to them. Before the project ended, the children had developed their own system of money with its own name and uses. By exchanging the goods and services they needed, they learned the basics of economics. Seven-year olds were routinely talking about "scarcity."

IMPLEMENTATION

Sony Corporation of America's most visible attempt to be a "good citizen" tackled the perception that the Japanese harbor racist attitudes toward black and Hispanic Americans. This problem was approached from a commercial angle by skillfully weaving together a strong, appealing advertising campaign with a corporate giving program. Sony wanted to base its campaign on its reputation as an innovative personal electronics manufacturer. The company views itself as a leader in foreseeing lifestyle changes and the marketing opportunities they present, such as the now-famous portable radio-cassette player, the Sony Walkman.

To reach blacks, Sony's strategy was to highlight cultural innovation within the black community. This perspective led executives to focus on black musicians in particular, as a way to build a bond between Sony products and consumers. A competition was devised to seek out innovative black musicians, with the reward being talent opportunities for young artists in Sony ads, and secondarily, to provide free professional-quality Sony musical equipment to record the works of black musicians. The first Sony Innovators awards were given in 1988. Sony officials conclude that the campaign was so successful that they continued it, with a focus on black film artists.

In one of the few areas today where they outdistance their Japanese counterparts, U.S. corporations have become astute participants in the foreign communities where they do business. In 1988 IBM gave more than $135 million to social, cultural, and educational programs throughout the world. The United Nations Environment Program received equipment worth $6.5 million to use in a global resource database, which channels environmental data from a variety of sources to people who investigate the health of the planet. To improve child health in Latin America, IBM made a grant to the International Child Health Foundation and established a partnership with the Instituto de Investigacion Nutricional in Lima, Peru. The objective was to train public health experts in the use of IBM computers to coordinate diarrheal disease programs, and to provide health education for parents in poor and rural areas. With IBM assistance, Japan's Braille Forum became a model for applying information technology to assist the handicapped. Researchers at the IBM Tokyo Research Laboratory, including a blind researcher, developed a software system that converts English or Japanese katakana characters into braille far faster than previously existing systems.

This role of American corporations grew out of a preoccupation with world economic leadership. Gradually aware of the toll their post-War expansion had taken on the overall health of the locations where their business was carried on, American companies in recent decades have conducted their profit-seeking activities with greater regard for the interests of the surrounding communities.

Early on, philanthropy in the U.S. supported by corporate wealth was a key element in solving problems of health, education, and welfare. The Russell Sage Foundation assisted the National Tuberculosis Association. The Rockefeller Sanitary Commission demonstrated that hookworm disease could be eradicated, thereby advancing the entire movement for establishing public health programs. The Carnegie Foundation for the Advancement of Teaching inaugurated pensions for college teachers, which led to pensions for other workers.

Since these beginnings of corporate philanthropy, American companies have invested so much imagination and such substantial resources into community projects that they have, in some cases, become unforgettable. One such company is Dayton-Hudson, whose ability to win local friends even before settling in a location established the retailer as an integral part of the Great Lakes area. Moreover, the department store chain took the lead in creating the Five Percent Club, persuading other corporations in the Twin Cities area to donate that amount of after tax earnings to community projects.

Even more sublime is the durable association of avant garde visual art with Philip Morris, the giant cigarette manufacturer. Heavily dependent upon package design, Philip Morris used sponsorship of new art to inspire its ascent to first place in the industry. Mobil Oil may have wrestled with problems inherent to the energy business, but faithful sponsorship of public television's "Upstairs, Downstairs" has gone a long way to soften the image of a predatory oil and gas giant.

Yet the notion of philanthropy is hardly an American invention. Aristotle spoke of the profound responsibility of giving away money. The concept of a charitable organization is drawn directly from the English common law charitable trust. Many charitable programs in pre-Revolutionary France were abolished during the Reign of Terror and replaced by more socialized services. Japan has its own philanthropic tradition, expressed by "on," an ideogram that refers to the obligation of the wealthy to "reciprocate kindness" to those responsible for their wealth. Drafters of the American Constitution wrote monographs supporting the role of organizations that occupy the middle ground between the state and public, thus ensuring the nation's plurality and containment of government interference. The rationale underlying tax exemption of private organizations serving community needs is that without these groups, government would bear the cost.

Ideally, a foreign company will include philanthropic activities as part of its overall strategic planning. For example, links to local nonprofit organizations provide good entry to the life of a host community. Harlan Flint, director of BP America's external affairs, points out that a common mistake is to make funding decisions "based on who comes through the door. This is a reactive style." Instead, companies need to be pro-active—go into the community, discover needs and then address them. This is especially important for foreign-owned companies that must overcome a community's sense of their "foreignness." Planning is especially important if a company does not have much money to give.

An inbound company generally should create a clear identity as soon as possible. Simply being a name in a long list of charitable supporters is not enough. A corporation must look for critical areas of interest where its support makes a real difference at the margin. Cosmair, the French cosmetics giant, discovered a unique opportunity. Its Lancome division contributed a sizable grant to a project for the American Cancer Society. In a video presentation entitled "Look Good, Feel Better," which is distributed to cancer treatment centers, Lancome demonstrates how cosmetic application can lift the spirits of patients undergoing chemotherapy.

How does the foreign corporation begin its philanthropic agenda? The first step is to identify and interview key community leaders. This gives a company a sense of what needs exist without making promises to address them. In addition to seeking the opinions of key leaders, potential outlets should be discussed with prospective or current employees. Employees also can be used to interview community leaders. This technique alone demonstrates the company's willingness to get involved, apart from increased visibility and potential relationships with important people.

In the United States, where so many worthy causes and so many social needs compete for assistance, managers of foreign subsidiaries can quickly become overwhelmed. In Japan, however, generally only educational programs are funded by private sources. Therefore, it is not surprising that Japanese corporations attempting to develop charitable giving programs in the U.S. are somewhat daunted by the wide array of possible recipients. American causes range from music education in the public schools, to the homeless, AIDS, child care, elder care, teacher shortages, shortages of minority teachers to serve as role models, job training, literacy, racism, teenage pregnancy, and drug abuse.

To its dismay, one Japanese corporate foundation discovered that local leaders did not possess the skills necessary to support the foundation's strategy. The foundation subsequently turned its attention to the entire nation, eventually locating communities appropriate to its philanthropic plans.

Established by a research and development company, the Hitachi Foundation funds programs that are long-term in scope, with investments to be realized in five, ten or twenty years' time. When Hitachi Foundation planners were forming their funding guidelines, they undertook lengthy discussions with people whose international business acumen provided critical insight to appropriate beneficiaries. Such discussions led to a funding theory based on preparation for a rapidly changing world—emphasizing new skills, new sensitivities, and respect for national differences. According to Delwin A. Roy, president of the foundation, "We are keenly aware of the impact of new international economics on local communities increasingly touched by changing global conditions." Translation? The Hitachi Foundation tackles programs that do not yield quick results—racism, voter rights, empowerment, and improvement of educational curricula.

It also is important at this stage to discover what other companies in the area are doing, and what other corporations in the same industry are doing. Next, the company must determine how to create the bridge from itself to the community groups it wants to get to know. One approach is for the company to review its own unique assets and resources as a starting point for what it can offer. In essence, what in the company's mission statement or product line can be used to focus on the type of program it has designed? Employees who have leadership positions in community groups throughout the selected issue areas can be very useful at this time.

A large British drug manufacturer decided to target its corporate giving to projects and organizations in the area around its North Carolina headquarters. While this may have seemed reasonable because the company was a relative newcomer to the area, small grants to state arts associations have not proved effective in extending the company's identity. Management now is rethinking its contributions policy and narrowing the program horizons toward projects more related to company expertise. Future funding will be directed toward training programs for pharmacists, research and other programs assisting sick children and elderly people.

In contrast, the Burroughs-Wellcome Fund has from the beginning limited itself to making grants across the country for research in clinical pharmacology and closely related fields. Their contributions manager explains that a niche allows a company "to make some waves—then you can't really go wrong." The Fund spent $1 million in 1989, primarily to educate health professionals on AIDS, and secondarily to help some AIDS care-giving organizations. (Burroughs-Wellcome developed a leading AIDS drug, AZT.)

Grant-making alone, however, misses the point. A comprehensive approach requires layers of activities including monetary contributions, employee (including top executives) voluntarism, cooperative projects with other companies or agencies, and cross-fertilization whereby community efforts are applied to internal practices and policies.

EVALUATION

A corporate philanthropy program will not be successful unless it has well-defined short-term and long-term goals, established control for its management and a policy for evaluation and re-evaluation. The American Honda Foundation, for example, seeks its results through success of its beneficiaries. Consequently, grant applications receive thorough and thoughtful review, and beneficiaries can depend upon the foundation for additional support if it means the difference between success and failure.

The staff assigned to the project should be acutely aware of community needs and must have strong planning skills. Most important, however, is the active participation of local managers and key executives in each community where the company operates. Businesses are realizing that a manager must understand his public role, and community relations is a suitable part of the manager's responsibilities.

Finally, full public relations potential of the program should be realized both inside and outside the company. Certainly employees take pride in working for an enlightened company. When gifts are made, basic fact sheets are directed to news agencies, the business and trade press. Investor newsletters are useful, and key political groups should be informed of the program's scope.

CONCLUSION

A company operating outside its nation of origin inevitably does more than simply fulfill its own economic purposes. If nothing else, the company carries its national cultural history with it. Philanthropy, as practiced by investors from different countries, goes even further. It promotes cross-cultural understanding by integrating people and resources at the corporation's foreign locations. What this suggests is the immense range of possibilities available to companies doing business abroad. Martin Meyerson, president emeritus of the University of Pennsylvania and a trustee of the Matsushita Foundation has predicted: "The great philanthropic country has been the United States. But in the next ten years, we will see Japan as the second great center of philanthropy." This attitude is clearly being promoted by the Japanese government, which sponsors the largest foreign aid program in the world—three times larger than the U.S. program.

International corporate citizenship holds great promise in the easing of frictions as economic forces hurtle toward true globalization. Few companies view the world as one great system whose human and material resources have been distributed unequally. Within that environment they have learned to plan, produce and market globally, allocating those resources irrespective of national frontiers in order to find the most effective patterns of worldwide production. The international company, as curator of its cultural heritage, must become a diplomat in the deepest sense. It is one of the best available means to smooth the rapidly increasing synthesis of world economies.

REFERENCES/SOURCES

Charitable Contributions by Corporations. Tax Management Portfolio 290-2nd. Washington: Bureau of National Affairs, 1986. Leonard L. Silverstein. Summary of tax aspects of various kinds of gifts made to exempt organizations by corporations.

Corporate Philanthropy. Washington: Council on Foundations, 1982. Collection of articles on philosophy, management and future trends in area of corporate giving in America.

The Foreign Investors' Handbook: Making Successful U.S. Investments. New York: Business International Corporation, 1989. In-depth analysis of business strategies used in market entry into the United States. Contains long chapter treating broad range of public affairs concerns including corporate philanthropy.

Jankowski, Katherine E., ed. *Directory of International Corporate Giving in America*. Washington: The Taft Group, 1989. Guide to the U.S. charitable giving of foreign owned companies. Detailed information of amounts, types and recipients of gifts.

Research Papers Volume I, History, Trends, and Current Magnitudes. Sponsored by The Commission on Private Philanthropy and Public Needs. Washington: Department of the Treasury, 1977. Wide range of research into philanthropy in the United States, including a chapter summarizing the doctrine of stewardship and the development of voluntary associations for educational, cultural and welfare purposes.

Carole S. George

Carole S. George is a practicing attorney specializing in business and estate planning. She frequently structures community relations programs for foreign corporate clients. She has served as Chairman of the American Bar Association Committee on International Property, Estate and Trust Law and is an active member of the Subcommittee on International Charitable Organizations. Through the Performing Arts and Public Media Program of the National Endowment for the Arts, George has advised the management of many regional arts organizations.

Index

Ad valorem tax
  tariffs, 155, 381
Adaptability screening (of managers), 759
Adapting Foreign Operations to Cultural Diversity, 811
Age perception of executives, 732
Agency for International Development, 439
Alaska (trade with Japan), 131
Alcohol
  abuse by expatriate managers, 783
  business gift, 160
Alliances
  China business, 65
  competition reduction, 868
  corporate strategic, 181
  culturally diverse, 263
  labor and government (Mexico), 651
  multinational, 228
  project defined, 261
  technology transfer, 236
Arbitrage, 471
Arbitration
  alternative to dispute resolution, 742
  GATT, 618
  joint-venture, 331
  NAFTA, 650
  small business, 601
  U.N. Convention, 568
  Vietnam, 101

Argentina
  cooperative market agreements, 153
  foreign debt, 375
  market opportunities, 11
  pipeline project, 158
  technology transfer laws, 184
Arthur Andersen approach (cultural influence), 723
Asia-Pacific Economic Cooperation (APEC), 118
Assessing Global Market Opportunities, 9
Bangladesh
  privatization of industry, 437
Barter, 190
Belgium (labor relations), 659
Big Bang (London market), 183
Bilateral investment protocols, 101
Black Monday (effect on foreign markets, 479
Block Currency Rule, 545
Bona fide resident (tax rule), 551
Brazil
  equity markets, 481
  negotiating contracts, 831
Business Environment Risk Intelligence (BERI), 348
Buy-back, 191
Call option, 470
Canada
  bartering, 192

909

Index

franchise laws, 303
NAFTA, 646
Vietnam projects, 90
Center for Privatization, 440
Centralization and Control (in the Global Organization), 173
Channel control strategy, 877, 882
Chile
   pipeline project, 158
Chile, 152
China, 87
China
   bureaucracy, 844
   cultural barriers, 820
   economic growth, xii
   foreign currency shortages, 844
   language obstacles, 843
   negotiating, 733
   negotiating obstacles, 822
   tariffs, 380
   technology exhange, 293
Choice of forum issues, 319
Choice of laws issue, 319
CIME, 662
Clearing Accounts, 191
Codetermination laws, 669
Committee on International Investment, 662
Compensation in International Settings, 800
Consensus
   decision-making, 730
   power structure, 738
Consulting Firms (for Japan), 142
Contract joint-venture, 321
Contracts
   Chinese, 76
   exchange rate (hedge), 466
   foreign, 594
   insurance (OPIC), 276
   Japan, 841
   Korea, 125, 792
   management, 586
   mistaken, 73
   spot market, 522
   tax considerations, 320
   turnkey, 335
   U.N. dispute resolution, 318
Contractual agreements, 452
   exporting arrangement, 453
Controlled foreign corporations, 538
Corporate Global Alliances, 181
Counterpurchase (in turnkey operations), 336
Counterpurchase, 190
Countertrade, 190
Countertrade
   avoiding quotas, 192
   Chile, 158
   Vietnam, 97
Country market analysis, 14
Country market environment assessment, 34
Credit assistance (developing nations), 441
Cross-cultural training, 759
Cultural Differences on Sexual Harrassment, 850
Cultural diversity
   corporate culture, 261
   defined, 811
   developing global vision, 261
   employee selection, 178
   personnel selection, 256
**Cultural Diversity
Adapting Foreign Operations to**

910

Index

Cultural Diversity, 811
Compensation in International Settings, 800
Cultural Keys to Successful Negotiating, 840
Cultural Differences on Sexual Harrassment, 850
Developing Global Perspective, 867
Ethical Dilemmas in Transacting Business Across Cultures, 820
Preparing Managers for Intercultural Assignments, 790
Profiling Your Negotiating Counterpart, 830
Cultural Keys to Successful Negotiating, 840
Cultural values, 455, 698, 804
Culture shock, 793
Deductions (on foreign income), 542
Delphi method (risk analysis), 352, 367
Denmark (labor disputes), 659
Department of Commerce, 10, 24, 50
 China, 85
 European Community, 637
 franchising specialist, 311
 licensing data, 402
 representative, 134
 risk analysis, 378
Developing Nations
 Public Sector Role (Export Marketing), 411
 Private Sector Role (Export Marketing), 431
 Management Infrastructure, 691
Design patent, 575
Direct exporting, 3, 452

foreign market entry, 4
Direct investment, 452
Directive ambiguity, 629
Dispute Resolution in International Business, 742
Dispute resolution, 330
Distribution license (export), 403
Domicile
 Joint-venture, 325
Doing Business in . . .
 China, 87
 Korea, 108
 Japan, 131
 Chile, 152
Dual-career, 713
Dual-directional communication, 815
Dumping (goods), 155
Econometric method (exchange rate forecasting), 509
Economic risk
 legal dimensions, 329
Economies of scale, 412
Economist method (risk analysis), 345
Ecuador
 exporting, 437
Egypt
 cultural sensibilities, 694
Entering Foreign Markets, 1
Equity Markets (Emerging), 477
Equivalent Reciprocity, 626
Ethical Dilemmas in Transacting Business Across Cultures, 820
European Community, 182
 codes of conduct, 657
 collective bargaining, 665
 labor relations, 670
 price support, 615
 sexual harrassment policies, 851

911

Index

European Free Trade Association, 384
European Labor Relations, 669
European Union
  tariffs, 384
European Union, 624
Exchange rate volatility, 374, 526
Excludable Income, 536
Expatriate Managers (Selecting), 755, 765
Expatriate managers
  adjustment to conditions, 765
  cultural adaptation, 790
  cultural adjustments, 765
  labor relations, 669
  returning home, 265
  salaries, 184
  socialization, 799
  women, 787
Expatriate personnel
  compensation, 553, 597
  cost of relocating, 776
  family training, 780
  respect for local culture, 872
  restrictions on, 397
  training, 795
  types of, 727
  value of overseas assignment, 874
Export Markets for Small Business (Locating), 22
Export Markets
  Assessing Global Market Opportunities, 9
  Entering Foreign Markets, 1
  Export Markets for Small Business (Locating), 22
  International Market Analysis Through Electronic Databases, 888

Niche Marketing for Small Business Exporters, 44
Export markets
  competition, 33
  Country Market Environment Assessment, 34
  screening, 30
  selecting target markets, 37
Export Marketing for Developing Nations
  Public Sector Role, 411
  Private Sector Role, 431
Export Restrictions, 401
Exporting, 3
  advantages to small business, 1, 22
  analyzing opportunities, 247
  assistance from agencies, 27
  Chinese strategies, 451
  Contractual agreements, 453
  developing countries, 411, 431
  difficulties, 53
  European Union, 624
  foreign direct investment, 453
  identifying opportunities, 12
  indirect, 452
  licensing, 296
  market research, 25
  NAFTA agencies for assistance, 653
  pass-through or re-exporting, 402
  profits, 462
  restrictions on, 237
  technology, 397
Expropriation
  defined, 364
  insurance, 280
  Latin America, 595
  negotiating contracts, 594
  OPIC guarantees, 100, 277

Index

Third World, 596
Farm subsidies, 384
Forecasting
  composite, 511
  fundamental, 496, 509
  judgmental, 496, 510
  technical, 496, 510
Foreign Assignees (Selecting), 775
Foreign Contract Agreements, 594
Foreign direct investment, 3, 453
Foreign earned income, 551
Foreign exchange
  avoiding host country restrictions, 462
  Chile, 158
  China, 70, 293, 844
  commercial banks, 375
  controls, 463
  developing countries, 461
  effects on exports, 248
  hedging, 471
  Korea, 114
  OPIC, 276
  Opportunity evaluation, 882
  terms of access, 405
  Vietnam, 95
Foreign Exchange Market, 489
Foreign Exchange Rates and Forecasting, 496
Foreign Exchange Reserve Act, 597
Foreign Markets (Entering), 1
Foreign Markets (Assessing), 9
Foreign personal holding company, 540
Foreign sales corporation, 533
Foreign tax deductions, 549
Foreign-earned income exclusion, 551
Forum

contractural disputes, 318
Forward contract (currency hedging), 468
Forward exchange, 518
Forward market hedge, 466
Forward rate, 503
Franchising, 303
Franchising, 880
  contractual agreements, 453
  Dept. of Commerce specialist, 311
  export method, 3
  market entry strategy, 3
Fundamental forecasting, 509
GATT (Impact on the Global Business Environment), 613
General Agreement on Tariffs and Trade (GATT), 613
  China, 70
  countertrade, 191
  Chile, 154
  Korea, 114
  tariff, 380
  tax incentives, 533
  developing nations, 422
  R&D, 211
General Agreements on Tariffs and Trade (GATT)
  technology controls, 396
General license (export), 402
Germany
  bilateral investment protocols, 101
  directive ambiguity, 638
  harassment, 856
  labor laws, 598, 672
  labor relations, 670
  nepotism, 704
  preformative liability, 315
  technology sharing, 226

Index

trade, 44
Ghana
  compensation of workers, 803
Global Alliances (Corporate), 181
Global Perspective (Developing), 867
Global Village
  transacting business, 820
Global Vision, 167
Gold card system
  export license, 404
Harmonization (European Union), 627
Harmony (Japanese management), 681
Headquarters and Foreign Subsidiary Communication, 729
Hedge
  money market, 466
  options market, 466
Hedging (currency)
  forward contract, 471
  option contract, 471
Human Resources Management (Decentralizing), 721
Human Resource Management, 326
  China, 77
  culture, 267, 817
  evolution of MNEs, 256
  Japan, 764
  legal considerations, 326
  market assessment, 49
  trust building, 229
  women managers, 787
Human Resources and Trust Building, 229
Human rights
  Arab, 658
  Chile, 153
  China, 386

South Africa, 821
Income exclusion (on foreign income), 551
Inconvertibility insurance, 280
India
  A.I.D. assistance, 438
  countertrade, 192
  emerging equity markets, 481
  infractions of trade policies, 384
  licensing, 291
  management restrictions, 201
  pension funds, 478
  restrictions after Bhopal, 322
  risk, 597
  subsidiaries, 328
  trade restrictions, 52
Indirect exporting, 3, 452
Individualism, 801
Industry analysis
  exporting, 15
Information sharing (labor relations), 673
Intellectual property
  Chile, 156
  China, 70, 384
  exploring market opportunities, 10
  Korea, 117
  NAFTA, 648
  patents, 617
  protecting, 578
  violations, 596
  World Intellectual Property Organization (WIPO), 577
  World Trade Organization, 613
Interfirm Collaboration for Technology Sharing, 224
International diversification (investment trend), 478

International Finance Corporation (IFC), 434
International Franchising, 303
International Franchise Association, 303
International Market Analysis Through Electronic Databases, 888
International Labour Organization (ILO), 657
International Monetary Fund, 10, 50, 191, 375, 515
International Personnel (Selecting), 755, 765
International Risk Analysis, 372
Iran
  cultural differences, 870
  fundalmentalism, 595
  risk, 292, 363, 375
  technology transfer, 203
Israel
  compensation of workers, 802
Italy
  technology transfer, 203
Japan
  controlling technology transfer, 395
  equity markets, 478
  expatriate managers, 755
  franchising, 306
  Gold Card system, 404
  imports, 24, 52
  licensing, 295
  management style, 681
  negotiating strategies, 841
  nepotism, 704
  patents, 576
  pension funds, 478
  reciprocity, 626
  tariff controversy, 382
  technology transfer, 226
  trade with Chile, 154
  trade with Korea, 91
  use of lawyers, 604
Japan, 131
Japan External Trade Organization (JETRO), 136
Japanese Management by Consensus, 681
Japanese Banks in the U.S., 141
Japanese Consulates, 138
Japanese Government, 143
Japanese Trading Companies, 139
Joint-ventures, 314
Joint-venture
  consortium, 323
  contract, 321
  corporation, 322
  domicile, 326
  EU countries, 635
  partnership, 320
  site of operation, 325
  tax considerations, 320
  terminating, 330
Korea, 108
Korea
  Industry Technology Cooperation Fund with Japan, 119
  Labor relations, 326
  codetermination, 672
  Denmark, 659
  information sharing, 673
  Works Councils, 671
Lawyers (Selecting and Managing Foreign), 603
Latin American Agribusiness Development Corporation, 438

Index

Legal Standards Imposed by International Organizations, 657
Licensing as an International Business Strategy, 290
Licensing
  EU countries, 635
  export method, 3
  foreign market entry, 5
  market entry strategy, 2
  Licensing-in/out, 295
Madrid Agreement (trademarks), 577
Management Infrastructure in the Third World, 691
Management by Walking Around, 685
Management Contracts, 586
Managing International Science and Technology Transfer, 261
Market expansion/channel control strategy, 877
Market Opportunities (Assessing), 9
Masculine vs. feminine cultures, 801
MERCOSUR (S. American alliance), 153
Money market hedge, 466
Multinational Investment Guaranty Agency, 320
NAFTA, 646
Nationalizing foreign companies, 280, 358
Negotiating
  China, 71, 821
  counterpart, 830
  cultural influences, 840
  performative liability, 315
  price, 147
  selecting the team, 845
  training, 683
  with OPIC assistance, 283

Nepotism in International Management, 704
Niche Marketing for Small Business Exporters, 44
Nonresident alien, 556
North American Free Trade Agreement, 646
Offset trading, 191
Operations strategies, 884
Opportunity/risk scanning strategy, 877
Option contract (currency hedging), 471
Options market hedge, 466
Organization for Economic Cooperation and Development
  selecting target markets, 50
Organization/operations strategy, 877
Outright rates, 504
Overseas Private Investment Corporation (OPIC), 275
Panama
  technology transfer, 201
Passive Foreign Investment Companies, 541
Patents and Trademarks, 574
Pension funds, 478, 486
Philanthropy as Strategy, 895
Philippines
  currency devaluation, 375
  emerging markets, 480
  little tiger, 246
  political uncertainty, 479
  private sector, 440
  stocks, 483
  technology transfer, 597
  women executives, 855
  worker compensation, 805

Index

Pipeline
  Argentina/Chile project, 158
Political Instability, 363
Political Risk
  legal dimensions, 327
Political variables (risk analysis), 346
Political Violence
  insurance, 281
  OPIC guarantees, 281
Possessions corporation, 537
Power distance
  subordinates, 801
Preformative liability, 315
Preparing Managers for Intercultural Assignments, 790
Private Enterprise Bureau, 436
Product Classification, 26
Profiling Your Negotiating Counterpart, 830
Profits from Foreign Operations (Managing), 461
Profits
  Branch profits tax, 560
  foreign exchange market, 498
  from foreign operations, 540
  renaming, 464
Quality control circles, 679
Quality of Work Life, 674
R&d Performed Abroad by U.S. Multinationals Abroad, 210
Reciprocity (in trade), 626
Repatriation, 760, 777, 781, 787, 793, 814, 874, 880
Resource Management
  family business, 712
**Risk Analysis
  Export Restrictions, 401
  International, 372**

Market Analysis Through Electronic Databases, 888
Political Instability, 363
Socio-political, 343
Tariff Barriers, 380
Technology Controls, 394
Ringi system
  Japanese management, 683
Risk analysis
  Delphi method, 367
  political instability, 363
Risk scanning strategy, 881
Rome (Treaty of), 569
Russia (tariff policies), 386
Screening
  adaptability of managers, 759
  for foreign assignments, 770
  foreign lawyers, 608
  market opportunities, 10, 23
  overseas suppliers, 421
  Peace Corps method, 766
  standardized testing, 779
Secondary Data Search, 28
Senegal (A.I.D. program), 442
Small Business Administration, 28, 149, 249, 570
Social variables (risk analysis), 347
Sourcing of income, 558
Southern Cone Common Market, 153
Small Business Exporting, 22, 44
Socio-political Risk Analysis, 343
Specific tax
  tariffs, 381
Spot exchange rate, 469
Spot Market, 518
Spot rate, 502
State Trade Offices, 136
Strategic Export Markets for Small

917

Index

Business, 22
Strategic Planning for the MNC, 877
Strategic vision, 167
Subsidiary Communication, 729
Subsidiaries, 52, 127, 168, 183, 211, 219, 239, 261, 276, 311, 322, 328, 365, 453, 464, 497, 509, 531, 538, 560, 587, 595, 635, 659, 673, 729, 776, 784, 802, 812, 868, 879, 903
  communication to, 171
  technology transfer, 183
  R&D, 211
Superstores (in Japan), 144
Swap rates, 503
Switch-trading, 191
Systematic Pattern Analysis (communications), 729
Taiwan, 45
  discrimination laws, 851
  emerging capital markets, 484
  emerging markets, 479
  investment capital, 62
  investments abroad, 89
  newly industrialized country, 433
  sales forecasting, 734
  trade, 68
Tariff Barriers, 380
Target markets
  selecting, 37, 49
Taxation
  U.S Corporations Doing Business Abroad, 531
  U.S. Citizens Doing Business Abroad, 548
  Non-resident Aliens and Foreign Corporations
Technology and Culture, 241

Technology Controls, 394
Technology Sharing, 224
Technology Transfer (Managing), 261
Technology Transfer Across Borders, 200
Technology transfer
  China, 72
  control of, 226
  controls on, 395
  government tolerance, 70
  importance of planning, 182
  legal assistance, 590
  licensing, 290
  to subsidiaries, 215
Tiananmen Square
  effect on foreign investment, 821
  stagnation of reform, 64
  symbol of backward leadership, 69
  symbol of repression, 386
Trade specialists (Dept. of Commerce), 2, 27, 134
Trademarks
  contractual agreements, 453
  discriminatory laws, 596
  GATT, 617
  Korean laws, 126
  management contracts, 589
  relation to franchising, 303
  relation to licensing, 291
Transaction Exposure (Managing), 466
Transaction exposure (exchange rate), 374
Transfer price, 536
Transfering funds (from country to country), 489
Treaties and Conventions, 565

Index

U.N. Convention on Arbitration, 568
U.N. Convention on Sale of Goods, 567
U.S. Embassy Commercial Section, 135
Uncertainty avoidance
  cultural differences, 801
Uniform Law for International Sales, 315
United Kingdom
  bilateral investment protocols, 101
  foreign contract agreements, 600
  information sharing, 674
  joint venture example, 568
  labor relations, 670
  privatization, 433
  trade with U.S. firms, 250
Validated license (export), 403
Value date, 502
Vulnerability indicators (risk analysis), 374
Works Councils (labor relations), 671
World Intellectual Property Organization (WIPO), 577
World Trade Centers, 138
World Trade Organization (WTO)
  China, 70